THE ODYSSEY of TEXAS RANGER JAMES CALLAHAN

THE ODYSSEY of TEXAS RANGER JAMES CALLAHAN

JOSEPH LUTHER

Introduction by Mike Cox

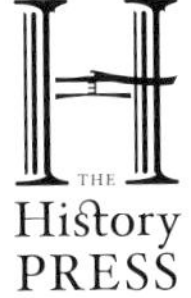

Published by The History Press
Charleston, SC
www.historypress.net

Front cover, top: Sketch by Lee Casbeer; *bottom*: *The Mexicans Attempted Two More Charges. From* With Crockett and Bowie; or, Fighting for the Lone-Star Flag: A Tale of Texas, *by Kirk Monroe and Victor Semon Pérard (New York: C. Scribner's Sons, 1898).*

First published 2017

Manufactured in the United States

ISBN 9781625858771

Library of Congress Control Number: 2016961490

Notice: The information in this book is true and complete to the best of our knowledge. It is offered without guarantee on the part of the author or The History Press. The author and The History Press disclaim all liability in connection with the use of this book.

To my son, Christopher Neal Luther.
Pass it on

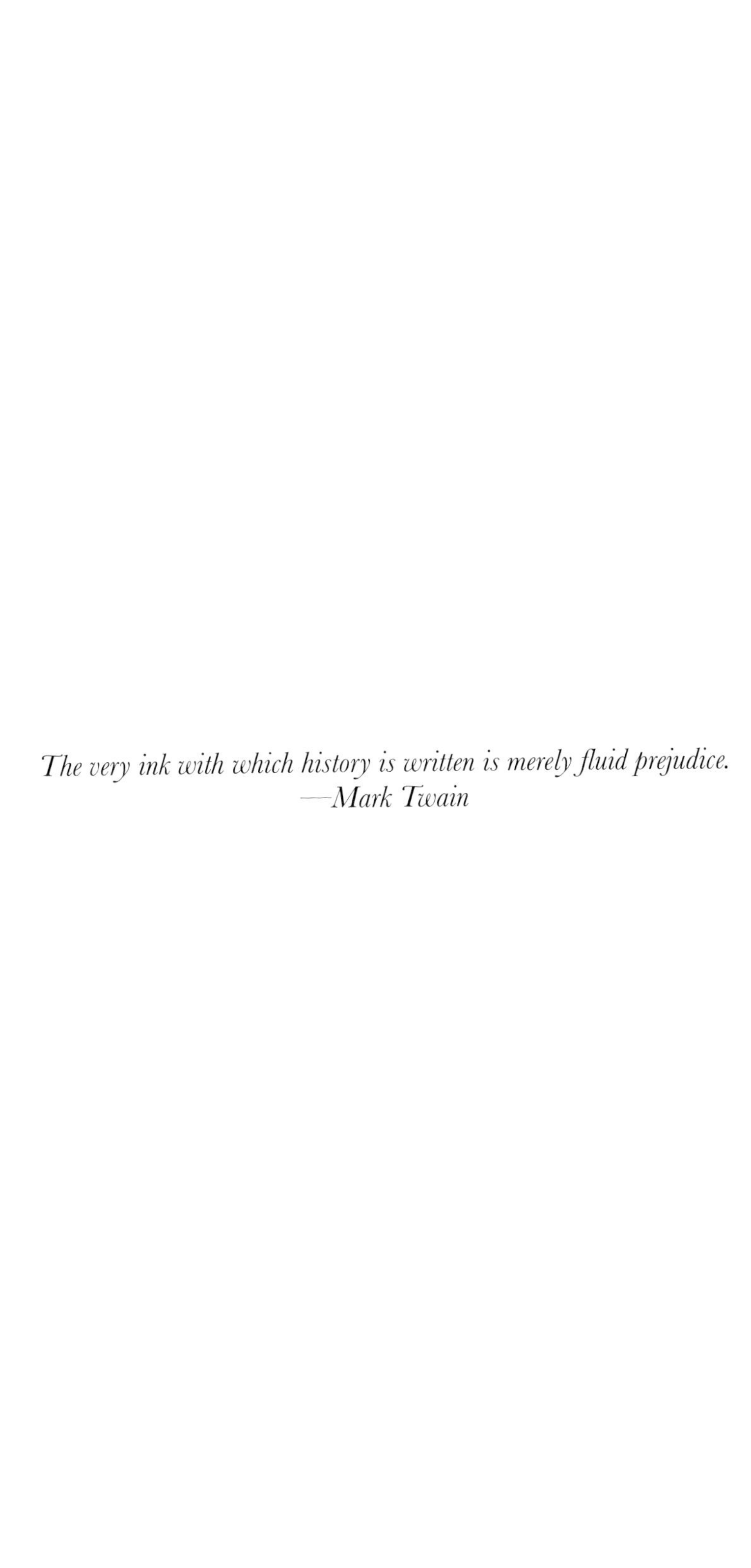

The very ink with which history is written is merely fluid prejudice.
—Mark Twain

CONTENTS

Acknowledgements 11
Introduction, by Mike Cox 13

1. The Georgia Battalion 15
2. The Fiery Crucible of War 19
3. Santa Anna's Campaign 29
4. Battle of Refugio 39
5. Battle of Coleto 55
6. Massacre at Goliad 63
7. Gonzales Rangers 72
8. Woll's Invasion 85
9. The Somervell Expedition 96
10. Seguin Ranger Station 101
11. Callahan's Expedition 109
12. A Tangled Web 114
13. Bandera 119
14. Rendezvous at Uvalde 128
15. Fort Duncan 136
16. Battle of Rio Escondido 142
17. Battle of Piedras Negras 147
18. The Return 157

Afterword	161
Notes	167
Bibliography	189
Index	217
About the Author	223

ACKNOWLEDGEMENTS

A special mention goes to Mike Cox for serving as my editor on this tale of Texas lore. My sincere appreciation for their kind consideration and cooperation is also given to the following individuals who provided inspiration, information, critique and support for this research: Craig H. Roell, Michael Collins, Tom Hester, Douglas D. Scott, Susan Dial, Jack Johnson, Sloan Rogers, Cliff Caldwell, Gary Carson, Ray Phillips, Julia Robb, Joe Enrique, Debra A. Vasquez, Javier M. Campos and Mike Edwards.

Thank you to the following organizations and individuals for their kind consideration and cooperation: Blanco Pioneer Museum, Callahan County Library Museum, Captain Shackelford's Company of Alabama Red Rovers, Daughters of the Republic of Texas, Dolph Briscoe Center for American History, Former Texas Rangers Association, Fort Martin Scott, Fort Velasco Restoration Society, Georgia Volunteer Battalion, Gonzales County Historical Commission, Institute of Texan Cultures, Kerr Regional History Center, Library of Congress, National Archives, National Cowboy and Western Heritage Museum, Refugio County Museum, Refugio Militia, Schreiner University Logan Library, Seguin–Guadalupe County Heritage Museum, Southern Texas Archaeological Association, South Texas Heritage Center at Witte Museum, Texas Archeological Society, Texas Beyond History, Texas Historical Society, Texas Ranger Hall of Fame and Museum, Texas State Historical Commission, Texas State Library and Archives, University of Texas Perry–Castañeda Library, Victoria Regional History Center and William P. Clements Center for Southwest Studies.

This book would not have been possible without Vicki Braglio Luther, my soulmate.

INTRODUCTION

Concise writing is good writing, but some stories simply deserve more detail. Only 462 words are devoted to the life of James Hughes Callahan in the *Handbook of Texas Online*, the venerable encyclopedia of Texas history—and five of those words are the entry's heading, which gives his full name and dates of birth (1812) and death (1856).

Of course, the brief entry in the Texas State Historical Association's digital handbook gets the job done in conveying the basic details of all the living and killing that constituted the Georgia native's forty-four years of existence. But after three years of research, historian Dr. Joseph Luther has written the full story of Callahan's action-filled yet controversial life and ultimately his ironic death.

Along with other volunteers from Georgia, Callahan came to Texas in December 1835, fought in the Texas Revolution and survived the March 1836 Goliad Massacre. Most men would have settled for just one brush with violent death and turned to more peaceful pursuits for the rest of their lives, but while he did marry, put down roots and have children, Callahan never seems to have turned down an opportunity to march out or saddle up to take on Mexicans or hostile Indians.

In addition to having taken part in the revolution that made Texas an independent republic for nearly a decade, Callahan served as a Texas Ranger or volunteer citizen-soldier from 1839 to 1842. He led Rangers in pursuit of Indian raiders in central and southwest Texas and fought Mexican irregulars and professional soldiers when Mexico twice unsuccessfully invaded Texas after the revolution.

During this time, he survived unscathed (at least, in the physical sense—we can only wonder what effect all that fighting and several close calls had on his psyche), and he developed a reputation. He had come to Texas a sergeant in a volunteer outfit from the Deep South, but he grew into a leader, usually serving as a captain, in his adopted home.

In 1855, he undertook one more campaign, this time as leader of a Ranger force ordered by Governor E.M. Pease to do something about Lipan Apaches raiding into Texas from their sanctuary in Mexico. He organized a punitive incursion that continues to bear his name, the Callahan Expedition. But was the foray he led really intended to punish hostile Indians?

Some historians have maintained that what really drew Callahan and his men to Mexico was not Indian fighting. Indeed, it has been asserted that Callahan's true motive was capturing runaway slaves for the reward money. In this groundbreaking work, Luther examines the evidence and lays out what he is confident is the true story.

Whatever his purpose, the captain did not succeed in realizing the publicly proclaimed mission objective. In fact, he and his command barely made it out of Mexico with their lives. The Texans had boldly splashed across the Rio Grande ostensibly to fight Indians and ended up facing well-trained and well-equipped Mexican soldiers. If they had intended to find slaves, they failed at that as well.

While his infamous invasion of Mexico was and continues to be controversial, there is no doubt that Callahan fought hard for Texas. As a volunteer soldier or Texas Ranger, Callahan successfully dodged bullets, cannonballs and Indian arrows while depopulating Texas of some of its enemies. But as any combat veteran of whatever generation can attest, repeatedly surviving close calls does not guarantee that you'll live a long life.

Following his disastrous expedition, Callahan made it home to wife and family, but as Luther ably demonstrates in the first-ever biography of this noted Texas Ranger captain, there is truth in the Greek dramatist's Aeschylus classic line, first spoken in 482 BC: "By the sword you did your work, and by the sword you die."

MIKE COX
Wimberley, Texas

1

THE GEORGIA BATTALION

"The cries of our fellow countrymen of Texas have reached us calling for help against the Tyrant and Oppressor" ran the headlines of the *Macon Messenger* of early November 1835. "Let all who are disposed to respond to the cry, in any form, assemble at the courthouse, on Tuesday evening next, at early candle light."

James Hughes Callahan was recruited for Texas in a town hall meeting in Macon, Georgia, on November 10, 1835. The atmosphere was electrically evangelistic. Lit by candlelight, the ambiance grew inflamed as orator after orator worked the crowd. Passionate speeches were shouted out and voiced in that old southern gospel style, exhorting the crowd to rise up, rise up to defend Texas.

Presided over by Levy Eckley, scores of local men crowded the meeting hall to consider Texas's ongoing effort to wrest itself from Mexican control. Seeing it as a struggle against tyranny, most of those attending—some of them sons or grandsons of men who had fought Great Britain in the name of liberty—stood ready to join the fight.

Thunderous applause rattled the old courthouse, and the drum beat of war stirred Callahan's blood. He immediately joined the phalanx of young men clamoring to fight in the new frontier. Thirty-two young men rushed forward and enrolled their names as volunteers; James was at the forefront. Callahan was glory bound.

U.S. Army lieutenant Hugh McLeod, recently from the Military Academy at West Point, "gave a spirit-stirring appeal, pledging himself to resign his commission and embark as a volunteer in the cause of liberty."[1]

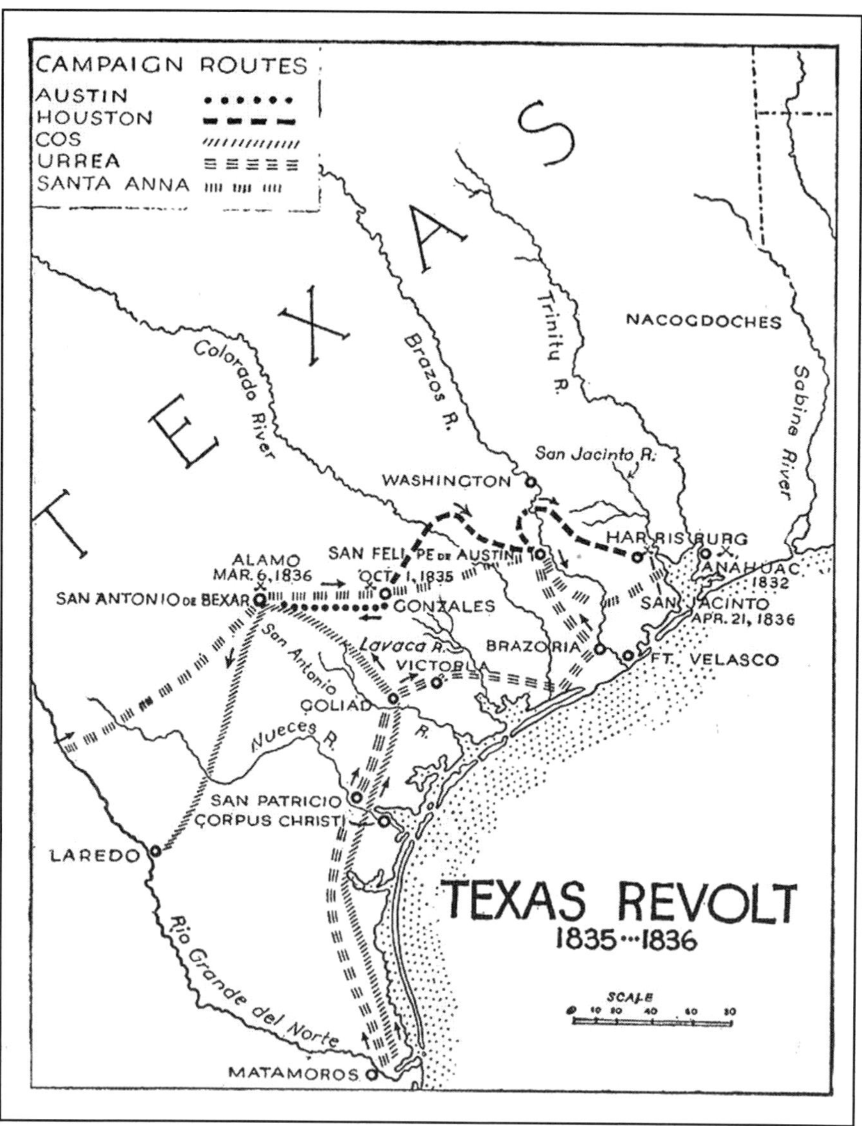

A map of the Texas revolt of 1835–36. *Courtesy of Texas State Historical Association.*

The resolutions finally agreed on by the "great concourse" of people declared that the citizens of Macon felt sympathy for the people of Texas "now struggling against tyranny and oppression," that they would give all aid not forbidden by the laws of their own country and that a committee of five should be appointed to correspond with the provisional government of Texas, receive donations and enroll the names of those disposed to "risk their lives, their fortunes, and their Sacred honor" in the support of a noble cause. Furthermore, the resolutions authorized the committee to correspond with all cities and towns in Georgia to solicit aid.[2] At this meeting, $3,141 was immediately subscribed to defray expenses of the trip to Texas. The volunteers were to be commanded by William Ward, the other officers to be chosen after the company's arrival in Texas.[3]

William Ward and Dr. Robert Collins held another public meeting in Macon two days later to organize an infantry battalion in answer to the plea from Texas to join the revolution. At the meeting, Ward recruited 120 men from Milledgeville, Columbus and Macon.

Here Callahan found himself among the Georgia Volunteers. From these young men, Ward formed three companies. With weapons and supplies from the Georgia State Arsenal, he armed and supplied the southern volunteers. He booked passage for them to Texas at his own expense.

The editor of the *Macon Telegraph* in the issue of November 26, 1835, published the following statement, headed "Texas Fever": "The Texas fever has treated us worse than the Cholera! Our office is completely swept! Journeymen and apprentices, men and boys, devils and angels, are all gone to Texas. If our readers get an empty sheet or no sheet at all, don't blame us."[4]

The material incentives to sign on for military service were not inconsiderable. These inducements were primarily in the form of land bounties, as the revolutionary government would have land aplenty if the revolt succeeded. These bounties gradually increased over time. In December 1835, the government authorized an award of 640 acres for each man who served through the duration of the war while those who signed on for three months were to receive half that amount. Otherwise, the volunteers would receive the same pay, provisions and clothing that U.S. soldiers had received more than twenty years earlier during the War of 1812—twenty dollars a month. If the volunteer was killed or died during his service, his heirs were entitled to his land plus an additional award of 640 acres.[5]

If truth be known, many of these volunteers went to war to find themselves.

The Macon volunteers, under the command of Ward, left Macon on November 18, 1835. Their first stop was at Knoxville (Georgia), and it was here on the steps of the Troutman Inn that Miss Joanna Troutman[6] presented the Lone Star flag to Lieutenant Colonel Ward for delivery to Lieutenant McLeod, who had gone on to Columbus to organize a company there.

A thoughtful and patriotic citizen, Miss Troutman took one of her silk skirts and designed and sewed the Lone Star flag.[7] The teenager made the banner with white silk. On each side of the flag, in the center, she sewed a large azure star of five points. Above the star on one side was the inscription "Liberty or Death" and, on the other, the Latin motto "Ubi Libertas Habitat Ibi Patria Est" ("Where Liberty Dwells, There Is My Country").

This Lone Star flag became the standard for the Georgia Battalion.

James Callahan was among the volunteers of the Georgia Battalion taking passage for Mobile, Alabama, on the steamer *Ben Franklin*. From Mobile, the Georgia Battalion embarked on the steamer *Convoy* for New Orleans. At New Orleans, Ward's company received some additional recruits, making it 150 men strong. The colonel laid in supplies, and then the Georgia boys sailed for Texas.[8]

The *Macon Telegraph* noted, "On Sunday, December 20, four schooners, the *Pennsylvania*, *Camancho*, *America* and *Santiago*, after being out eleven days, were landed at Velasco having on board 220 volunteers in the cause of liberty, from the State of Georgia."[9] Velasco, on the Texas Gulf Coast, was at the mouth of the Brazos River.[10]

The same day that Callahan disembarked at Velasco, the Texans at Goliad signed a declaration of independence from Mexico. The enacting clause resolved that the former department of Coahuila y Tejas ought to be a "free, sovereign, and independent State," and the signers pledged their lives, fortunes and honor to sustain the declaration.[11]

2

THE FIERY CRUCIBLE OF WAR

This is the kind of a mess I like to have my spoon in.
—*Davy Crockett*[12]

As Callahan leaned against the rail of the schooner *Pennsylvania*, looking at the dock in Velasco, he saw his destiny before his eyes. Standing there were Stephen F. Austin, James W. Fannin, William H. Wharton and Branch T. Archer. Someone informed Callahan that these men were the founding fathers of Texas. In 1821–24, Austin led a group of American settlers, known as the Old Three Hundred, who negotiated the right to settle in Texas with the Spanish royal governor of the territory.[13]

Fort Velasco had been built here in 1831–32 by a Mexican garrison that was defeated by Texan forces in a battle here on June 26, 1832. This was a prelude to the Texas Revolution and probably the first case of bloodshed in the relations between Texas and Mexico to take place. The fort stood about 150 yards from the Gulf shore, overlooking the Brazos River.[14] The fortification consisted of two concentric circles formed by upright posts 10 feet high.[15] To Callahan, Fort Velasco seemed like a formidable place of defense, with a four-pounder cannon on a fortified mound.

Callahan was now an American volunteer attached to the Texan army. The term Texan or Texian was generally used to apply to a citizen of the Anglo-American section of the province of Coahuila y Tejas or of the Republic of Texas.[16] Encamped at this beachhead, the Georgia Battalion was prepared for combat. For the boys in Callahan's company, excitement ran high. Most of these volunteer soldiers were adolescents, and some were even in their early teens. At twenty-three, Callahan was older than most. As a sergeant, he was quickly identified and followed as a leader.

On December 30, 1835, just after Ward and his Georgians arrived in Texas and with many more Americans on the way, the Mexican government, with Santa Anna's sponsorship, passed what came to be called the Tornel Decree.[17] It took its name from the man who issued it, José María de Tornel y Mendivil. He was, at the time, the Mexican equivalent of a secretary of defense. He was also one of Santa Anna's most ardent supporters. The document essentially stated that any foreign persons caught armed on Mexican soil with the intent of attacking or challenging Mexico or the Mexican government would be treated as a pirate. Likewise, anyone on Mexican soil who armed such persons would be treated the same.

The punishment for piracy in Mexico was death.[18] Given that they had come to Texas to fight Mexico, the men of the Georgia Battalion, and all like them, were considered pirates by the Mexican government. The boys on the beach that day had no knowledge they were already considered guilty of a capital crime.

Coahuila y Tejas was one of the constituent states of the newly established United Mexican States under its 1824 constitution. General Antonio López de Santa Anna, a centralist and two-time dictator, approved the *Siete Leyes* (Seven Laws) on December 15, 1835, a radical amendment that institutionalized the centralized form of government.

Americans in Coahuila y Tejas became increasingly frustrated with the Mexican government:

> *Many of the Mexican soldiers garrisoned in Texas were convicted criminals who were given the choice of prison or serving in the army in Texas. Mexico did not protect Freedom of Religion, instead requiring colonists to pledge their acceptance of Roman Catholicism; Mexican Law required a "tithe" paid to the Catholic Church. The American settlers could not grow what crops they wished, but as other citizens of Mexico were required to do, grow which crops Mexican officials dictated, which were to be redistributed in Mexico. Growing cotton was lucrative at the time, but most settlers were not permitted to grow it and those that did were sometimes imprisoned.*[19]

The tipping point for Americans in Texas was Santa Anna's annulment of the Federal Constitution of 1824. The Texans feared they would live under a

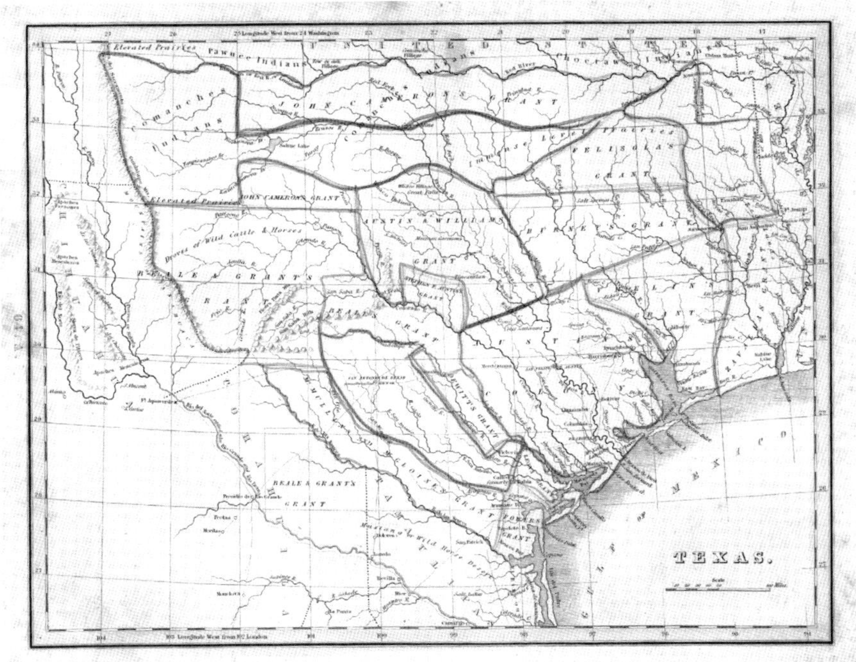

A map of Texas in 1835. *Courtesy of Perry-Castañeda Library Map Collection.*

tyrant with no representation at all. When Santa Anna suspended the 1824 constitution, civil war spread across Mexico, and three new governments declared independence: the Republic of Texas, the Republic of the Rio Grande and the Republic of Yucatán. The Texans opting for independence chose David Burnet as ad interim president and Lorenzo de Zavala as vice president on March 17.

Callahan became part of the new Provisional Regiment of Volunteers, organized at Velasco and made up of the Georgia Battalion under Major Warren J. Mitchell and the LaFayette Battalion under Major Benjamin C. Wallace. The Lafayette Battalion contained troops from U.S. volunteer units such as the New Orleans Greys and former Texan members of the Matamoros Expedition who had abandoned it to join Fannin at Goliad. Colonel James W. Fannin of the LaFayette Battalion was designated as regimental commander. William Ward of the Georgia Battalion was promoted to lieutenant colonel, making him second in command of the regiment. Warren J. Mitchell, surgeon of the battalion, became major and commander of the Georgia contingent.

The four companies of Ward's Georgia Battalion included:

(1) The "First Company," under Captain William A.O. Wadsworth, enlisted at Columbus, Georgia (hometown of Colonel Fannin and of future Republic of Texas president Mirabeau B. Lamar), but was much enlarged by recruiting at New Orleans and en route.
(2) The "Second Company," under Captain Uriah J. Bullock, enlisted at Macon, Georgia, and vicinity. When this company left the Brazos River on January 24, Captain Bullock was sick with measles and unable to travel. He never rejoined the unit or exercised command.
(3) The "Third Company," under Captain James C. Winn, formed in Gwinnett County, Georgia. This company was also enlarged at the mouth of the Brazos or en route, the additions being, for the most part, Mississippi volunteers. Callahan was a sergeant in this company.
(4) The "Alabama Greys," under Captain Isaac Ticknor, recruited by Edward Hanrick, at Montgomery, Alabama. This company arrived at the mouth of the Brazos only a few days before Colonel Fannin sailed.[20]

Winn's Company was completed in November 1835, with J.C. Winn as captain.[21] Captain Winn's company was staffed by Lieutenants Chadwick, Hughes and Brooks; Sergeants Bates, Thorn and Callahan; and Corporals John M. Gimble, Walter Davis, Abraham Stevens, J.M. Powers and Ray. Official Texan military rosters list Callahan as "3rd Sergeant, Mechanic."

Joseph Chadwick, who came to Texas from Illinois and who had spent two years at West Point, was made sergeant major, and John Sowers Brooks of Virginia, with one year's experience in the U.S. Marine Corps, was made adjutant of the Georgia Rifleman. Lieutenant Colonel Ward's two companies were armed with U.S. model 1817 common rifles, "yagers," from the Georgia armory.[22] As Callahan proudly marched out of Macon, he shouldered his splendid new yager.

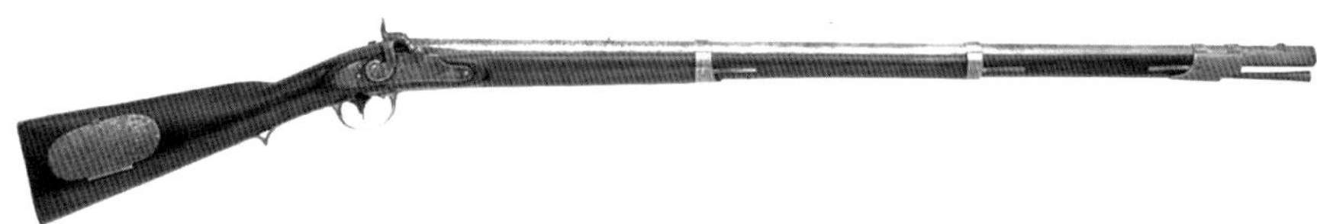

An 1817 common rifle. Robert P. Broadwater *A Most Uncommon Rifle, The Model 1817 U.S. Flintlock. Military Trader,* http://www.militarytrader.com/military-trader-news/model_1817_us_flintlock.

At the time that Callahan arrived at Velasco, he was told the Texan strategy was to invade the Mexican port city of Matamoros at the mouth of the Rio Grande. As the Mexican government transitioned from federalism to a centralized government under Santa Anna in 1835, many federalists offered armed opposition. In Mexican Texas, settlers had launched a full rebellion in October 1835. Matamoros, in the state of Tamaulipas, was an important source of revenue and, if seized, could be used to defray the cost of the rebellion.

At Monclova, Coahuila, in the spring of 1835, the federalist governor and the legislature of Coahuila and Texas illegally sold 1,500 to 1,600 leagues of public land in Texas in an attempt to finance the cost of opposing Santa Anna's centralist forces. Among the buyers, some of whom were interested as *empresarios*, were Ben Fort Smith, Green DeWitt, Benjamin R. Milam, Thomas J. Chambers, Haden Edward, James Grant, Francis W. Johnson, Robert R. Peebles, Samuel M. Williams and John T. Mason, the last of whom was working through José Antonio Mexía. Land speculation, in due course, influenced what Sam Houston called "Matamoros Fever."

Soon after arriving in Texas from his native Georgia, Fannin became an activist for the Texas Revolution. On August 20, 1835, the Committee of Safety and Correspondence at Columbia appointed him to use his influence for the calling of the Consultation (convention).[23] On August 27, Fannin wrote to a U.S. Army officer in Georgia requesting financial aid for the Texas cause as well as West Point officers who might be interested in a command in the nascent Texas army.

Sam Houston served as a delegate from Nacogdoches to the Consultation of 1835, which deliberated in Columbia in October and at San Felipe. On November 12, the Consultation appointed Houston major general of the Texas army. He would be required to raise his army afresh rather than take over the volunteer force already commanded by Stephen F. Austin.

The provisional Texas government—referred to as the Council—hearing reports that other Mexican states were near revolt, on December 25 authorized an expedition to Matamoros. Driven to carry out the Matamoros project, the Council on January 7 had appointed Colonel Fannin as "agent" of the volunteer expedition, authorizing him to call on Texas merchant Collin McKinney[24] for provisions, transportation and munitions. Inexorably, Callahan felt drawn to this exciting prospect. He soon became part of Fannin's regiment, which was preparing to march on Matamoros. Francis (Frank) W. Johnson became commander of the volunteers.

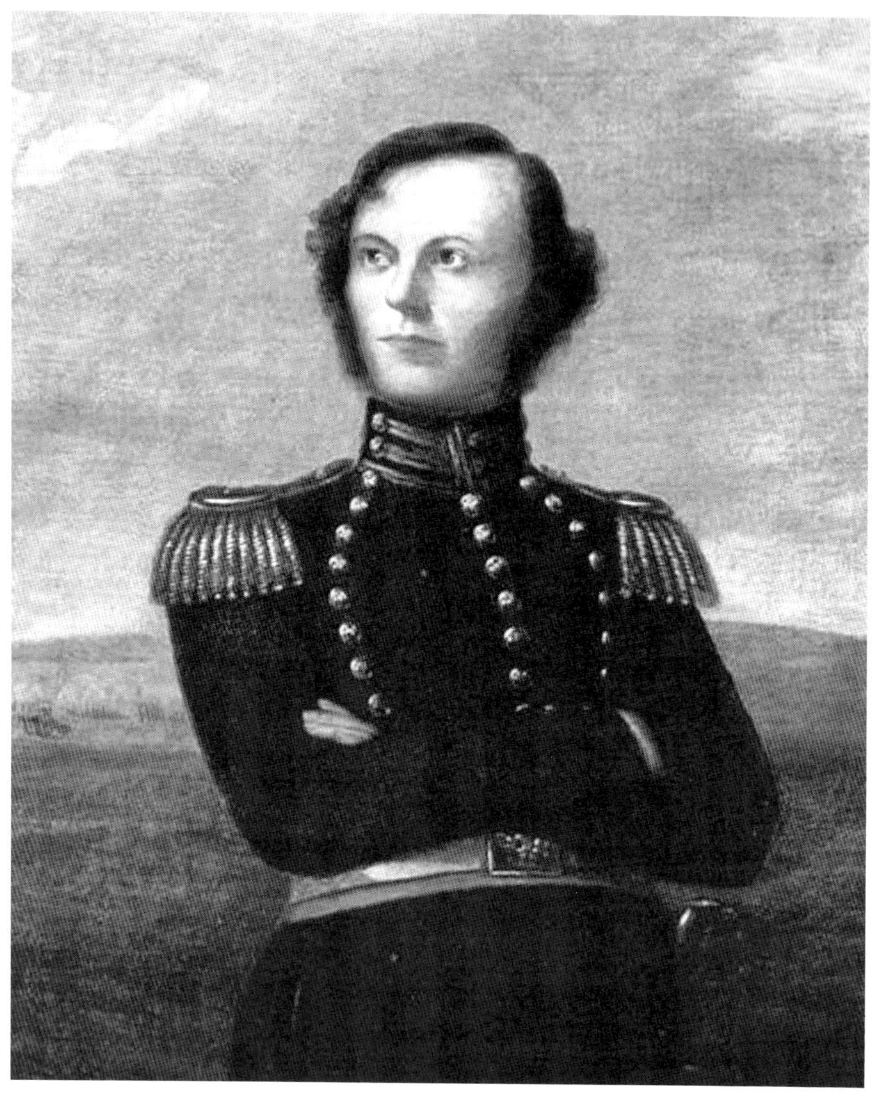

James Walker Fannin. *Courtesy of Dallas Historical Society.*

In late December 1835, the Texas provisional government named Johnson co-commander of the Matamoros Expedition. By late January, the Council had named several others as heads of the Texan army, and there was confusion in the army and the public over who stood in charge. For several months, it was unclear if James Grant, Fannin, Johnson or Houston was in charge of the Texan army.[25]

Callahan remained at Velasco until February 1, 1836, when the Georgia Battalion received orders to move to Copano, a port on the mid-Texas coast that dated back to Spanish colonial times. Intent on an expedition to Matamoros, Fannin would meet them there. Fannin's recruitment policy had included a proclamation that the volunteer force "should be paid of the first spoils taken from the enemy." This ancient tradition of "to the victor go the spoils" was a customary practice among Texas troops and, later, the early Texas Rangers.

Callahan and the men of the Georgia Battalion knew little of these international intrigues. As soldiers of the line, all their intelligence came from the top down or by hearsay. The young Georgian only knew that there was a scheme afoot to invade Matamoros.

Fannin sailed from Velasco on January 24, 1836, and landed at Copano on February 2 with about two hundred men, including Ward's Georgia Battalion. Supplies from McKinney, Williams and Company had not yet arrived from New Orleans, so Fannin pressed them from the stores of three vessels then in port, the *Columbus*, the *Flora* and the *Invincible*.

Callahan and his comrades boarded the schooner *Columbus*, a U.S. vessel. They received supplies from the government that included four pieces of artillery: two six-pounders and two four-pounders.[26] The Georgia Battalion arrived at the door to the interior of Texas, landing on Copano Bay.[27]

The boys from Georgia were immediately dispatched to an old Spanish edifice, Nuestra Señora del Refugio Mission at Refugio, on the north bank of the Mission River.[28] They traveled on an old military road that went north fourteen miles to the abandoned mission.[29]

The Georgia Battalion was officially organized upon its arrival at Refugio on February 14, 1836. By then, Ticknor's company of the Alabama Greys had been added to the unit. Attached to Ticknor's company was Luis Guerra's artillery company, a remnant of José Antonio Mexía's expedition against Matamoros during the summer of 1832.[30]

On February 7, Fannin learned through Plácido Benavides that Santa Anna was moving to invade Texas and suppress the rebellion at Goliad and San Antonio. Furthermore, the general intended to use Matamoros as a trap to defeat the planned Texas expedition, of which he had knowledge.

Fannin's response to this news bordered on panic. Taking a newly fortified and forewarned Matamoros was out of the question. Houston himself had increasingly begun to doubt the advisability of a campaign against Matamoros.[31] This was particularly so because, if Benavides's information was correct, Santa Anna's plans hinged on such a move.[32] Fannin would be a fool to march into such a trap. The warning caused the colonel to abandon the Matamoros project and begin to remove his headquarters to Goliad.[33]

Three weeks after their arrival at the mission at Refugio, the Georgia Battalion marched to Goliad, some twenty-seven miles distant. Looking like a proper military unit, the Georgia Battalion formed into a column of fours. Snare drums rattled, and their Lone Star flag snapped in the breeze as James Callahan stepped out on the road to Goliad. Marching to a drum "beaten into them" at Velasco, the Georgia boys shared a common identity. They had become "the corps."

Fannin was elected colonel of the Georgia volunteers at Goliad on February 7, 1836, and from February 12 to March 12 acted as commander in chief of the Texan army. Fannin had chosen Goliad as his headquarters because of its defensible position at the presidio of La Bahía and its strategic location near the Texas coast. The old Spanish fortress stood on high, rocky ground overlooking the San Antonio River. Captain Phillip Dimmitt had captured the place during the Cos invasion of 1835,[34] and it was currently commanded by Captain Ira J. Westover. He had a small number of men and several cannons.

It was sleeting when Callahan caught his first sight of the presidio in mid-February. La Bahía was the third and last of a series of mission-fort combinations to bear variations of the same name. The Spanish, perhaps

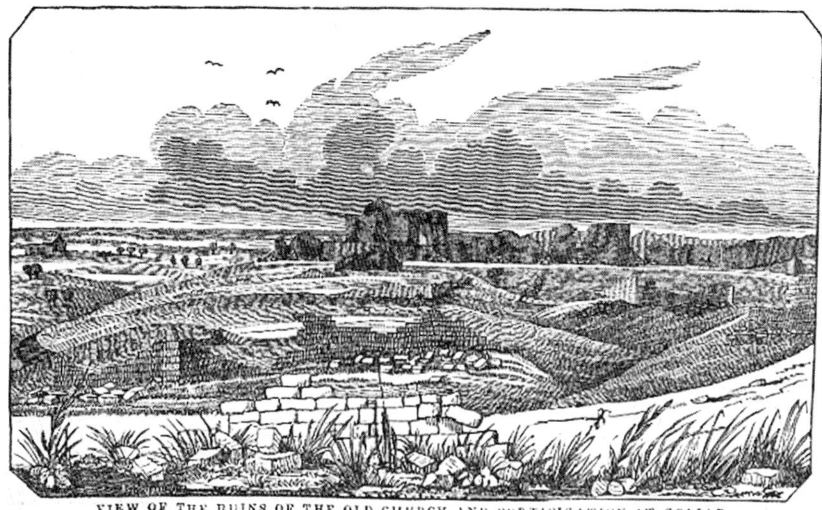

Old La Bahía. *Taken from the larger work* The twelve months volunteer; or, Journal of a private, in the Tennessee regiment of cavalry, in the campaign, in Mexico, 1846–7; *courtesy of Rice University.*

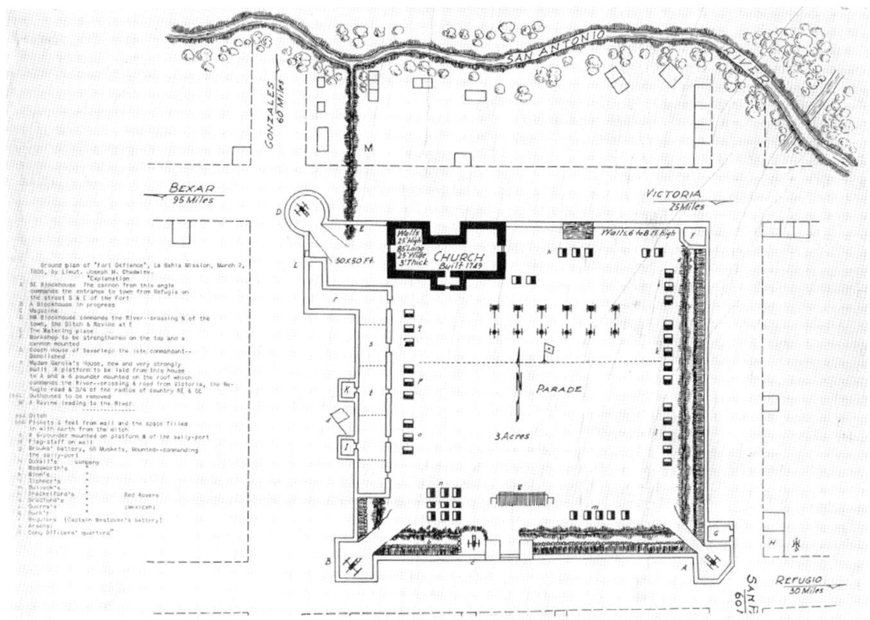

Fort Defiance at Goliad. *Courtesy of Texas State Library and Archives Commission.*

out of habit or for sentimental reasons, continued to call it Presidio La Bahía, although it lay at least thirty miles from the coast. Unlike many of the old Spanish missions in Texas, the site at Goliad was intended from the beginning as not just a mission but also a stronghold.

Constructed on high ground, the presidio was the most imposing structure within eighty miles or more. Its chapel on the north wall featured a tall bell tower that served as an excellent lookout post. Bastions for artillery marked the corners of its eight-foot-high walls, which enclosed an area of about three acres. Inside were barracks and other structures, including blockhouses for storing ammunition and other provisions.

Fannin immediately put the men to work on making the fort more defensible. Callahan's skills as a mechanic were soon much in demand. The stone walls were already three feet thick, but the Georgia soldiers further reinforced them with dirt, additional stone and pilings.

Where required, the walls were repaired. Soil from a ditch excavated around the interior perimeter was used to shore up the walls. Fighting positions, or bastions, for artillery were reinforced and new ones built. Outside the walls, shacks and other structures were burned or pulled down so that they couldn't be used for cover by an attacking force. Importantly, the men built a covered trench to the nearby San Antonio River, thus ensuring that the presidio would have access to water in the event of a siege. Joseph M. Chadwick, Fannin's adjutant, supervised the strengthening of the fort. In all appearances, the garrison newly named Fort Defiance seemed impregnable.[35]

Fannin's regiment now numbered 450 men.[36] By contrast, the Texan command at the Alamo in San Antonio de Bexar consisted of, at most, only 257 volunteers.

At Goliad, the Georgia Battalion was again augmented by Captain Amon B. King's Kentucky volunteers. King's company had reached Nacogdoches on December 8, 1835. They marched on to Washington-on-the-Brazos and reported to General Houston on December 25. As a result of disagreements over the Matamoros Expedition of 1835–36, King and his company were sent to Refugio the first week in January 1836 to garrison the old mission there. They remained until ordered to Goliad. There, on March 1, they were mustered into the Georgia Battalion as "auxiliary volunteers."

3

SANTA ANNA'S CAMPAIGN

Such is Santa Anna, whether good or bad, what his country has made him.
—Fay Robinson, 1847

In February 1836, General Santa Anna led a large invasion force to reclaim Texas.[37] The veteran general and president intended a nationalistic campaign to restore Mexican territorial integrity and political centralism. In his own words, he hoped to subordinate "those turbulent, insolent North Americans" and threatened that if the colony resisted, "all their property will be confiscated."[38]

Santa Anna also threatened to "convert Texas into a desert." The Mexican expeditionary army consisted of more than 6,000 soldiers, including infantry, cavalry and artillery, and was organized into three combined-arms brigades of more than 1,500 men each. Two brigades of light cavalry, one of 400 men and the other with 600, allowed tactical mobility for the cumbersome force.[39]

As a student of Napoleonic warfare, Santa Anna maneuvered his army according to a conventional European military strategy that emphasized speed of march and surprise attack. He accordingly elected to penetrate Texas from the south with two simultaneous flying columns targeting San Antonio and Goliad.[40] More than five hundred miles south of San Antonio, Santa Anna assembled his troops at San Luis Potosí. After resting at Saltillo, the Mexican army started across the desert of Coahuila for San Juan Bautista Mission (Presidio Rio Grande).[41]

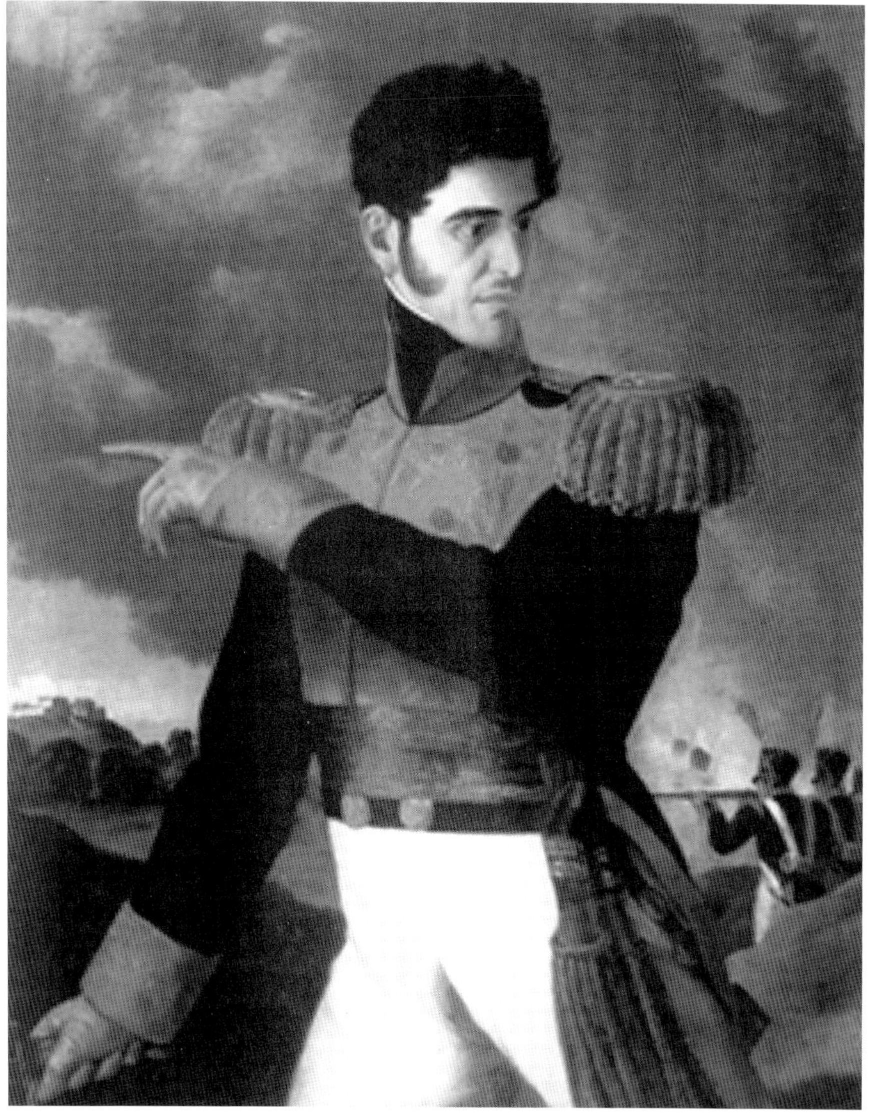

Antonio López de Santa Anna. *Texas State Historical Association.*

Santa Anna collected 1,800 pack mules, thirty-three four-wheeled wagons and two hundred two-wheeled carts for the overland haul from the Rio Grande. The army's only hindrance was a want of forage, especially between the Nueces and the Medina Rivers, where the Texans and the Indians had burned the grass.

The average distance covered by Mexican troops on a day was only about seven leagues, or just under twenty miles. Records indicate that the most common distance marched was about six leagues, or sixteen miles.[42]

Due to limited supplies, Santa Anna's troops advanced in stages. General Joaquín Ramírez y Sesma's Vanguard Brigade arrived in Laredo on December 26 to join forces with General Martín Perfecto de Cos, later moving up to Presidio Rio Grande[43] to join with the rest of Santa Anna's forces. General José de Urrea and his cavalry left Saltillo in another direction, moving down to Matamoros in late January and combining there with the Yucatán battalion of Mayan Indians.[44]

Initially, Urrea's forces consisted of only cavalry units, "choice troops from the interior…armed, everyone, with lance, musket, pistols and sword."[45] Soon, however, his command was strengthened with three hundred infantry at Matamoros. These were, however, poorly trained conscripted Mayan Indians from the Yucatán Activo Battalion at Tampico.[46]

The Texans began to receive reports in mid-January of the advance of Santa Anna's army, though most still considered a winter campaign across the desert by a large army implausible. Nevertheless, Santa Anna's *soldados* made the march, though suffering en route from winter storms and from raids by Comanches on their supplies and stragglers. Finally, on February 16, 1836, Santa Anna, with his Vanguard Brigade, began crossing of the Rio Grande. The invasion of Texas had begun.

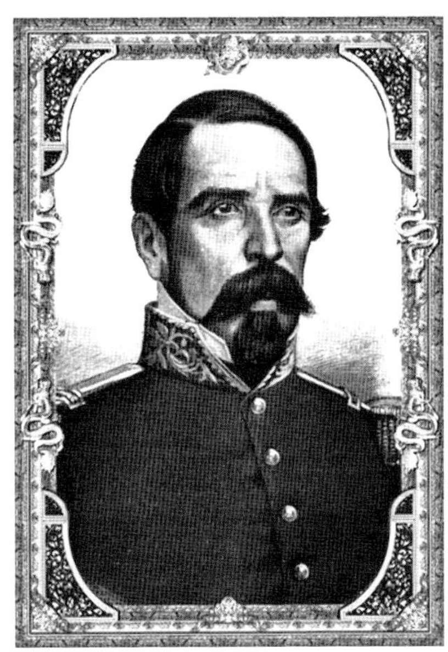

General José de Urrea. *Texas State Historical Association.*

As Santa Anna entered Texas, General Urrea advanced to Matamoros, just as Robert C. Morris had warned Fannin. On February 18, Urrea pushed north into Texas at the head of 650 cavalry and infantry. The general had learned that the Johnson and Grant expedition had continued toward Matamoros against General Houston's personal admonitions. General Urrea was determined to destroy Matamoros Expedition.[47]

Through the first part of February 1836, Santa Anna's army marched north into the face of a freezing rain across the barren Texas thorn scrub plains. It was the time of the "Little Ice Age,"[48] and bitter cold would be a common nuisance for all combatants in the coming battles. Enduring the grueling demands of a four-hundred-league march through inhospitable terrain, the Mexican army received support and comfort from the inhabitants of the province. Despite that, the army had to contend with scarce supplies, Indian attacks, sickness and the harsh climate.

On February 13, a "norther" hit with rain, then freezing rain and finally snow. The Mexican soldiers and followers, many without shoes or adequate clothing, suffered, and some perished. Especially hard hit were the Mayan Indians from the south of Mexico. The adverse conditions debilitated livestock as well, with many oxen and mules dropping along the trek.[49] Comanche warriors continually harassed the soldiers and the camp followers. Like wolves, these raiders sought out stragglers, making slashing jabs, killing all they found and looting their goods.

The Texan troops, under the commands of Grant and Johnson continued their quest toward Matamoros. As co-commanders, with about seventy to one hundred men, they had gone to San Patricio to gather horses for the expedition. There Grant learned that Mexican captain Nicolas Rodríguez and a small company formerly from Fort Lipantitlán were in the area.[50] The Texas commander confronted and overtook them, confiscating their horses and taking the men prisoners. Within a few days, the prisoners had escaped, alerting nearby Mexican forces.

Urrea commanded the army marching north out of Matamoros. Well informed by Mexican locals, he approached San Patricio from the south at the head of his column of cavalry and infantry. While Grant was gone, Urrea led a surprise attack on San Patricio early in the morning on February 27. The Mexicans killed most of Johnson's men, but Johnson narrowly escaped.

Splitting into smaller groups, the Texans searched for mounts and supplies, proceeding all the way to Santa Rosa Ranch, near the site of present-day Raymondville. While busy foraging, Grant and his men were attacked by a contingent of Urrea's cavalry. On March 2, 1836, the Mexicans ambushed Grant's party of twenty men at Agua Dulce Creek, about twenty-five miles south of San Patricio. Grant died in what came to be called the Battle of Agua Dulce.

Plácido Benavides, *alcalde* of Victoria in Grant's command, was among those who escaped. He hurried to Goliad and brought to Fannin the first news of the immediate approach of General Urrea.

Mexico's easy routing of the Matamoros Expedition constituted a major failure on the part of Texas's provisional government, leaving the rebellious Texans virtually paralyzed by inaction and indecision.[51]

On February 25, 1836, Callahan and many of the other Georgians saw a rider galloping toward Fort Defiance. They later learned the horseman carried a message from the Alamo, an urgent plea from Colonel William B. Travis to their Fannin for help:

> *We have removed all our men into the Alamo, where we will make such resistance as is due to our honour, and that of the country, until we can get assistance from you, which we expect you to forward immediately. In this extremity, we hope you will send us all the men you can spare promptly. We have one hundred and forty-six men, who are determined never to retreat. We have but little provisions, but enough to serve us till you and your men arrive. We deem it unnecessary to repeat to a brave officer, who knows his duty, that we call on him for assistance.*[52]

After days of dithering, Fannin ordered his three-hundred-man regiment to march to the Alamo on February 25. They were only ninety miles away. Then the unimaginable happened. Fannin's rescue column traveled less than one mile before turning back. While the desperate men at the Alamo held fast, Fannin quit.

To acting governor James W. Robinson, Fannin reported:

> *Yesterday (Feb. 25) after making all preparations possible, we took up our line of march (about three hundred strong and four pieces of artillery) toward Bexar, to the relief of those brave men now shut up on command of this post. Within two hundred yards of the town (Goliad) one of the wagons broke down, and it was necessary to double teams in order to draw the artillery across the river, each piece having but one yoke of oxen. Not a particle of bread-stuff, with the exception of half a tierce of rice, with us no beef with the exception of a small portion that had been dried, and not a head of cattle, except those used to draw the artillery, the ammunition, etc., and it was impossible to obtain any until we should arrive at Seguin's Rancho, seventy miles from this place. After crossing the river, the troops encamped. This morning while here I received a note from the officers commanding the volunteers, requesting in the name of the officers of this command a Council of War on the subject of the expedition to Bexar, which, of course, was*

> *granted. The council of war consisted of all the commissioned officers of the command, and it was by them unanimously determined, that inasmuch as a proper supply of provisions and means of transportation could not be had, and as it was impossible, with our present means to carry the artillery with us, and as by leaving Fort Defiance without a proper garrison, it might fall into the hands of the enemy, with the provisions, etc., now at Matagorda, Dimmitt's Landing, and Cox's Point and on the way to meet us; and as by report of our spies (sent out by Col. Bowers), we may expect an attack upon this place, it was deemed expedient to return to this post and complete the fortifications, etc., etc., J. W. Fannin.*[53]

In the field, Sergeant Callahan immediately went to work repairing the wagons. That done, the Georgian volunteers spent six hours crossing the waist-deep water of the San Antonio River. By the time they reached the other side, it was dark, and Fannin ordered a stop for the night. A cold front blew into Goliad that evening, leaving the scantily outfitted soldiers "chilled and miserable" in a driving rain on that bald prairie.

On awakening, Fannin discovered that all the oxen had wandered off during the night. It took most of the day for the men to round them up. The colonel also found that his men had neglected to pack food for the journey. After two days of travel, Fannin's men had not even ventured one mile from their fort at La Bahía.

Many of Fannin's men lacked shoes and clothing. Yet the volunteers faced a well-provisioned and trained enemy of superior numbers. Fannin's aide-de-camp, John Sowers Brooks, wrote, "We cannot rationally anticipate any other result to our Quixotic expedition than total defeat."[54]

Accordingly, Fannin decided that it would be better to return to Goliad and continue to bolster the old presidio's defensive works. Safely back in Fort Defiance, Fannin wrote: "I will never give up the ship, while there is a pea in the ditch. If I am whipped it will be well done." By March 1, the fortifications of Fannin's Fort Defiance were nearly complete. "I am pretty well prepared to make battle," Fannin reported to Robinson.[55]

Robinson added to the confusion when he wrote to Fannin, "Use your own discretion to remain where you are or to retreat as you may think best for the safety of the brave Volunteers under your command."[56]

During the siege of the Alamo, newly elected delegates from across Texas met at Washington (now called Washington-on-the-Brazos).[57] On March 2, the delegates declared independence, forming the Republic of Texas.[58]

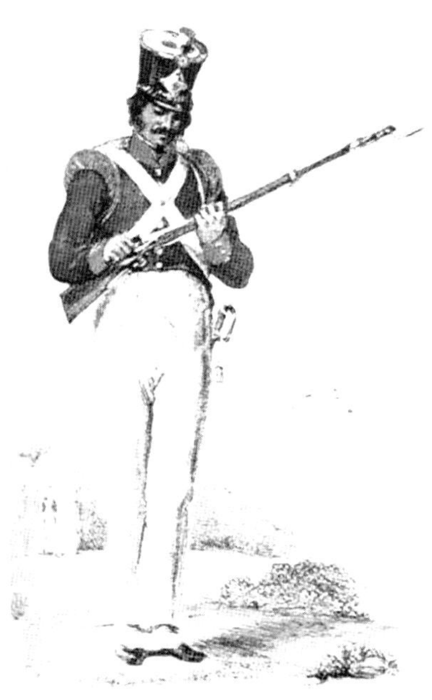

A Mexican soldier. *Painting by Claude Linati, 1835.*

On March 4, the Convention appointed Sam Houston commander in chief of the entire regular, volunteer and militia troops. Houston attempted to take over Fannin's command and issued to him the long-awaited order to retreat, but by then, Fannin had already engaged General Urrea. Two days later, Houston departed for Gonzales[59] to join the main force of the revolutionary army. When he arrived, he found that army consisted of 374 poorly dressed and ill-equipped men. Most had no guns or military experience, and they had only two days' rations. Before Houston could prepare his troops to rush to aid the Alamo defenders, however, word arrived that Santa Anna had defeated them.

Just after 5:00 a.m. on March 6, 1836, Santa Anna's troops charged the Alamo. Twice the Texans repulsed the attacks. Santa Anna called in his reserves and ordered the bugle call of *degüello*, meaning no quarter would be offered.[60] This time, the Mexicans overran the north wall, and Travis fell early in the fighting. David Crockett is reported to have fallen defending the palisade on the south side. Jim Bowie died inside the main structure or the low barracks. All the defenders were killed.

Prevailing at the Alamo proved to be a costly victory for Santa Anna; he lost some six hundred soldiers that day to roughly two hundred rebellious Texans. But the Mexicans had proven that they intended to crush the Texan attempt to wrest Texas from their control. They would offer no quarter, viewing the Texans not as soldiers but a band of pirates. On March 15, news of the fall of the Alamo finally reached the Convention at Washington and, according to one witness, "spread like fire in high grass," causing "complete panic." One delegate had lost a son at the Alamo; another lost a brother. Heartsick and fearful of invasion by enemy troops, yet focused on the task ahead, the men remained for another two days and completed the task of electing ad interim officials. Finally, on March 17,

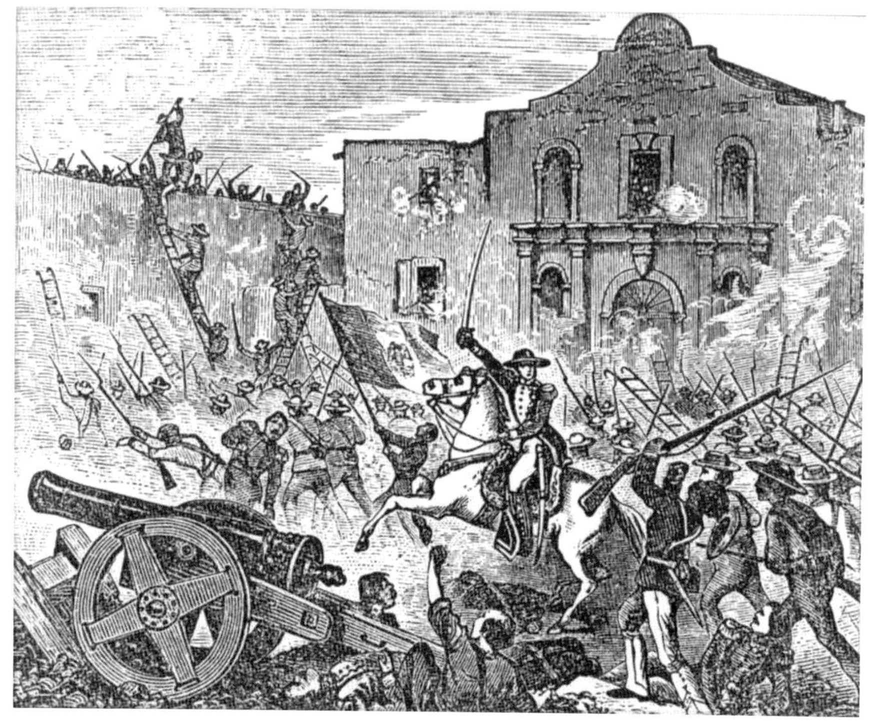

The storming of the Alamo. *Courtesy of National Park Service.*

the delegates, along with the citizens of Washington, fled Santa Anna's advancing troops.[61]

Scouts reported that Santa Anna's troops were heading east toward Gonzales. Unprepared to confront the Mexican army with his poorly trained force, Houston began a series of strategic retreats that later became known as the "Runaway Scrape."

Writing from his field headquarters in Gonzales, Houston informed Fannin of the Alamo's fall. Fannin received the order on the fifteenth.

Head Quarters, Gonzales, March 11, 1836.
Houston to Fannin.
To James W. Fannin,

Sir: upon my arrival here this afternoon, the following intelligence was received through a Mexican, supposed to be friendly, which, however, was contradicted, in some parts, by another who arrived with him. It is, therefore, only given to you as a rumor, though I fear a melancholy portion of it will be found too true. He states that he left Fort San Antonio on Sunday, the 6th inst; that the Alamo (citadel) was attacked on that morning at the dawn of day, by about 2,500 men, and was carried a short time before sunrise with a loss of 520 men, Mexicans, killed and as many wounded. Col. Travis had only 150 effective men, out of his whole force of 187. After the fort was carried, seven men surrendered, and called for Gen. Santa Anna and quarters. They were murdered by his order. Col. Bowie was sick in his bed, and was also murdered. The enemy expect reinforcements of 1,500 men under Gen. Cordiles, and 1,500 reserve to follow them. He also informed us, that Ugartechea has arrived with two millions of dollars, for the payment of the troops, &c. The bodies of the Americans were burnt after the massacre, in alternate layers of wood and bodies. Lieutenant Dickinson, who had a wife and child in the fort, after having fought with desperate courage, tied his child to his back, leaped from the top of a two story building, and both were killed by the fall. I have but little doubt that the Alamo has fallen. Whether the above particulars are all true may be questionable.

Sam Houston.

P.S. The wife of Lieut Dickinson is now in the possession of the officers of Santa Anna. The men, as you will perceive fought gallantly, and in corroberation [sic] *of the truth of the fall of the Alamo, I have ascertained that Col. Travis intended firing signal guns at three different periods of each day, until. succor should arrive. The signal guns have not been fired since Sunday; and a scouting party have just returned, who approached within five or eight miles of the fort, and remained for eight hours. S.H.*

When Fannin shared the message from Houston with his command, Callahan and the other Georgians listened with outrage. Some likely felt shame that their colonel had abandoned his attempt to assist the Alamo garrison. On the other hand, it must have sunk in on them that they well might have died had they succeeded in reaching San Antonio de Béxar. Clearly, fighting for Texas independence would be no lark.

Houston's next dispatch to Fannin was an order, not the transmittal of information:

Sir: You will, as soon as practicable after the receipt of this order, fall back upon Guadalupe Victoria, with your command, and such artillery as can

> *be brought with expedition. The remainder will be sunk in the river. You will take the necessary measures for the defense of Victoria, and forward one-third of your effective men to this point* [Gonzales], *and remain in command until further orders.*[62]

Houston then set forth his concerns about protecting the helpless and the need to not leave anything that could be of aid to the enemy. "Previous to abandoning Goliad, you will take the necessary measures to blow up that fortress; and do so before leaving the vicinity. The immediate advance of the enemy may be confidently expected....Prompt movements are highly important."[63]

With that, Houston ordered the town of Gonzales burned to the ground. Rear guard troops under Captain John Sharpe with two groups working their way from north to south torched the village.[64]

4

BATTLE OF REFUGIO

Infuriated by the tremendous losses they had sustained the day before, the soldiers rushed upon the wounded Texian soldiers and their care-takers and bayoneted them with brutal cruelty.
—Henry Scott's narration

General Urrea and 1,500 centralista soldiers were on the march from Matamoros to Refugio and Goliad. Urrea took the Atascosito Road and marched northeast from the southern tip of Texas. While Santa Anna was stalled at the Alamo, Urrea continued toward Refugio.

On March 7, Lewis Ayers brought Fannin news from Refugio, twenty-five miles south of Goliad. The week before, the *victoriana guardes*, a group of *tejanos* (native Mexican residents) who supported centralism, had ransacked the town. After destroying much property, the *guardes*, under the command of Carlos de la Garza, made camp just outside Refugio. Several pro-independence Anglo families, including Ayers's wife and children, remained in the village. These families worried that if they stayed, they would be captured by the Mexican army. But if they left, they feared Garza's men.

Despite Houston's warning against sending out small parties when the Mexican army under Urrea was so near, Fannin dispatched at least two. The first sortie, led by William C. Francis of Shackelford's company, left on March 10 for Carlos de la Garza's ranch to deal with him. The second party, commanded by Captain Amon B. King, left on March 11 for Refugio.

King led a company of infantry (twenty-eight men) and most of the wagons to evacuate the settlers. The company arrived on the evening of

March 11 and camped for the night at the old mission. Some of the Anglo families had taken refuge there, but others were scattered elsewhere in the vicinity.[65]

The next day, while collecting the scattered families, King chose to punish some local *rancheros* who had been plundering Refugio. Instead, the captain blundered upon one of Urrea's advance cavalry outposts at Esteban López's lower ranch.[66] King managed to gather the scattered families and, pursued by a Mexican force of fifty or sixty men, retreated with the families into the mission. Significantly outnumbered, King sent word to Fannin for help. Meanwhile, the Mexicans made haphazard attacks and milled about while awaiting reinforcements.[67]

When King's men took refuge in the old mission, they prepared fortifications. The Texans cut loopholes in the walls, barricaded all the doors and windows and made preparations for a static defense. Like the Alamo, the abandoned mission lay in ruins. Most of the buildings—including workshops, a granary and living quarters for the padres, the Indians and the mission's few soldiers—had been constructed of driven poles with adobe walls and thatched roofs. Only the church and the blacksmith shop were of stone. The chapel was 100 feet long and 35 feet wide with a tile floor. The ceiling was 20 feet high, with a wooden roof. The stone walls were 3 feet thick. A stockade surrounded the mission and helped protect the soldiers and inhabitants during times of Indian attack. The outer wall of the stockade was 150 feet on a square.[68]

Under cover of darkness, King's messenger rode swiftly for Fort Defiance, reporting the dire state of affairs at Refugio and begging for help. Captain Jack Shackelford reported on the recklessness of King's venture:

> *About midnight, on the 14th, King's express reached Goliad, and Col. Fannin immediately dispatched Col. Ward's Battalion to his relief. This was the beginning of our trouble; and the only act for which I ever blamed Fannin…an unworthy prejudice which has been created in the minds of many, that Fannin wished to forestall Houston in the command of the army, and therefore disobeyed his orders.…He committed an error in separating his forces. Had he not done this, we should have been prepared to fall back on Victoria, as ordered, with a force sufficient to contend with every Mexican we might have encountered. Fannin's great anxiety alone, for the fate of Ward and King, and their little band, delayed our march…not the result of any wish to disobey orders.*[69]

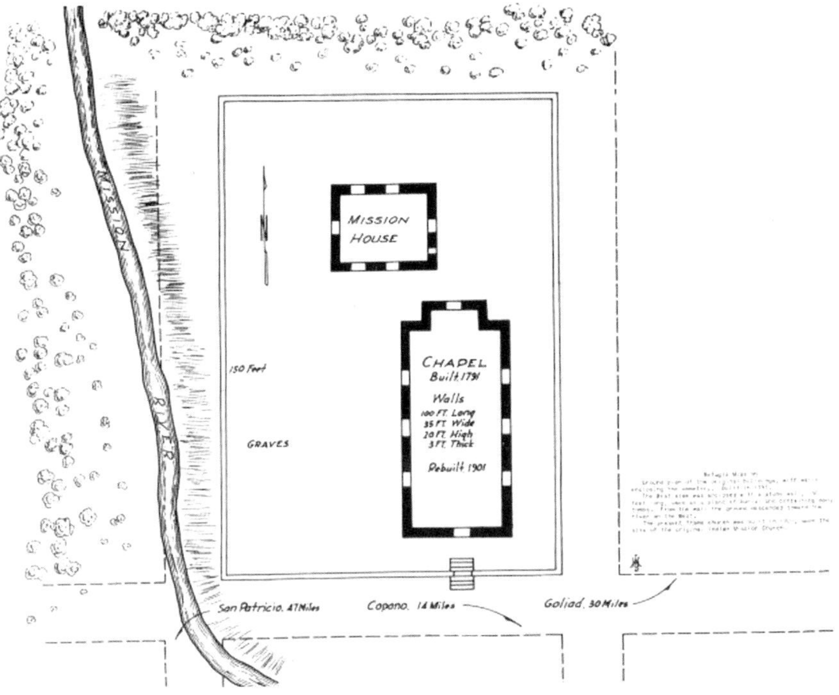

Nuestra Señora del Refugio Mission. *Ground plan of Fort Defiance from March 2, 1836, by Lieutenant Joseph M. Chadwick.*

Fannin received King's plea at 1:00 a.m. on March 13 and ordered Lieutenant Colonel Ward and the Georgia Battalion, along with a portion of Peyton S. Wyatt's company, to King's relief. Ward may have been Fannin's second in command, but like most of the Goliad garrison, he was wholly inexperienced. Fannin subsequently dispatched veterans John Sowers Brooks and Joseph M. Chadwick to ensure Ward's success.[70] But their guides got lost in the dark and their force returned to Goliad.

Ward started his column of 120 men for Refugio several hours before daylight on March 13. The soldiers, on foot, double-timed south down the dark road to Refugio. The prairie was wet, and the going was difficult. Yet the men covered the twenty or so miles in six hours, arriving late that afternoon. Callahan struggled, as did others, with the pace of the march to Refugio. With rifles at port, knapsacks on their back and full combat gear, the Georgia boys gamely puddle jumped their way to war: "We marched at 3 o'clock in the morning, and arrived at the Mission about 2 o'clock of the same day; and as we expected, found Capt. King and his company in the Church and a large company of Mexicans in sight across the river. We succeeded in getting to the Church where we remained till night."[71]

The battalion arrived in Refugio around 2:00 p.m. Sergeant Callahan and the other Georgia boys fought their way through a Mexican cavalry company. When he learned that the Georgia Battalion arrived at Refugio, Urrea sent Captain Rafael Pretalia's cavalry unit, along with Guadalupe de los Santos's local *rancheros*, to hold Ward there until the main Mexican army could arrive. Pretalia had a small party of soldiers and thirty fellow townsmen to advance against and hold the enemy.[72]

Details are scant, but it appears that Ward's formation was much larger than the group of Mexicans that had Captain King's company forted up at the mission. Nothing more than a "single salute from their rifles served to drive off the enemy, who had invested King in his position." The ensuing mayhem caught the besieging Mexicans completely by surprise. Indeed, a fully saddled, panic-stricken horse nearly ran into the church where the huddled families were cooking their evening meals.

Urrea advanced his forces from the Aransas River to Refugio. He commanded 180 infantry and 100 cavalry and had one artillery piece.[73] Colonel Francisco Garay recorded in his diary:

> [March] *13. I marched towards Goliad and was informed enroute that the enemy had dispatched a strong detachment to occupy the port of Cópano and that they would halt at Refugio Mission. I dispatched a picket commanded by Capt. Pretalia and thirty civilians headed by Don Guadalupe de los Santos with instructions for the first group to hold the enemy at the mission until I arrived with my division. I selected 100 mounted men and 180 infantry; and, with our four-pounder, continued the march during the night, leaving the rest of our troops encamped on the Aranzazu Creek.*[74]

Urrea's force was followed by what he described in his diary as "a convoy of children and women who without fail, pillage, destroy and annihilate everything in sight, so that by the time the poor soldier, who happens to remain true to his duty, arrives at camp, can't even find water to drink because of this rabble, like locusts, have left nothing."[75] Greg Dimmick wrote of the sea of mud, where "more than 2,500 Mexican soldiers and 1,500 female camp followers foundered in the muddy fields of what is now Wharton County, Texas.[76]

The general recorded that when he reached the mission, the Texans "opened up a lively fire." The Georgians' hasty shooting proved their undoing.

Ward and King had arrived at Refugio with insufficient ammunition for a daylong encounter.[77] The fight lasted from one to two hours before the Mexicans withdrew. After this initial skirmish, Ward decided to rest his men overnight before returning to Goliad.

Once he arrived at the mission at Refugio, Ward disobeyed Fannin's orders. Rather than collecting the various families and immediately returning to Goliad with King, he marched twenty-five miles during the day, most of the way over a soaked prairie with ankle-deep water; the men of the Georgia Battalion were too fatigued to think of returning the same night.

Ward let the volunteers off the leash on the evening he arrived. He gave Isaac Ticknor permission to mount a quick foray against one of the nearby Mexican camps. What practical purpose the lieutenant colonel intended to achieve is unknown. At any rate, Ticknor led fourteen men beyond the mission's walls toward the Mexican positions. He and his party, as related by Joseph W. Andrews, "crept up slyly upon the enemy; and firing on them & keeping it up for a few rounds, retired in safety to the mission without the loss of a man or having one wounded." Regardless of the raid's purpose, its execution was a success.[78]

After posting sentinels, the men were permitted to "sleep on their arms." Certainly, Ward's men were tired, and unquestionably it would have taken time to get the families ready for the march. But the need to get to safety was urgent. Returning the wagons and oxen to Goliad was even more critical than resting, and time was running out. Orders were given to commence the return march to Goliad at daybreak.

Ward and King wasted time arguing. Their clash was another example of the discord and petty rivalry typical of the Texas army. Without so much as a nod to chain of command, King declared that he was familiar with the area and knew the military situation best. He then asserted that Ward should give up command of his men to him. Of course, Ward outranked King and refused. Meanwhile, Urrea's army continued to close in on Refugio.[79]

Sergeant Callahan was incredulous at the bickering of the two senior officers. As a consequence, these combined forces did not immediately depart for Goliad. Neither Lieutenant Colonel Ward nor Captain King had planned on remaining in Refugio. They were lightly armed and had a short supply of provisions and only thirty-two rounds of ammunition per man. By morning on March 14, Ward and King had still not agreed how to join or lead their forces. A withdrawal to Goliad was not the priority.

Taking his own company and eighteen of Wyatt's men, King sallied forth on his own punitive expedition to López's lower ranch while Ward sent Major Warren J. Mitchell to reconnoiter the enemy and waited at the mission for their return. After torching some deserted ranches, the small group began to take fire while refilling a pair of barrels from the Mission River that ran nearby. Suddenly, Urrea's army appeared. Mitchell saw the Mexicans, and he and his men raced back to the mission, just in time for the assault by Urrea's main body of troops.[80]

On that morning of March 14, Urrea's army was approaching from the south. Any prospect of Ward returning to Goliad with the families or even his battalion was now gone. It appeared the Georgia Battalion was now limited to the static defense of the Mission Refugio and of the people in it.

The Georgia boys fortified all the entrances to the church with benches, pews or anything available to provide protection. The mission was an old stone ruin vulnerable to assault from three sides, and on the fourth side, there was a wall around an old cemetery. Captain Bullock's Company of thirty-five men (Bullock was not there) was deployed in the cemetery, and the remainder of the battalion occupied the ruins of the mission. The Mexicans advanced on the mission, but the accurate fire of the battalion drove them back.

At eight o'clock in the morning, the Mexicans advanced briskly to assault from all points. When they reached musket-shot distance, the attackers fired on the unenclosed sides of the building. On the side of the churchyard, the defenders discovered the *soldados* marching slowly and silently in close column, intending to draw up unperceived while most of the defenders were trying to repel the attack from the other sides.

Callahan watched with awe as the Mexican troops deployed onto the battlefield. It was as he had always imagined Napoleon's army, bright-red tunics of the cavalry topped with gleaming silver helmets. Even the very basic infantrymen were dressed in white uniforms and displayed excellent discipline while executing military maneuvers.

Colonel Francisco Garay reported:

> *I immediately ordered a column of infantry to make the charge, protected by the fire of our cannon which had been moved forward sufficiently to destroy the door of the church. With our cavalry covering our flanks, our advance was so successful that the infantry arrived within ten paces of the cemetery without a single man being wounded. The enemy, coming out of its lethargy, opened up a lively fire upon our men. The troops, being mostly recruits from Yucatán, stopped spellbound the moment their first impetus was spent, and all efforts to force them to advance were unavailing, for the*

greater part of their native officers who a moment before had been so eager disappeared at the critical moment. These men were, as a rule, unable to understand Spanish, except in a few cases, and the other officers, not being able to speak their language, were handicapped in giving the commands. The infantry took refuge in a house and corral situated about fifteen paces from the church. I ordered a part of the cavalry to dismount in order to encourage the former by their example. Not succeeding in making them advance, and the dismounted cavalry being insufficient to take the position of the enemy, the moments were becoming precious, for at that very moment another party, coming from Cópano, was threatening my rear guard. I, therefore, ordered a retreat.[81]

The Mexican soldiers kept firing as they crossed the river and marched to within one hundred feet of the mission. At that point, Lieutenant Colonel Ward ordered his men to open fire, which drove the Mexicans back and left the ground corrupted with dead and wounded.[82]

The Mexicans made four valiant charges with both cavalry and infantry that day. Callahan and his comrades were awed by the discipline and formal majesty of the Mexican soldiers.

Callahan killed his first man during this battle. Without thinking, he had been firing at the masses of Mexican soldiers. Suddenly, he saw one of the men—a boy actually—stop and grab the bloody stain spreading across his chest. The soldier collapsed to the ground. It was all in slow motion. Callahan watched in fascinated horror as the youth's legs pounded the soil, as if running away, even as he lay dying on the ground. Callahan stood transfixed, held in thrall by the death throes of his enemy. Now, he knew what it was to kill a man.

Attacking in columns, the Mexican soldiers maintained their ranks as row after row was cut down by the grapeshot and volley fire of the Georgia Battalion.

They came up bravely for a while, received our rifle balls, fell, and were carried off, and others took their place. But after a while we could see that it was with great difficulty the officers could whip up their soldiers with their swords to make a charge. This continued until near evening, when they retired a short distance, but not out of sight. We then started an express to Col. Fannin, to let him know we were nearly out of ammunition—having only taken thirty-six rounds from Goliad.[83]

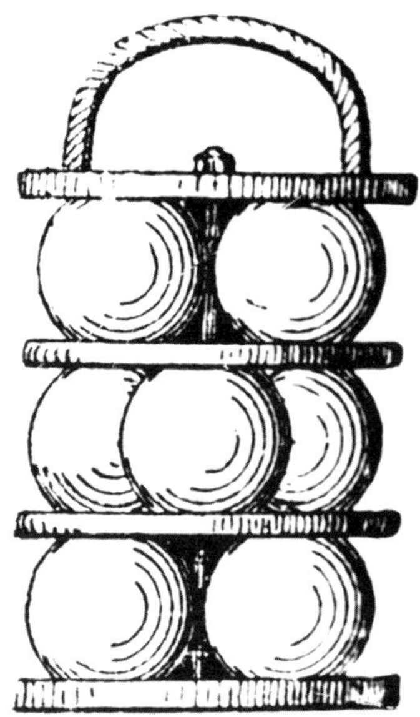

Grape shot. *http://etc.usf.edu/clipart/70200/70226/70226_grapeshot.htm.*

Ward had ordered his men not to hazard an ineffectual shot, telling them to reserve their fire until sure of their aim, and he was obeyed to the letter. At the first discharge of rifles from the building, the advancing line of Mexicans bit the dust. This produced confusion in the Mexican ranks, and one or two parties retreated. But others recovered and made a rush towards the building.

A second discharge, no less fatal than the first, cut down the foremost ranks and put the survivors to flight. Meanwhile, the contest had begun on the side of the churchyard. The Mexican column had pressed forward as soon as the firing commenced on the other quarters; at less than one hundred yards, they received the fire of the Georgia Battalion, until then concealed behind the wall. Several of the front ranks fell, almost as if one body—as many, perhaps, from the panic as from the bullets. The remaining ranks fell back a few yards, but a farther retreat was stopped by the efforts of a few brave officers.

The column now deployed, as well as detachments from the two wings, advanced to attack the yard in flank, while the center once more moved forward over the bloody mud to the attack in front.

Callahan and the other Georgians stood undaunted, pouring quick and deadly volleys on the front, regardless of the threatened attack on their flank. Having then driven the first attackers beyond the reach of their muskets, they were at full leisure to attend to the attack on that quarter, and the flankers, now falling rapidly from their oblique fire and unrestrained by the presence of any superior officer, fled like frightened deer beyond the reach of danger. Still, every attempt to reach it proved ineffectual.[84]

About ten o'clock that morning, a party of fifteen Texans was sent to the Mission River, about two hundred yards off, with oxen and cart to bring two barrels of water into the fort. The men had just filled the water barrels and were leaving the river when they were fired on from an open prairie on the other side.

Though they had water, the Georgia volunteers had run out of something more precious at the moment—ammunition. With the supply exhausted, Ward faced either retreat or surrender.

Lieutenant Colonel Ward dispatched two messengers, Corporal James B. Murphy of Milledgeville and J.B. Rodgers from Wadsworth's Company, to Fannin with a request for more ammunition and more men. But the messengers were quickly captured by the Mexicans.

A message finally came through from Fannin, brought by Edward Perry, ordering Ward to abandon the church, blow up the fortifications and retreat to Victoria. There, Fannin would join him.[85]

Sometime during the afternoon, the Mexicans brought up another small cannon. The Georgia volunteers feared that the attackers would load the gun with "hot shot" to start the roof of the church blazing. To counter this threat, the order went out to concentrate fire on the *soldados* tending the cannon. From the church's belfry, the Georgia sharpshooters shot and killed the Mexican gunners.

The Texans then stormed the Mexican lines to bring back the cannon. Out they went over heaps of dead Mexicans while their comrades in the belfry were dropping more Mexicans thick and fast around the field piece. Taking it without losing a single man, they rolled it into the church as a yell went up that seemed to shake the rafters of the sanctuary.[86]

By now, Callahan had learned what it sounds like when a man gets shot—a sharp whack as if someone had slapped a horse's rump. He also had become acutely aware of the other expressions of combat: the discharge of numerous rifles and cannons at the same time, the smell of gunpowder, the awful sound of wounded men and boys squealing like stuck pigs. Callahan would never forget a wounded man's high, quavering scream like an Italian opera singer. It was as if Callahan's senses had suddenly come alive as men died before his eyes. The adrenaline coursing through his blood gave him almost superhuman abilities. In this fiery furnace of individual combat, Callahan had never felt so alive. He had found himself.

In the moment, Callahan became aware of the Mexican artillery hammering the thick stone walls of the old mission. He saw round shot as it plummeted through the roof and bounced around inside. The Texan firing positions were constantly raked with grapeshot, chain shot and canister shot—all lethal to any Georgia boy caught in their sweep.

Suddenly aware of his circumstances, Callahan took stock of his situation. He was safely sheltered by the mission's wall. He had his rifle, cartridge box, bayonet, pistol and knife. His canteen and knapsack were lost. He had only a few rounds left.

The members of the Georgia Battalion, having resisted this attack so gallantly and successfully and with such terrible effects to the enemy, flattered themselves that they would remain unmolested for the remainder of the day. But they were mistaken. The pride of the Mexican officers, many of whom had long been in service, was obviously wounded by the result of the failed assault. Given the great inequality in numbers, they took it as a disgrace to the Mexican arms.[87]

The Mexican loss in the first attack had been devastating, yet it was followed up in two hours by a second attack. Still later, Urrea ordered a third attempt to dislodge the hundred volunteers from their mission fortress. No matter the general's determination to prevail against the rebellious Anglos, each assault was less vigorous than the previous, and none found success. The only satisfaction Urrea could take was that his casualty rate decreased with each charge.[88]

The Mexicans, for a number of hours, had pounded the mission chapel with artillery fire. Seventeen cannonballs had penetrated the roof, but the old mission walls were too stout to be battered down. In the first attack on the mission, the Texans had not lost a single man; in the second charge, Thomas Weeks, a lad from Mississippi, took a mortal wound to the chest. In the third charge, there was no harm done to the defenders, though Ward was slightly grazed on the head by a musket ball. This Mexican effort continued until nightfall, when the enemy withdrew. To keep the besieged mission lighted, Urrea's troops placed fires around the structure about one hundred yards apart and four hundred yards from the mission.

As more of Urrea's troops arrived, the fighting with Ward's men continued. Mexican bugles continued to sound throughout the day and into the night of March 14. The Georgia Battalion repelled four assaults, killing eighty to one hundred Mexican troops and wounding fifty.

Following his raid on Lopez's lower ranch, Captain King had led his company back toward Refugio earlier that day. When he and his men heard gunfire from the direction of the town, they knew that Ward was under attack. What they did not know was just how close to the Mexican army they had ridden. Less than a mile from the mission, they stumbled into the rear of Urrea's command.

With flight the only option, the captain and his men raced for a wooded area near the Mission River, not half a mile distant. Reacting quickly, Mexican cavalry gave chase but were unable to catch the volunteers before

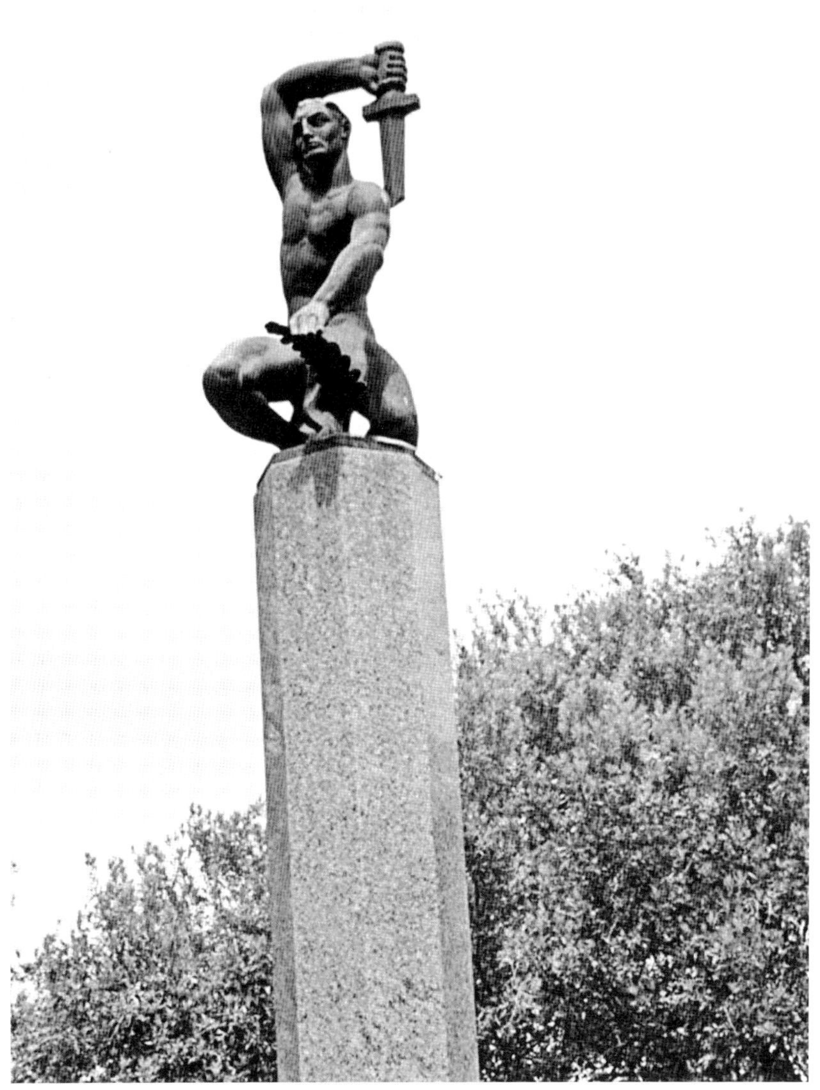

King Monument, Refugio. *Texas State Historical Marker No. 152; sculpture by Raoul Josset.*

they reached the woods. Under cover of the trees, the rest of the volunteers hastily went to ground, took up defensive positions and prepared for the Mexican attack. It came soon enough.

Colonel Gabriel Núñez's cavalry and Colonel Francisco Garay's infantry pressed the assault. King and his small company put up a plucky fight that lasted from late morning until night. During the engagement, a musket ball shattered one of King's arms. One of his men was killed, and four were wounded. After months of wishing for a real fight, King and his men were fighting for their lives.[89]

Ward's Georgia Battalion—itself under siege—heard the shots as King and his men were taken under fire. A hurried relief force was organized, and the would-be rescuers sallied forth from the mission. Almost immediately, the main body of Urrea's formation intercepted them while a unit of cavalry maneuvered to cut them off from the safety of the mission. With nearly one thousand troops between them and King and their escape route back to the mission in jeopardy, they recognized the rescue attempt was foolhardy. Accordingly, Ward ordered them back to the mission. King and his men were on their own.[90]

Because the day's fighting had nearly exhausted their supplies of gunpowder, King ordered his men to escape that night by swimming across the Mission River. What powder they did still have was ruined in the crossing. They succeeded in making it across the river, but local Mexicans reported the Texans' location to Urrea. King and thirty-two men soon surrendered to Carlos de la Garza's *rancheros*.

The men were tied two by two with a single rope and marched approximately eight miles back to Refugio. Lashed by the vengeful *rancheros*, King's men were forced to march across prickly pear cactus with their bare feet when they were returned as prisoners of war to the Refugio Mission.[91] Six hours after, King and his men were executed on orders from Urrea. [92]

With no cavalry at his disposal, Fannin was virtually blind. Worse, the captured Texan messages had informed Urrea of Fannin's situation, strength and intentions. So far, the Mexicans had suffered more casualties, but they clearly had the strategic advantage.

Ward waited in suspense that night to hear from Fannin, to whom he had sent for reinforcement. When he finally did get news, it was not good. Colonel Garay, commander of the Mexican infantry, sent captured courier Edward Perry, an Irish colonist, with a message for the besieged Georgians. Perry had been carrying Fannin's reply to Ward when he was caught. Garay, presumably to make certain that the volunteers knew that the Mexicans were now aware of Fannin's plans, forwarded the message to Ward. In the dispatch Fannin related that he had orders from General Houston directing him to destroy the fortifications at Goliad and retreat to Victoria. Ward knew that he could expect no help from Fannin.[93]

The Irishman told Ward that he had been instructed by Urrea to say that he would be reinforced the next day with heavy artillery and would batter down the mission. If Ward did not surrender, Perry related, he and his command would be shown no quarter. Ward dismissed the Irishman, telling him to say to Urrea that he would not surrender and that the Georgia Battalion would sell their lives dearly.

Despite his bravado, Ward did not want to continue to fight against impossible odds. The colonel decided after a consultation with his officers to escape into the night.

The men prepared to leave, but there was no water for the few wounded men whom they were going to leave behind. In the dark, a sortie was launched to a spring located within the Mexican lines. They ambushed several *soldados* guarding the rivulet and killed four of them while several others fled into the night. Water gourds were filled and taken to the wounded, who were wrapped in blankets taken from slain Mexicans.

Incredibly, another Georgia man by the name of Samuel Woods, believing that he was being awakened for guard duty, refused to get up. He was left to his fate. There was in this mission at the time of retreat six to eight women and five or six children. Ward made a heartbreaking decision to leave the women, children and wounded men behind in the mission. Ward would not allow them to be awakened for fear that they would start screaming. From these women, it was afterward ascertained that the wounded and sleepy Mr. Woods were put to death. Having done as much as they could for their wounded comrades, Ward and his men departed "with tears and sobs" and slipped away from the mission into what had become a rainy night.[94]

Quietly and in the dark, the men of the Georgia Battalion stealthily made their way out of the old chapel. Callahan and the other men climbed out a window and disappeared into the night. No voices called after them. Amazingly, the Mexicans surrounding the mission did not detect the escaping Anglos.

At dawn on March 15, when Urrea's forces stormed the mission, the lack of return fire told them the Texans had fled. They found four of Ward's wounded and caregivers who had chosen to remain. Also in the ruins were the sheltered families of the local colonists.

Colonel Urrea later wrote in his diary:

> *March 15. This day at dawn, as I approached the church, I noticed the absence of the enemy and ordered the place to be occupied. Six wounded*

> *men, four others, some colonist families and several Mexicans who had been commandeered were found. Having reinforced the detachments that, I had* [collected] *on the road to Goliad and El Cópano, I ordered all the available cavalry to pursue the enemy.*[95]

In his account of the event, Henry Scott wrote, "Infuriated by the tremendous losses they had sustained the day before, the soldiers rushed upon the wounded Texan soldiers and their care-takers and bayoneted them with brutal cruelty."[96]

The Georgia boys wandered all night and, in the course of their roaming, encountered but successfully evaded Mexican troops three times. About an hour before daybreak on March 15, they found a bridge across Melon Creek and, for the first time, ascertained where they were. At this bridge, they could tell that the enemy had crossed in pursuit of them. They then had to change their direction and, instead of making for Copano, struck across the prairie, hoping to reach Victoria.[97]

The Texans made slow progress but did so without interruption. By the third day, March 17, the men had begun to suffer greatly for the want of water. David Holt and seven men were dispatched to find water, but they got lost and never rejoined the battalion. Eventually, they all escaped to Texas settlements to the east.[98]

On the fourth night, the Georgians encamped on the San Antonio River, below Fagan's Ranch, some twenty or more miles above Copano.[99]

During this time, Fannin led his forces out of Fort Defiance at Goliad, bound for Victoria to rendezvous with Ward. The Texans marched for only a short distance before becoming engaged in the Battle of Coleto on March 19 and 20.[100]

On March 19, the fifth day since they had escaped the mission at Refugio, Callahan and the Georgia Battalion heard the gunfire at the Coleto Creek, roughly ten miles away. After losing valuable time trying to join Fannin at Victoria, the Georgia Battalion returned to the Guadalupe River that night.

Urrea, knowing that Fannin expected reinforcements and that Ward planned to rejoin his commander at Victoria, already had dispatched the *rancheros* of Carlos de la Garza and others who knew the land well to prevent Ward and his men from reaching Fannin.

On the night of the sixth day, Ward's command again stayed on the Guadalupe River. Sam Mays, Joseph Wilson and Joseph Tatum went on to Victoria and were captured.

The remnants of the Georgia Battalion were hungry, dispirited, footsore and without ammunition. A number of them deserted and escaped. The Georgia boys lay hidden in the marshy river bottoms until night.

At 10:00 p.m. on March 21, Ward roused his remaining men and sought to march by night to Dimitt's Landing on Lavaca Bay. General Urrea, however, controlled that area as well.

The morning of March 22 found the starving Georgia troops searching for food. The ragged band halted within two miles of its destination to slaughter a "beeve" and reconnoiter. ("Beeve" is an old Texas word for beef.) While some of the men butchered the bovine, others in the command shouted that the Mexicans were coming. Ward sent two men to reconnoiter. Both were quickly captured. The two prisoners called out to the Texans and told them that the Mexicans had them outnumbered. At the urging of their captors, the prisoners asked that Ward talk with General Urrea regarding terms of surrender.

Accordingly, accompanied by Major Mitchell and Captain Ticknor, Ward met with General Urrea. The general told them that if the battalion would surrender as prisoners of war, the men would be marched to Copano and from there shipped to New Orleans or be retained as prisoners of war and be exchanged.[101]

On returning to the camp of the Texans, Ward advised his men of the proposition. Undaunted, Ward told them he opposed surrender. He was emphatic that resistance was better than surrender. If they gave up, he feared they would be executed. The colonel put the matter to a vote, and the majority of his men favored surrender. Accepting their decision, Ward declared: "If you are destroyed, do not blame me."[102]

Again accompanied by Major Mitchell and Captain Ticknor, Ward returned to parlay with Urrea, and the terms of capitulation were quickly agreed on.

Placed under a strong guard, the men were marched in line and ordered to turn their arms over to the Mexican officers. At the time of the surrender, Ward had about 83 of the approximately 119 men he had with him when he left the mission at Refugio.[103]

Somehow, the Mexicans learned that Sergeant Callahan was a mechanic and pulled him from the line of prisoners. His valuable skills were needed by the Mexican army. General Urrea had left Colonel Telesforo Alavez in charge of Victoria and the prisoners. Señora Francita Alavez, "Angel of Goliad," intervened with her husband in their behalf to make sure the captive laborers' lives would be spared.[104]

On March 24, at the village of Victoria, the following men were selected to build boats to ferry the Mexican men and materiel across the Guadalupe River: Callahan; Tom Smith and John C.P. Kennimoreof Columbus, Georgia; Pierce Hammock and William Cubelo Wilkinson of Macon, Georgia; James B.F. Mordicai of Savannah, Georgia; James Neely; Thomas Stewart; and others.

Under the supervision of Lieutenant Colonel Juan José Holzinger, the laborers were immediately put to work constructing the boats. All later escaped, including Callahan. Eight other men had been separated from Ward's forces and stayed in the swamp. They were eventually picked up by Houston's scouts and fought in the Battle of San Jacinto.

5
BATTLE OF COLETO

We will march at the dawn of day tomorrow with 320 men and 4 pieces of artillery—2 sixes and 2 fours. We have no provisions scarcely, and many of us are naked and entirely destitute of shoes. But something must be done to relieve our country.

—John Sowers Brooks

Callahan's agonizing experience at Refugio and Victoria unfolded at the same time that Fannin was engaged in a desperate battle on the plains at Goliad. Callahan, at that time, was close enough to hear the Coleto gunfire. The Battle of Coleto occurred near Coleto Creek in Goliad County on March 19–20, 1836.

Fannin learned of King and Ward's defeat in the Battle of Refugio from Hugh McDonald Frazer on March 17. The colonel told his command that they would evacuate Fort Defiance the following day.[105]

Mexican scouts were already encamped within three miles of Goliad, awaiting General Urrea's arrival. Anticipating an immediate attack by Urrea, Fannin stayed put. But with characteristic indecision, Fannin changed his mind and ordered the cannon buried before he abandoned La Bahía. Then he instructed the men to dig up the guns. The colonel's command thus occupied, the oxen needed for hauling the regimental supply wagons and artillery went without feed or water throughout the day.

As instructed by General Houston, Fannin destroyed everything in and about the Fort Defiance that he could not take with him. Anything that would burn was torched. The grain and food they could not haul away in

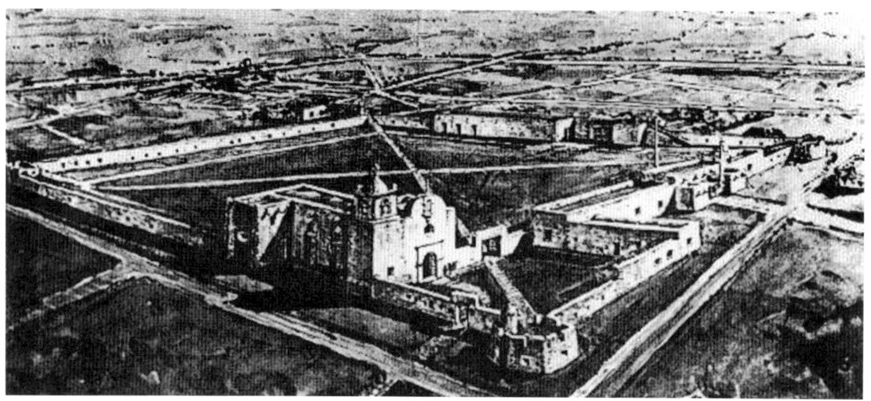

Mission La Bahia Perspective. *Celtic Cowboy Company, http://celticowboy.com/RvTx6a.htm.*

the carts were dumped in the chapel and set on fire. Walls of the fortification were torn down, and all houses outside the walls were burned or otherwise destroyed. Nine cannons and several cartloads of ammunition, baggage and supplies were taken along as the Texans left their stronghold.

A heavy fog lay over the land as both the Texan and Mexican camps went about their morning routines that March 19. But Fannin and his men were off to a slow start, not finishing breakfast until nearly 10:00 a.m. They had to load the carts with the cannons, artillery and soldiers' baggage. Still more time was consumed while they hitched up the oxen. Other men spiked the guns they would leave behind. Despite all those time-consuming preparations, they forgot to load food.

Fannin and around three hundred men finally took up the road to Victoria. With nine cannons, an ammunition cart and at least two baggage carts, they trundled through the lingering fog, the billowy clouds cloaking their departure from the Mexicans. Jack Shackelford's Red Rovers led the march, and Burr Duval's Kentucky Mustangs provided the rear guard.[106] With the exception of Colonel Albert Clinton Horton's Company, all the men were afoot.

Setting out across the prairie, the Texans quickly discovered that the ox teams were weak and easily tired. That necessitated frequent rest stops, an expenditure of time Fannin's command could ill afford.

Almost immediately, the Texans had to ford the San Antonio River at a point flanked by high banks. It would not be easy getting the heavily loaded carts from one side to the other. Men stood in waist-high water and slid in mud as they manhandled the carts down and up the steep slopes. Some of the carts had to be unloaded and then reloaded. More time was lost.

The men now noticed that the carts and their teams were not up to the task of moving everything that had been loaded. Soon the heaviest, bulkiest and least necessary items had to be jettisoned.

As Herman Ehrenberg recounted:

> *The way was strewn with objects of all kinds and here and there a wagon that was left standing or knocked to pieces. The rest of the baggage remained standing a mile from Goliad on the romantic banks of the San Antonio or was dropped in haste into the clear water to the river. Chests filled with muskets, provisions or the belongings of the soldiers disappeared in the waves.*[107]

Fannin was well aware of the risk of this march to Victoria, which had begun by being sloppy, disjointed and incremental. He knew that the countryside was filled with Mexican troops and that many of them were cavalry. His column was moving, at best, about two miles an hour. Victoria lay almost thirty miles northeast of Goliad. Fannin realized he had more than fifteen hours of travel in front of him. He also had to know that, moving as slowly as he was, an engagement with Urrea's army was inevitable.

Two couriers, David Kent and Benjamin Highsmith, arrived at Fannin's headquarters at Goliad on March 13. They delivered a communique from General Houston that ordered Fannin to forward one-third of his men to join the army's main body and then fall back to Victoria. "Previous to abandoning Goliad, you will take the necessary measures to blow up the fortress," Houston wrote. Fannin's reply said a lot in a few words: "Tell him I will not give up Fort Defiance." Fannin's decisions to this point may have been late, ill considered, unpopular or even plain stupid, but his misjudgment hadn't necessarily doomed his men. His next decision, however, did. Shortly after crossing Manahuilla Creek, he stopped the column in the middle of the grassy prairie so that the men and animals could eat and relax.[108]

Behind the column, as well as ahead and to its left, Mexican cavalry appeared. The Texans sounded an alarm, but the Mexican horsemen quickly encircled Fannin's men. Colonel Albert Horton's Mobile Greys had worn out their horses in a series of skirmishes with Urrea's scouts throughout the day.[109] Finding the remainder of Fannin's army surrounded by hostile forces, Horton and his patrol fled—an action that saved his life but haunted his later political career.

Fannin's troops quickly unlimbered the six-pounder cannon. The Texans managed to fire three rounds at the Mexicans, but the shots fell short.

The Texas troops should not have been surprised. Colonel Horton had left four of his men in the rear of the Texans' line of retreat to keep a lookout for the Mexican army. Instead, the four dismounted to rest and fell asleep. Consequently, the enemy was on them before they knew it. Hastily mounting their horses, they wildly fled for their lives, passing about one hundred yards on the right of the Texas army. The panicked lookouts did not look back on their dismounted colleagues, but they probably heard the shouted curses as they galloped by hoping to save their own lives.[110]

Caught in a valley some six feet below its surroundings, Fannin tried to reach the more defensible higher ground about four to five hundred yards distant. More calamity reared its head when the Texans' ammunition cart broke down. Fannin called a council to determine the feasibility of taking what ammunition they could and reaching the timber. Urrea, seeing his advantage, attacked.

Observing the threat, Fannin formed his men into a Napoleonic-style moving square. In this defensive formation, Fannin's men continued toward the timber of Coleto Creek, which flowed less than two miles away. About 1:30 p.m., the Mexican commander ordered his cavalry to block Fannin's advance toward the protective trees.

The hollow square was three ranks deep, each man having three to four muskets and many having bayonets, rifles and pistols. From that position on the open prairie, Fannin and his men fought for two days.[111]

General Urrea took time to plan a professional, coordinated attack. He assigned Colonel Juan Morales to attack the north side of the hollow square and ordered Colonel Mariano Salas to attack the front, or west side. Urrea himself took the south edge of the square and directed Colonel Gabriel Núñez to lead his cavalry against the Texans' rear.

The fighting began in earnest. More than one thousand Mexican soldiers had Fannin's three hundred men pinned down.[112]

The Mexican cavalry led the initial charge. Urrea's horsemen spurred their mounts into a gallop as a battle cry went up from the Mexican soldiers. The men waiting in the hollow square felt the ground shudder under the pounding of the animals' hooves, but they held their fire. They knew that musket fire at a distance created a lot of smoke and noise but had little effect on the enemy.[113]

Outnumbered as they were, the volunteers had to make every shot count. Fannin shouted at the men to hold back.[114]

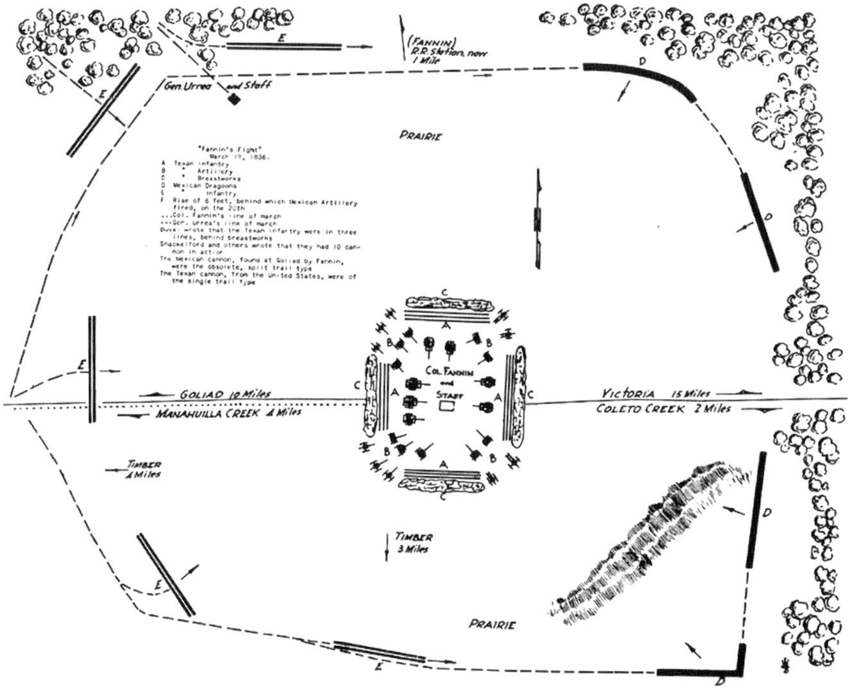

Fannin's hollow square defense. *Texas State Library and Archives Commission.*

When the Mexican cavalry closed to well within one hundred yards, Fannin gave the order to fire, and the corners and sides of his hollow square exploded in gunfire. The combined effects of the rifle and musket rounds and of the artillery grapeshot tore into the Mexicans. Many of the cavalrymen were shot out of their saddles. The bloodied limbs of man and beast alike tumbled through the bedlam.

Fannin's inexperienced soldiers fought like lions. Surrounded on the prairie, without food and water, the Texans made a heroic defense until the full weight of all their disorder fell on them.

The Texas position became critical during the night because of the lack of water. Their inability to light fires made treating the wounded impossible. The situation was made even more unbearable by yet another cold and rainy weather front. The cries of the wounded demoralized everyone. The lack of water, which was required to cool and clean the cannons during fire, also guaranteed that the artillery would be ineffective the next day, especially considering that the artillerists had sustained a high number of

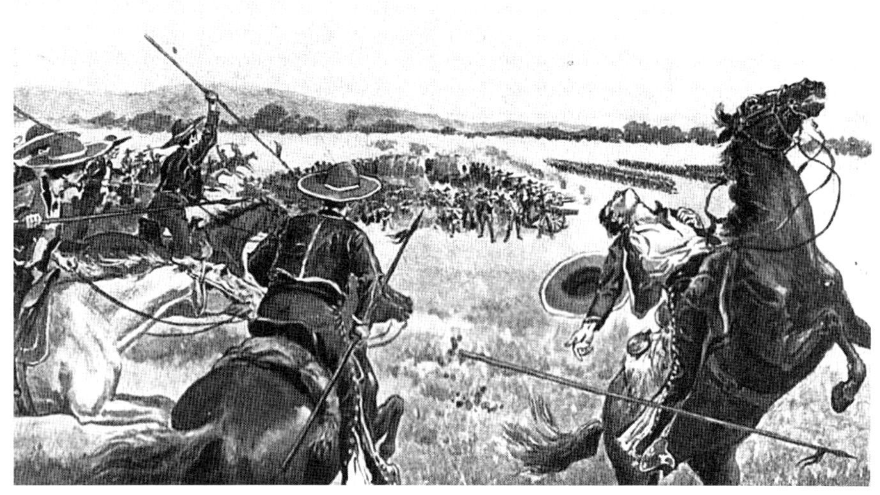

The Mexicans Attempted Two More Charges. Artwork in With Crockett and Bowie; or, Fighting for the Lone-Star Flag: A Tale of Texas *by Kirk Munroe and Victor Semon Pérard (New York: C. Scribner's Sons, 1898).*

casualties. Furthermore, ammunition ran low. Even so, the Battle of Coleto lasted until after sunset that day. Fannin's men had made effective use of their bayonets, multiple rifles and muskets and nine cannons. The defensive square remained unbroken, but Fannin realized his position was hopeless. It was time to negotiate.

The Texans suffered 10 deaths and 60 or more wounded. Urrea's forces lost more, perhaps some 50 killed and 140 wounded. Reports vary widely.

Captain Benjamin Holland and perhaps one or two others rode out from the hollow square to meet a Mexican delegation to discuss surrender. The parties met roughly halfway between the two formations. The meeting, by all accounts, was short. Colonel Morales quickly returned to the Mexican side with the message that the volunteers wished to capitulate. Morales was sent back to the negotiation with the message that Urrea would accept nothing other than unconditional surrender. This meant that the Texans would have no rights or guarantees.[115]

"Well then," Fannin declared, "I have no water; my wounded need attendance, I particularly recommend to you those unfortunate men and will deliver myself up to the discretion of the Mexican Government."[116]

Urrea then ordered Captain Salas Andrade, his secretary, to draw up two copies of the surrender terms, at discretion. Urrea directed him to write one copy in Spanish, to be held by the Mexicans, while the other was to be composed in English

Lieutenant Colonel Holzinger assured Fannin that there was no known instance in which a prisoner of war who had trusted in the clemency of the Mexican government had lost his life.[117] Holzinger went on to say that he would recommend to General Santa Anna acceptance of the terms proposed by Fannin's men and that he was confident of obtaining Santa Anna's approval within a period of eight days. There was little else that Fannin could do.

Urrea had received reinforcements, including artillery, that would have devastated Fannin's troops had he kept fighting. Fannin accepted Urrea's proposals but did not inform his men of their conditional nature. On the other hand, Holzinger, a German soldier of fortune, allayed their suspicions by entering the Texan lines with the greeting, in English, "Well, gentlemen! In eight days, home and liberty!"[118]

The Terms of the Capitulation were then read two or three times by officers who could speak and read both languages.[119] The instruments were then signed and interchanged in the most formal and solemn manner. In substance, they were as follows:

> *1st. That we should be received and treated as prisoners of war according to the usages of the most civilized nations.*
> *2d. That private property should be respected and restored: that the side arms of the officers should be given up.*
> *3d. That the men should be sent to Copano, and thence to the United States in eight days, or so soon thereafter as vessels could be procured to take them.*
> *4th. That the officers should be paroled and return to the United States in like manner.*

Captain Jack Shackelford's account of the surrender noted:

> *I assert most positively, that this Capitulation was entered into without which a surrender never would have been made. I know that when Santa Anna was a prisoner he flattered many into a belief, that no Capitulation was made; and those who were disposed to distrust the solemn asseverations of their unfortunate and much injured compatriots, in arms, and take the bare word of an unprincipled tyrant as blood-thirsty as ever foully disgraced the annals of civilization, are welcome to all the benefit of such confidence and credulity. After our arms had been given up and the necessary arrangements made, all*

> *who were not so badly wounded as to prevent their marching, were posted off to Goliad under a strong guard. We reached there a little after sunset, and were driven into the church like so many swine. We were compelled to keep a space open in the centre for the guard to pass backward and forward, and under the penalty of having it kept open by a discharge of guns. To avoid this, we had literally to lie one upon another. Early in the morning, their soldiery commenced drawing the blankets from our wounded. I resisted an attempt of this sort near me, and had a bayonet drawn and thrust at me.*[120]

After the conditions of surrender were agreed to, Fannin's regiment had to undertake the physical act of giving up. Holzinger was put in charge of this drill. The rebels were marched a short distance out from their ad hoc fortifications under heavy guard. There, they put their muskets and rifles in a pile. The officers' weapons were tagged with their names and boxed. This carefully organized procedure was intended to safeguard the personal property of the officers and lends credence to the surrender agreement as Fannin had related it to his men.

Many of the men, Mexicans and rebels alike, smoked cigars as they moved around the hollow square. It was almost ironic that it was after the fight when the biggest explosion occurred. A great roar rolled over the prairie as Fannin's ammunition wagon went up in a sheet of brilliant flame. The prairie grass caught fire, and hundreds of unspent paper-wrapped powder and ball that had been dropped and lost in the grass during the fight now exploded with sharp cracking reports. The first large blast and the subsequent smaller detonations sent men racing across the prairie and away from the fire. Order was restored soon, and none of Fannin's men took the opportunity to escape.[121]

After handing over their arms, including five hundred spare muskets, Fannin's command—230 to 240 men, including about 50 wounded—were marched back to Goliad over the next two days and imprisoned in the chapel at La Bahia.

The Battle of Coleto was one of the most significant engagements of the Texas Revolution. The battle, however, cannot properly be considered as isolated from the series of errors and misfortunes that preceded it, errors for which the Texas commander, James W. Fannin Jr., was ultimately responsible.[122] One historian refers to the Goliad campaign as "a burlesque tragedy."[123] Sam Houston, on hearing of Fannin's plight while at his defensive position on the Colorado River, said to his aide, "There is the last hope of Texas. We shall never see Fannin nor his men."[124]

6

MASSACRE AT GOLIAD

The second Sunday morning, they were brought out in squads and massacred, it was beautiful early summer
The work commenced about five o'clock and was over by eight.

None obeyed the command to kneel,
Some made a mad and helpless rush, some stood stark and straight,
A few fell at once, shot in the temple or heart, the living and dead lay together,
The maimed and mangled dug in the dirt, the new-comers saw them there,
Some half-kill'd attempted to crawl away,

These were dispatched with bayonets or battered with the blunts of muskets,
A youth not seventeen years old seiz'd his assassin till two more came to release him,
The three were all torn, and covered with the boy's blood.
—*Walt Whitman,* Song of Myself

On Palm Sunday morning, Callahan and other survivors of the Georgia Battalion continued to labor as prisoners in Victoria, building boats for the Mexican army. Survivor Samuel T. Brown wrote a letter to Ward's brother describing the events at Refugio:

> *I saw four of the Macon company who had been detained there after the surrender, on account of their being mechanics: William Wilkinson, John Kinneman, Barwell and Callahan….I was then taken to Goliad where I*

> *remained five days and saw the places where the four divisions of prisoners had been butchered; some of the carcasses remained, many burnt and others mangled; all so disfigured that I could recognize no particular person.*[125]

While Callahan survived at Victoria, the Texans at Goliad were far less fortunate. A Mexican officer called out to awaken the prisoners at La Bahia in the early morning on March 27. He ordered the men to form into a file so that they could be counted.[126]

The prisoners were told a variety of stories—they were to gather wood, drive cattle, be marched to Matamoros or proceed to the port of Copano for passage to New Orleans. Fannin cheerfully reported to his men that the Mexicans were making arrangements for their departure. The night before, the troops had sung "Home Sweet Home" as their Mexican guards looked on.

Benjamin Franklin Hughes later recounted, "We were called out and told to hurry up and get in line to march to a place of embarkation, and we got into line rather hopping and skipping with joy at the thought of soon being home."[127] Callahan's companions of the Georgia Battalion were formed in a column, carrying their knapsacks. When Hughes asked where they were going, the Georgia boys replied—with great excitement—that they were going to Copano in order to be shipped back to the States.

The Mexican command selected places on each of the three roads leading from Goliad, from one-half to three-fourths of a mile from the presidio. Unsuspecting prisoners were marched out, believing they were going home. On each road, the groups were halted. The guard on the right of the column of prisoners then countermarched and formed with the guard on the left. At a prearranged moment, or upon a given signal, the guards fired into the prisoners at a range too close to miss. Nearly all were killed at the first fire. Survivors who bolted were pursued and slaughtered by gunfire, bayonet or lance.

Survivor John C. Duval testified, "The first intimation I had of what was coming was given by someone near me saying, 'Boys, they are going to shoot us,' and at the same instant I heard the clicking of the musket locks; and before I fairly comprehended the situation the soldiers fired and killed nearly every man in the front rank of our division."[128]

Captain Jack Shackleford, a survivor with the Alabama Red Rovers, gave this account of the massacre:

> *27th March—Palm Sunday—Never whilst the current of life rushes through this poor heart of mine, can I forget the horrors of this fatal morning. At dawn*

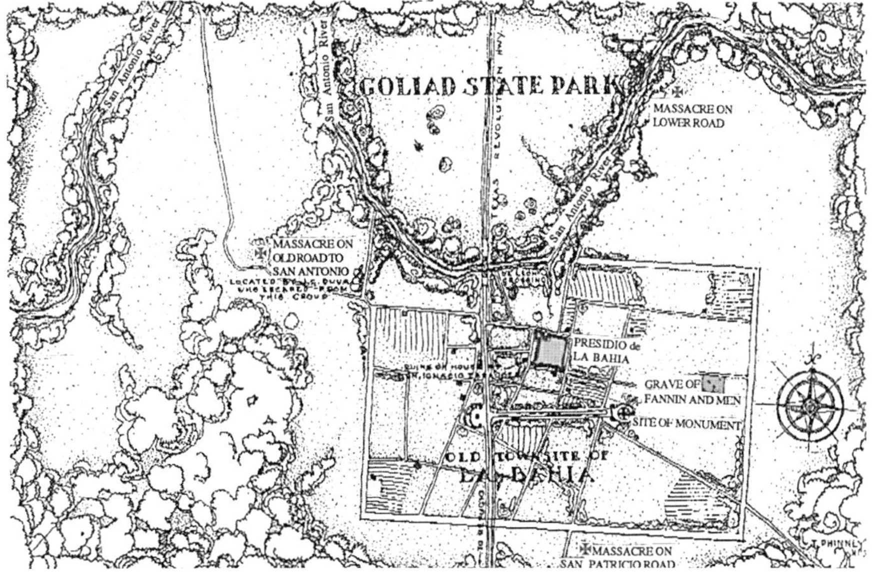

A map of the Goliad Massacre. *From* Ehrenberg: Goliad Survivor, Old West Explorer *(Dallas: Texas Heritage Press, 1997), a translation of Ehrenberg's memoir published in 1844:* Der Freiheitskampf in Texas im Jahre 1836.

> *of day we were awakened by a Mexican officer calling us up, and saying, he "wanted the men to form a line, that they might be counted."…Young Fenner rose on his feet, and exclaimed, "Boys, they are going to kill us—die with your faces to them, like men!" At the same moment, two other young men, flourishing their caps over their heads, shouted at the top of their voices: "Hurrah for Texas!" Can Texas cease to cherish the memory of those, whose dying words gave a pledge of their devotion to her cause?*[129]

Lieutenant Colonel Ward's Georgians and the Kentucky Mustangs were marched northwest toward San Antonio. Captain Benjamin Holland was part of that group. Just as the Mexicans halted the formation, the sound of musket fire and shrieks exposed the slaughter to the southwest. Holland suggested to Major Benjamin C. Wallace that "it would be best to make a desperate rush." Wallace replied that they were too heavily guarded: each prisoner was flanked on each side by a *soldado*. Holland then called on several more of his comrades to make a break, "but none would follow."[130]

Captain Holland gave the vivid testimony that so maddened Callahan and the other survivors of the massacre:

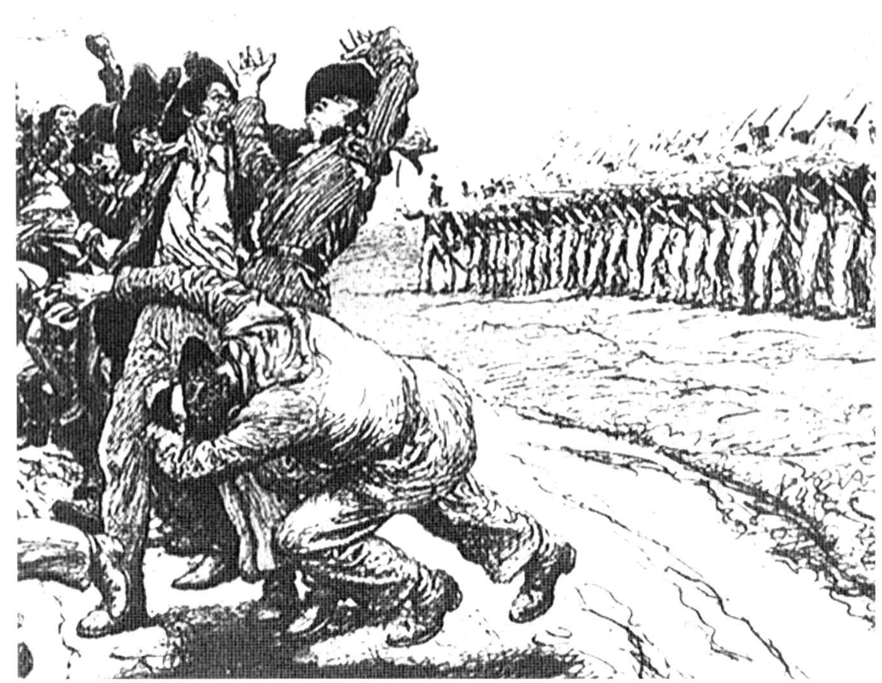

Goliad executions. *Texas State Library and Archives Commission.*

> *I heard our companions shrieking in the most agonizing tones "O God! O God! Spare us."…It was then we knew what was to be our fate.…Major Wallace…sprung, and struck the soldier on his right a severe blow with his fist: they being at open files, the soldier at the other file attempted to shoot him; but being too close, was unable. The soldier then turned his gun, and struck the writer a severe blow upon the left hand. I then seized hold of the gun and wrenched it from his hand.…The central one raised his gun to fire—I still ran towards him in a serpentine manner in order to prevent his taking aim—I suddenly stopped—dropped my piece, fired, and shot the soldier through the head and he fell instantly dead.…*[I] *immediately ran and leaped into the river.*[131]

The Mexican version of this incident is found in the diary of Colonel Nicolás de la Portilla:

> *March 27. At daybreak, I decided to carry out the orders of the Gen.-in-chief because I considered them superior. I assembled the whole garrison and ordered*

the prisoners, who were still sleeping, to be awaked. There were 445. (The eighty that had just been taken at Cópano and had, consequently, not borne arms against the government, were set aside.) The prisoners were divided into three groups and each was placed in charge of an adequate guard, the first under Augustín Alcerrica, the second under Capt. Luis Balderas, and the third under Capt. Antonio Ramírez. I gave instructions to these officers to carry out the orders of the supreme government and the Gen.-in-chief. This was immediately done. There was a great contrast in the feelings of the officers and the men. Silence prevailed. Sad at heart I wrote to Gen. Urrea expressing my regret at having been concerned in so painful an affair. I also sent an official account of what I had done, to the Gen.-in-chief.[132]

With savage barbarity, the Mexican soldiers checked the bodies of the fallen and deliberately bayoneted those who yet survived. The cruel butchery, however, was not yet over.

Mexican soldiers then marched to the barracks, where the wounded Americans lay. They dragged the men outside the presidio and flung them to the ground. Those wounded who could do so struggled to their feet or their knees. Most of the wounded men lay helpless on the earth and were simply shot out of hand. One firing squad commander noted:

Palm Sunday…a day of most heartfelt sorrow. At six…the execution of four hundred and twelve American prisoners…continued till eight.…At eleven…burning the bodies.…What an awful scene…when the prisoners were executed, and fell in heaps! And what spectator could view it without horror!…All young, the oldest not more than thirty, and of fine florid complexions…unfortunate youths.…Lamentations and the appeals which they uttered to Heaven…with extended arms, kneeling or prostrate on the earth, were such as might have caused the very stones to have cried out in compassion.[133]

Lieutenant Colonel Ward and about eighty of his men of the Georgia Battalion were added to the Goliad prisoners on March 25. General Urrea, in compliance with his promise, wrote to Santa Anna from Guadalupe Victoria, informing him that Fannin and his men were prisoners of war "at the disposal of the Supreme Mexican Government" and recommended clemency.

General Urrea described how he deliberately returned prisoners to Goliad. Ward's men were among these, as were William P. Miller's troops.

Urrea said that he did it "in the hope that their very numbers would save them, for I never thought that the horrible spectacle of that massacre could take place in cold blood and without immediate urgency, a deed proscribed by laws of war and condemned by the civilization of our country."[134]

One of these Tennesseans, a Mr. Coy, told S.T. Brown of how his beloved commander, William Ward, had died: [135]

> *After all the men had been shot the time of the officers came. Col. Ward was ordered to kneel, which he refused to do; he was told if he would kneel his life would be spared. He replied, they had killed his men in cold blood, and that he had no desire to live; death would be welcome. He was then shot dead.*

Shackelford's account noted:

> *I saw Ward's men in line, with their knapsacks on…stated that they were to march to Copano and…home!…Could* [later] *hear their screams.… Col. Guerrear* [Garay] *appeared…were* [they] *murdering our men? He replied that "it was so"—but that he "had not given the order; neither had he executed it."…*[He had] *done all in his power to save as many as he could; and that if he could have saved more, he would have done so.*[136]

William Ward, a plucky soldier, died with words of contempt and bitter reproaches for the treachery of his executioners on his lips. With him died the Georgia Battalion.[137]

The ragged roar of musket fire that marked the massacre of his men brought the wounded Fannin out of his bed and out into the yard of Fort Defiance. There Fannin spotted the ranks of his wounded, waiting for their own deaths.

At the same time, a Mexican captain ordered Joseph H. Spohn, spared as an interpreter, to escort Fannin to the northwest portion of the yard. There were six *soldados* with the officer, and Spohn asked outright if they were going to kill Fannin. The officer answered, yes, without hesitating.

Gary Brown in his book *Hesitant Martyr of the Texas Revolution: James Walker Fannin* wrote:

> *When Spohn approached Fannin, the Col. asked what was that firing, and when he told him the facts he made no observation, but appeared resolute and firm, no visible impression on Col. Fannin, who firmly walked to the place pointed out by the Mexican Captain placing his arm upon the*

> *shoulder of Spohn for support, being wounded in the right thigh, from which he was very lame.*[138]

On reaching that point, Spohn reported that he was ordered to translate the following statement: "That for having come with an armed band to commit depredations and revolutionize Texas, the Mexican Government was about to chastise him."[139]

On hearing the statement, Fannin immediately asked to see the Mexican commander. The captain refused him but asked why he had made the request. Spohn said that Fannin produced a gold watch that he declared belonged to his wife and that he "wished to present it to the commandant."

The Mexican captain would have none of it and asked Fannin for the watch. "Col. Fannin told him he might have the watch if he would have him buried after he was shot, which the Captain said should be done—'*con todas las formalidades necessarias*'—at the same time smiling and bowing."[140]

Following this promise, Fannin pulled a "small bead purse containing doubloons" from his right pocket. The clasp on the purse was damaged, and Fannin took time to explain to the Mexican that it had absorbed part of the impact from a musket ball before the round tore into the flesh of his thigh, taking some of his handkerchief into the leg with it. The purse with the gold was handed over to the captain. Fannin then reached into the left pocket of his India rubber overcoat and pulled out a canvas-wrapped "double handful of dollars." He also gave this money to the officer.

Spohn was ordered to blindfold his commander. Fannin passed him his pocket handkerchief: "He [Spohn] proceeded to fold it, but being agitated he done it clumsily, when the officer snatched it from his hand and folded it himself." The officer told Fannin to sit down on a chair that was near and, stepping behind him, bandaged his eyes, saying to Fannin, in English, "Good, good?"—meaning if his eyes were properly bound—to which Fannin replied, "Yes, yes."

That task complete, the captain ordered his *soldados* to detach the bayonets from their muskets and come near Fannin. Fannin, ever mindful of his person, told Spohn to ask the Mexicans not to place their weapons so close to his face that they would scorch it when they fired. The Mexican captain directed his men to approach Fannin so that their muskets were within two feet of Fannin's face.

On his signal, they fired, and "poor Fannin fell dead on his right side on the chair, and from thence rolled into a dry ditch, about three feet deep, close by the wall."[141]

Contrary to his last wishes, Fannin had been shot in the face.

Captain Jack Shackleford provided another account of Fannin's execution:

> *Major Miller, who knew Fannin informed me that the next day he saw him lying in the prairie among a heap of wounded; and that he was shot in the head! We were marched into the Fort about 11 o'clock, and ordered to the Hospital. Had to pass close by our butchered companions, who were stripped of their clothes, and their naked, mangled bodies thrown in a pile. The wounded were all hauled out in carts that evening; and some brush thrown over the different piles, with a view of burning, their bodies. A few days afterwards, I accompanied Major Miller to the spot where lay those who were dear to me whilst living; and whose memory will be embalmed in my affection, until this poor heart itself shall be cold in death;—and Oh! what a spectacle! The flesh had been burned from off the bodies; but many hands and feet were yet unscathed—I could recognize no one.—The bones were all still knit together, and the vultures were feeding upon those limbs which, one week before, actively played in battle.*[142]

A man-by-man study of Fannin's command indicates that 342 were executed at Goliad on March 27. Only 28 escaped the firing squads, and 20 more were spared as physicians, orderlies, interpreters or mechanics, including James Callahan, largely because of the entreaties of Francita Alavez, the "Angel of Goliad," and the brave and kindly intervention of Colonel Garay. Many of those who eventually escaped were recaptured on their first attempt but later managed a second escape. Two physicians, Joseph H. Barnard and John Shackelford, were taken to San Antonio to treat Mexican wounded from the battle of the Alamo; they later escaped.

The death of at least 182 men at the Alamo and the slaying of 342 unarmed prisoners at Goliad inflicted a powerful psychological wound on both Texas society and American sympathizers. The resulting collective rage provided intense motivation for enlistment, galvanized Texan military resistance and gained financial, materiel and volunteer support for the Texas cause from the United States. Stephen F. Austin called it "a war of barbarism against civilization" and claimed that the American "West and South" were "up and moving in favor of Texas." These atrocities, though claimed by Santa Anna to be legal under Mexican law as it applied to captured rebels and pirates, significantly hardened the Texan rules of engagement.[143]

Until this incident, Santa Anna's reputation had been that of a skillful and cunning man rather than a cruel one. Together with the fall of the Alamo, the Goliad Massacre branded both Santa Anna and the Mexican people with a reputation for cruelty and aroused the fury of the people of Texas, the United States and even Great Britain and France, thus considerably promoting the success of the Texas Revolution.[144]

Callahan later heard many stories told by the survivors of the Goliad Massacre. Each of these macabre narratives stoked the fire hatred burning in his heart. Callahan's unrepentant fury flowed from the cruel lies that were told to the Texan soldiers. This hard-favored rage was catalyzed by the way the Mexicans had malevolently slaughtered the unarmed and unsuspecting prisoners.

7
GONZALES RANGERS

Imagine…men dressed in every variety of costume, except the ordinary uniform, armed with double-barreled shotguns, squirrel rifles, and Colt's six shooters, mounted on small, wiry, half-wild horses, with Spanish saddles and Mexican spurs, unshaven, unwashed, undisciplined, but brave and generous men, riding pell-mell along roads, over the prairies, and through the woods, and you will be able to form a correct conception of a squad of Texas Rangers on the march.
—Willis L. Lang, planter and Texas Ranger, writing in his diaries

When settlers began returning to the Gonzales area after the victory at San Jacinto, nothing remained of the former town but one charred building. The Comanches had reestablished their claim to the area and posed a serious threat for all returning settlers. There was a clear and compelling need to protect these residents of Gonzales County.

Callahan received an honorable discharge from military service on June 6, 1836, and the war-weary Georgian joined other men streaming home from the battlefields. No longer a foot soldier, he at last had a horse. He would never have to walk to war again.

Gonzales and DeWitt Colony residents had begun to return soon after the victory at San Jacinto. Gonzales, left in ashes on General Houston's order three months earlier, lay derelict. Of all the structures that had been present there, only Adam Zumwalt's kitchen and Andrew Ponton's smokehouse remained standing.

For the next several years, the "resources of the place," as German naturalist Ferdinand von Roemer assessed them, remained "in keeping with

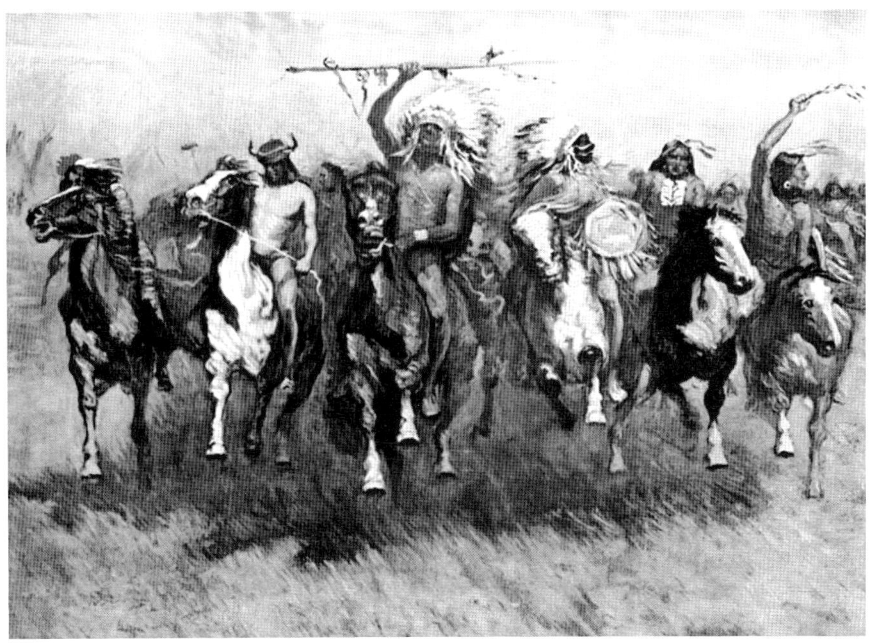

Victory Dance. Frederic Remington.

its cheerless aspect." Roemer found that "no sugar, coffee or other necessities could be bought in the entire place—nothing but bad whiskey."[145]

However, eventually many residents returned to begin the slow task of rebuilding the infrastructure of Gonzales and surrounding homesteads in the DeWitt Colony. Records describing proceedings of the Gonzales town council began again on March 26, 1839. The town was eventually rebuilt on the original site, with construction continuing throughout the early 1840s. Resurrection of the town was concentrated on the original town site near the Guadalupe River.

For his service during the revolution, Callahan was awarded 640 acres of land by the Republic of Texas near present-day Seguin, in what was then Gonzales County. In 1838, the area included what is now Guadalupe, DeWitt, Caldwell, Lavaca and Gonzales Counties. Bounty grants were issued to soldiers according to the length of their service in the army of the republic. The first bounty act was passed by the provisional government of Texas and promised 640 acres to those who served in the regular army for two years or throughout the war.

Robert Hall told the story of the founding of Seguin.[146] "In the fall of '38, fifty of us clubbed together and bought half a league of land from old Joe

Martin and laid off the town of Seguin. I was one of the chain carriers. The deer were so plentiful that they would hardly get out of our way. They acted as if they were not at all afraid of us."[147]

Soon most of the land around the town site of Gonzales was all owned. None were more aware of this than the returning Texas soldiers, who had made a camp before the war at a place called Walnut Springs, on the banks of Walnut Branch Creek in present-day Seguin. The area lay in the middle of Umphries Branch's 1831 league purchase. This had been a meeting place for the local militia during their patrols against malicious Indians, and by 1837, Callahan had settled there.[148]

A.J. Sowell described the scene:

> *In the spring of 1839, Captain Ben McCulloch and H.E. McCulloch, had an efficient company of minute men, and kept their scouts in the field from time to time. Their encampment was up the Guadalupe, at Walnut Springs. The friendly Indians, the Lipans and Tonkaways, frequently encamped at Gonzales, and in one or two instances co-operated with the McCullochs in pursuing other hostiles. On one occasion, the Indians were encamped just below town, on the river, driving a pretty brisk trade in ponies, deer-skins and trinkets.*[149]

Several of Callahan's friends and neighbors were patriotic *tejanos* holding land in or near the Seguin. They included José Antonio Navarro, signer of the Declaration of Independence and prisoner at Santa Fe; Luciano Navarro, brother of José Antonio; Erasmo Seguín, postmaster general of the Department of Béxar, friend of Stephen F. Austin and supporter of the revolution; Juan Seguín, mayor of San Antonio, republic senator and cavalry commander; the Manuel Flores family, large landholders in Floresville who fought for Texas independence; the Rodrigues family, landholders and supporters of the Texas Revolution; the Veramendi family, landholders and supporters of the Texas Revolution; and the Garza family, landholders and supporters of the Texas Revolution.[150]

Joseph S. Martin, although not an original settler of Gonzales, had been able to purchase the 1831 Mexican-granted Umphries Branch league for three hundred pesos. Martin was known to be a sound businessman and was held in respect by his contemporaries. As a result, three men, along with Martin, founded a corporation to establish a town site at Walnut Springs. These men were James Campbell, Arthur Swift and Matthew Caldwell.[151] They agreed to buy half of the Umphries Branch league and sell shares for

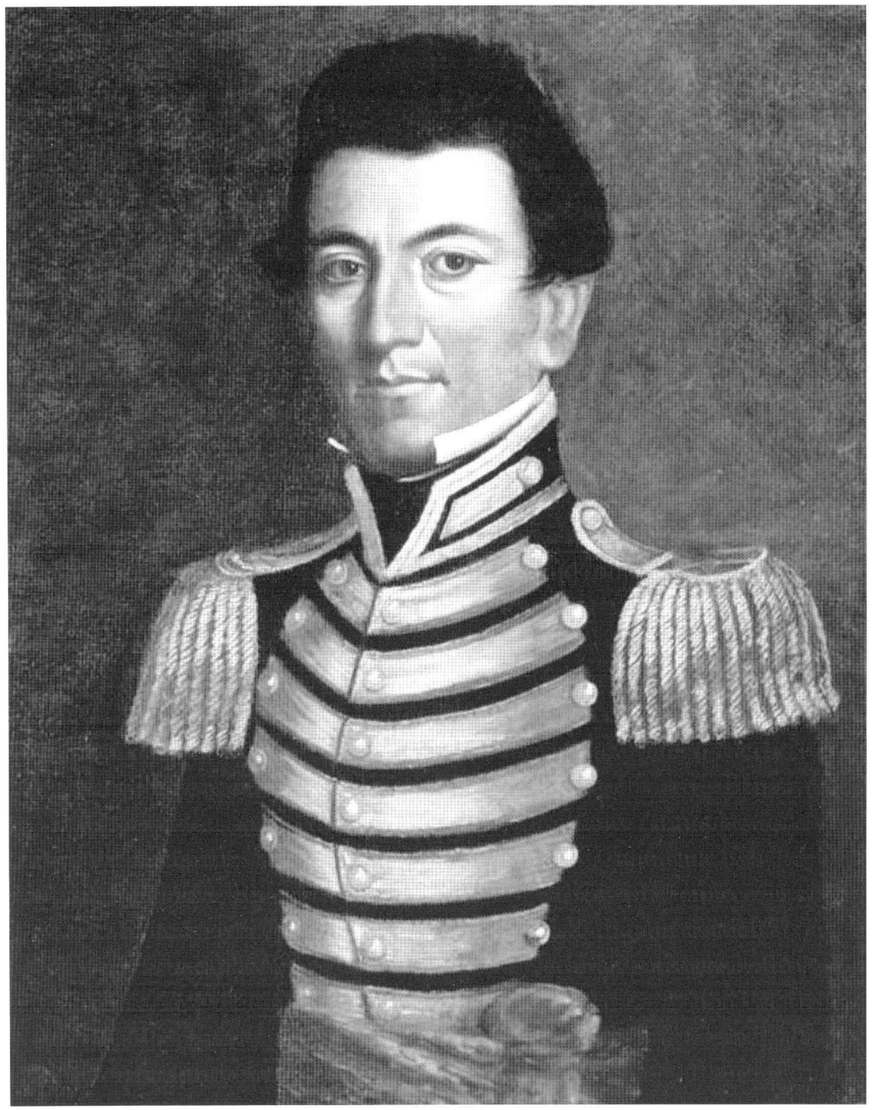

Juan Nepomuceno Seguín. *Courtesy of San Jacinto Museum of History.*

the purpose of building a town. Matthew Caldwell became a close friend of James Callahan and served as his commanding officer in several adventures.

On August 12, 1838, the corporation bore fruit, for that is the day Walnut Springs was founded. There were forty-four shares: thirty-three sold to thirty-three men and eleven reserved for Martin to dispose of as he saw fit.[152]

By the time of the town meeting of February 25, 1839, a majority of the shareholders was dissatisfied with the name "Walnut Springs" and voted to rename the town. The names "Tuscumbia" and "Seguin" (in honor of Colonel Juan N. Seguín of revolution fame) were suggested. "Seguin" won by a vote of eighteen to seven.[153]

Matthew Caldwell established the Gonzalez County Militia, which soon after became a company of Texas Rangers. Callahan appears on the muster roster of this organization in 1839—the year he became a Ranger.

Callahan rode with legendary figures of Texas history, Rangers such as John Coffee Hays, Ben and Henry McCulloch, Matthew Caldwell, Robert Hall, James Wilson Nichols, A.J. Sowell and James Milford Day.

James M. Day married Martha Nichols, daughter of George Washington Nichols and sister to James Wilson Nichols. In 1838, Day moved his mother, Sarah, into a house in Seguin. Mother Day's home site would be used extensively by the Rangers and become known as the Seguin Ranger Station. Here Day joined Matthew Caldwell's Gonzales-Seguin Rangers in January 1839.

In 2011, a historic marker was placed at the site of the old Ranger Station (the former Day home) in Seguin.[154] The 1820s log structure, which had stood for almost two hundred years, was razed about 2000. A brief message on the marker tells of the Days' contributions to the birth of Texas.

Matthew "Old Paint" Caldwell served as the first law officer or sheriff of Gonzalez County. He is said to have acquired the nickname because of white spots in his hair and beard and on his breast that made him look like a paint horse. On February 1, 1836, he was elected as a delegate from the Gonzales Municipality to the Convention at Washington-on-the Brazos, where he was a signer of the Texas Declaration of Independence. In 1838, Caldwell formed a frontier Ranger company of twenty-nine men. Charles Lockhart became first lieutenant, and Robert Hall joined as his second lieutenant. Within a short time, Callahan was riding with Captain Caldwell. President Lamar would appoint Caldwell, on January 15, 1839, as a captain, to recruit a company of Gonzales rangers. Two months later, he had raised his company of Rangers, and on March 23, 1839, Caldwell became captain of a company in the First Regiment of the Infantry of Texas.

Sequin was home to the celebrated Captain Jack Hays, perhaps the most famous Ranger of all. It is said that Hays became the exemplary Ranger leader, and he and his cohorts—John S. "Rip" Ford, Ben McCulloch and Samuel H. Walker—established the Ranger tradition. Hays joined the Rangers in the formative years of their roles as citizen soldiers. His Rangers gained a reputation as mounted troops with revolvers and individually styled uniforms; they marched and fought with a noticeable lack of military discipline. This rough-and-ready image of an irregular force left its imprint on the chronicles of Texas Ranger history.[155]

Jack Hays taught Callahan everything about being a mounted Ranger. No more infantry—the young veteran from Georgia had become hell on horseback.

James Wilson Nichols described a routine training sessions for Rangers (original spelling retained):

> *We put up a post about the size of a common man, then put up another about 40 yards farther on. We would run our horses full speed and discharge our rifles at the first post, draw our pistles and fire at the second. At first thare was some wild shooting but we had not practised two months until thare was not many men that would not put his balls in the center of the posts. Then we drew a ring about the size of a mans head and soon every man could put both his balls in the circul. We would practics this awhile, then try rideing like the Comanche Indians. After practisng for three or four months we became so purfect that we would ran our horse's half or full speede and pick up a hat, a coat, a blanket, or rope, or even a silver dollar, stand up in the saddle, throw ourselves on the side of our horses with only a foot and a hand to be seen, and shoot our pistols under the horse's neck, rise up and reverse, etc.*[156]

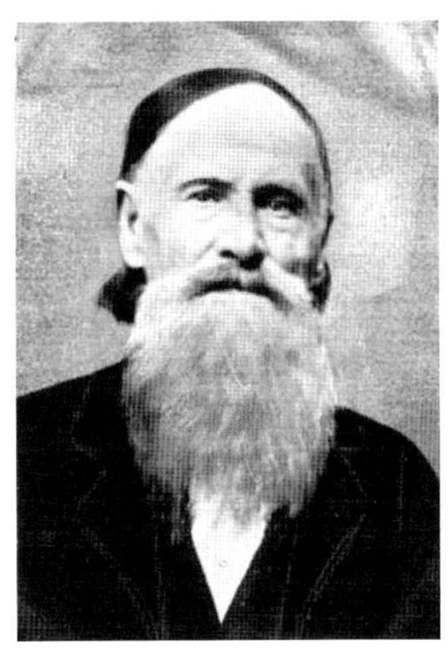

James Wilson Nichols. *Courtesy of Nichols family photographs.*

By the end of 1838, there were at least four marauding gangs south and west of the Nueces River engaged in plundering the towns and ranches in that region. The citizens were said to be "exceedingly exasperated on this account," believing that while this system of border pillage continued, they would be subjected to the "incursions of similar parties from the settlements on the Rio Grande, who would endeavor to retaliate for the injuries received from their bandit countrymen."[157]

That was not all. Even more distressing were marauding parties of American outlaws. In May 1839, Assistant Secretary of War Charles Mason informed General

Albert Sidney Johnston, "Col. Henry W. Karnes gives a deplorable account of the west; and I believe thinks, of the two, the marauding parties of the Americans are worse than the Mexicans or Indians. This, of course, will be relieved by the command of Captain Shapley P. Ross."[158]

Captain Ross rode with Hay's Rangers in 1842 and went on to serve as an Indian agent from 1855 to 1858. He became the father of famed Ranger and later governor Lawrence Sullivan Ross.

The "white land pirates," reported Colonel Karnes at Houston on July 6, robbed the Mexican traders from the Rio Grande, who were permitted by the government to come in to trade. Their robberies, he declared, were principally confined to the Mexican traders, and they were by no means particular about what they took; anything in the way of plunder seemed acceptable. The desolation of the depopulated counties of the southern and southwestern frontier and the ruin of many individuals who had struggled for the independence of the country were in no small degree traceable to the government's neglect of the western frontier. A small garrison on the lower Nueces would do much to ensure that protection so necessary for the peace, tranquility, settlement and development of the lower country.[159]

In the fall of 1839, there began to appear on the Rio Grande frontier two marauding parties of Mexican bandidos. One was headed by Agatón Quinoñes and the other by Manuel Leal.[160] They held themselves out as government customs guards but were really bandits and cutthroats, banded together for the purpose of pillaging and robbing the unguarded trader, who, according to Mexican law, was a smuggler engaged in illicit traffic.[161]

Among the lawless frontiersmen were "cowboys" who operated from 1838 to 1841 and made it their business to steal livestock being driven eastward for sale. These rustlers numbered not fewer than three or four hundred. They were regarded as murderers and merciless villains.[162]

Callahan served as a first lieutenant in Matthew Caldwell's company during Major George Howard's 1840 Indian expedition into the Comanche country.[163] Major Howard had been ordered to march from San Antonio with men through the Cañón de Uvalde to "scout the country in that direction."[164]

On September 11, the major spread the word for volunteers. Caldwell was the first to raise a small group of men from Gonzales on September 25. He named them the Gonzales Rangers. A muster roll for the Gonzales company shows that Caldwell's senior officers included twenty-eight-year-old first lieutenant Callahan.[165]

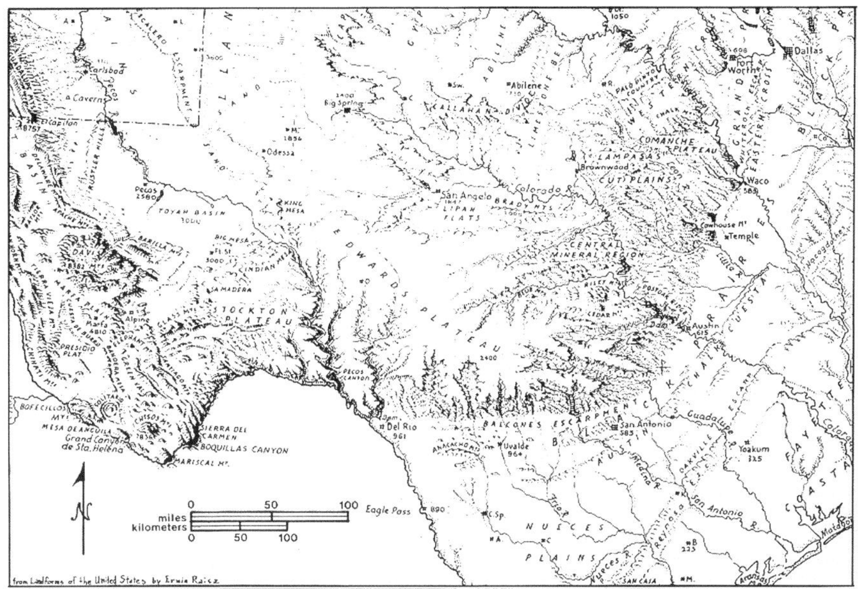

Landforms of the Edwards Plateau. *Erwin Raisz, with permission.*

The men from Gonzales rode west along the base of the Balcones Escarpment, penetrating country that Callahan had never seen before. James noted that the great wall of the escarpment was deeply frayed by westward-tending canyons. These canyons, fashioned by the rivers, are lined with sinkholes, caves and seeps created by ground water flowing through the limestone. At that time, profuse springs on the bluffs were festooned with long drapes of ferns, like hanging gardens, glistening with spring water. The water was exultant, dancing among the rocks of the riverbeds.

For the American Indians, this was a paradise full of wildlife, plants and shelter. Indigenous people had been living here for more than fourteen thousand years. By the nineteenth century, this was Apacheria and Comancheria. Callahan saw the many signs of their presence in the "Indian mounds" and "arrow heads" that lined the river and creek banks.[166]

During the expedition, Callahan explored the old Spanish missions on the upper Nueces River. They camped far upstream, in the rocky canyons of future Real and Uvalde Counties. These were the "El Cañón" missions, San Lorenzo de la Santa Cruz and Nuestra Señora de la Candelaria, founded in 1762

Along the upper Nueces, Callahan was involved in a skirmish with the Comanches when the Rangers attacked a large village near the headwaters of Las Moras Springs.[167] Although most of the Comanches had fled the village, Major Howard captured about 125 horses and mules, as well as numerous rifles. The Texans also destroyed the encampment's winter quarters and provisions.

Callahan's expedition moved out of the Indian village on October 14 and undertook what amounted to a grand tour of what would become known as the Texas Hill Country. From the head of the Nueces River, they rode to the head of the Frio River and then the upper reaches of the Guadalupe River. The area was open country with scattered trees. Grass was stirrup high. This was very rough country, and the rocky surfaces and slopes caused many problems for their horses and mules. Each rider was responsible for his own mount.

At the head of the north fork of the Guadalupe River, among the deep canyons, the Lipan Apaches had maintained an encampment since the early 1700s. The site became known as the "Boneyard" because it contained the bones of as many as four thousand head of cattle, which were neatly stacked there by Indians during a great rendezvous in 1782. The Lipans hosted a trade fair that year with other Texas tribes. More than two thousand Apaches arrived with three thousand horses. They were joined by six hundred Tonkawas and about three hundred Tejas, Bidais, Cocos and Mayeyes.[168]

From the Boneyard, Callahan rode with the expedition to the head of the South Llano River.[169] Major Howard's party then rode to the Pedernales River. When he learned that Colonel John Henry Moore was operating in this area, Major Howard elected to return his expedition home.

The Texans now rode along the old Pinta Trail to San Antonio.[170] The ancient road passed a place that is now Fredericksburg and then southeast to Leon Springs and San Antonio.[171] Callahan and the rest of Caldwell's company arrived in Seguin on November 16, 1840.

Callahan rode as a private in Captain Henry McCulloch's company in May 1841.[172] Callahan had already been made a captain of the Gonzales Minutemen Company, based out of Seguin, on April 7. He was probably in Gonzales when McCulloch assembled the volunteers for this campaign.[173]

McCulloch's company found an Indian trail where it crossed the San Marcos River at the mouth of Mule Creek. They followed this trail northwest to the head of York's Creek. They then rode into the Hill Country to the Guadalupe River and along that watercourse to the site of present-day Kerrville.[174]

This area was well known, having been traversed and mapped by the Spanish, commencing with Martín de Alarcón in 1718. The Spanish called this area Lomería Grande, "the big hills." The range was subsequently named the Guadalupe Mountains. This was the old Spanish trail to the Mission Santa Cruz de San Sabá and beyond.[175]

In 1828, French naturalist Jean Louis Berlandier and Lieutenant Colonel José Francisco Ruiz departed San Antonio on a hunting and exploration expedition to the Hill Country. They were escorted by thirty dragoons of the Alamo de Parras company and traveled with a party of "fifty to eighty Comanches" led by Chiefs Quelluna (Keiuna) and El Ronco.[176] Berlandier recorded the presence of a large camp of a Comanche chief at the location of present-day Kerrville.[177]

McCulloch had Berlandier's map of this region. More importantly, he had Stephen F. Austin's 1840 map of Texas.

Callahan was well aware that this region was homeland to the Tonkawas, Lipan Apaches and Comanches. These headwaters were located at the upper ends of the canyons that provided historic encampment areas for the annual buffalo hunt out on the plains of the Edwards Plateau and Llano Estacado.[178]

The country became increasingly rugged as McCulloch's men rode up today's Johnson Creek to the headwaters—beyond what is now Mountain Home.[179] Following the historic old trail, the expedition crossed and recrossed Johnson Creek fourteen times. They crossed the topological feature known as "the Divide" and rode down present-day Kimble County's Johnson Creek to its convergence with the Llano River. The Rangers set up camp at the confluence.[180] This was near present-day Junction.

The next morning, they scouted for hostiles and soon raided a nearby Comanche camp. They killed five Indians, and half of the remaining Indians were wounded, with only eight escaping. The Comanches abandoned their equipment as they fled, and the Rangers were able to capture horses, saddles, blankets, robes and even moccasins.[181]

The Republic of Texas was in constant fear of a Mexican invasion because of Mexico's refusal to recognize the independence of Texas after the Treaties of Velasco. The fear assumed reality on January 9, 1842, when General Mariano Arista issued a statement from Monterrey telling the Texans that it was hopeless for them to continue their struggle for independence and promising amnesty and protection to all who remained neutral during his planned invasion.

On March 5, 1842, some seven hundred Mexican troops, led by General Rafael Vásquez, occupied Goliad, Refugio and Victoria and then captured

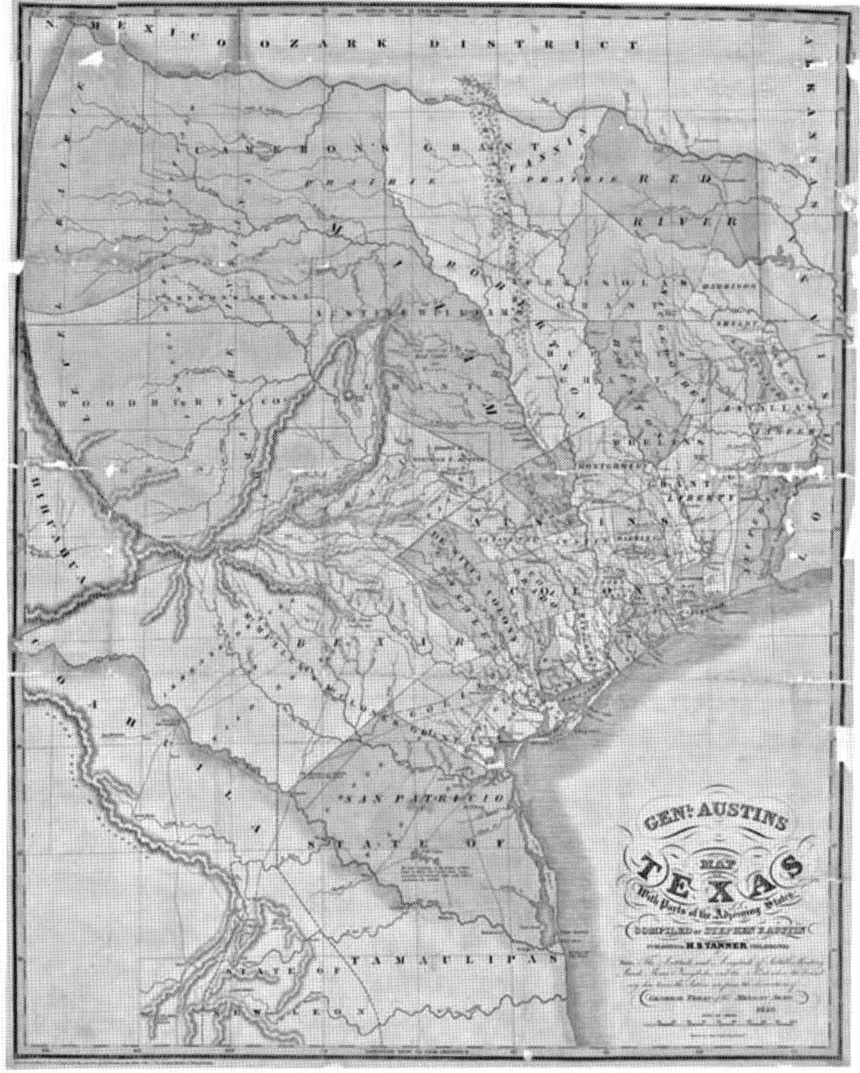

Austin's 1840 map of Texas. *Texas State Library and Archives Commission.*

San Antonio. The surprised Texans, who were without a large enough force to defend the town, fled to Seguin without a fight.

The Mexican flag was raised once more over San Antonio, and the city was held by the invaders for a few days. Vásquez declared Mexican laws in effect, but on March 7, he vacated San Antonio with Texas forces not far behind. The general crossed the Rio Grande and returned to Mexico.[182]

In retaliation, 400 Texan volunteers, including Callahan, assembled near Goliad for an expedition against Matamoros. Before the expedition could get underway, however, Mexican expatriate Antonio Canales, who had become a strong supporter of the central government, crossed the Rio Grande near Mier with an army of 539 men. Canales rode north to attack a camp of Texans in a bend of the Nueces River at Lipantitlán, north of present-day Banquete.[183] After an indecisive battle, Canales retreated to the Rio Grande, claiming a great victory.

The Vásquez Expedition was one of the events that led to retaliations by the Texans through the Mier Expedition and Somervell Expedition.

Less than a month later, the Texas Congress authorized the raising of a company of fifty-six Rangers, with officers appointed by the president, to protect Gonzales County for three months. Eight days later, three additional companies of mounted volunteers were assembled for immediate service against the hostile Indians on the Bastrop, Robertson and Milam County frontiers. Their authorization was on the same terms as the eight companies organized the preceding December. The term of enlistment here, however, was to be for six months, "unless sooner discharged." In the new companies, the men were to elect their own officers, and then the men and officers were to choose a major to command them.

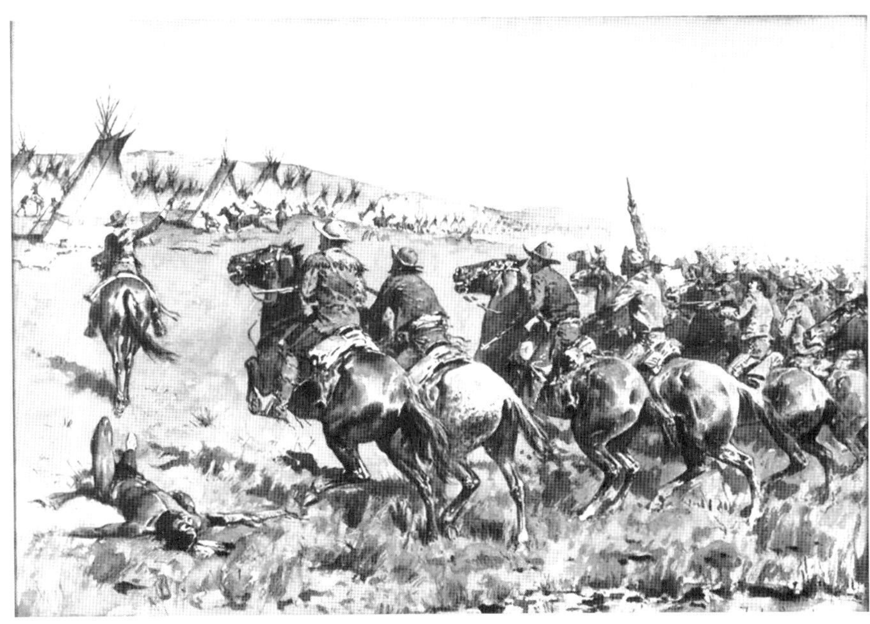

We Struck Some Boggy Ground. Frederic Remington.

On January 26, the republic's congress approved an act to create a Ranger corps, consisting of two companies of fifty-six men each, for the protection of the counties of San Patricio, Goliad and Refugio. These two companies were to be composed of volunteers enlisted for six months, and their officers were to be appointed by the president. Lawmakers appropriated $15,000 to cover the necessary costs. The pay of privates and noncommissioned officers was to be $25 per month, and the men were to furnish their own horses, arms and equipment.[184]

Callahan became a captain of a minuteman company. Most captains and their companies based their operations out of the region where they lived, sometimes joining forces with other regional companies in larger military actions when necessary. Therefore, the composition of the different companies was largely those individuals living in the specific sector. Captains Bird and McCulloch focused on and recruited from the immediate vicinity around Gonzales town and covered security of current Gonzales County east into Fayette County; Captain Matthew Caldwell, who used Gonzales town as a base, covered a broad area of the colony and beyond from San Antonio to the Rio Grande; Captain Callahan operated and recruited from Seguin, covering the northern sector of the colony from the western frontier across Guadalupe and Caldwell Counties; Captain John J. Tumlinson operated out of current Cuero, covering the Guadalupe River area south of Gonzales and into Victoria County; and Captain Adam Zumwalt focused on the Lavaca River area. Captain Ewen Cameron operated outside the colony area in the Victoria-Goliad areas.

Callahan served as captain of the Gonzales Minuteman Company from May 7 to December 30, 1841. His orders were to range the frontier to maintain the safety of the citizens. Callahan's company operated out of Sequin.[185]

Callahan's minuteman company conducted patrols, maintained scouts and fought Indians and Mexicans accused of stealing horses. Many of Callahan's men were veteran Rangers and Indian fighters. There are few reports to detail the actions of Callahan's company during this period.[186]

8

WOLL'S INVASION

The news spread like wildfire and once more the gallant Caldwell, Hays, Callahan, the McCullochs, Fryer, Bird, and others, whose gallantry has never been sullied, rallied their chosen and ever ready and willing.
—James Wilson Nichols

Callahan was once again confronted by his old nemesis, the Mexican army, the essence of his nightmares. Just as he was settling into life in Seguin, he was called to action to repel another invasion from Mexico.

General Adrián Woll crossed the Rio Grande with the Second Division of the Mexican Army Corps.[187] Leading a force of one thousand regular infantry, five hundred irregular cavalry and two pieces of artillery, Woll reached San Antonio on September 11, 1842. On that morning, the residents of San Antonio were surprised by the sounds of musket and cannon fire. Within two hours, Woll had control of the town.

District Court had been in session that week, attended by many officials and lawyers from as far away as Gonzales. They had no choice but to surrender to Woll's forces under conditions that they would be treated as gentlemen. After five days, about fifty-five prisoners were told that they would have to march to the Rio Grande where they would be handed over to Woll's superior, General Isidro Reyes, and set free.

In his report to General Reyes, Woll later wrote:

> *Most Excel. Sir: In the afternoon of the 18th inst., the Division under my command should have started out on its march to Rio Grande and*

> *San Fernando; we had taken this city (Bejar) by force, compelling its presumptuous defenders to surrender unconditionally; 150 horsemen had scouted the Guadalupe River up to the Gonzalez River, without any other incident than putting to death three Texans who tried to defend themselves against our skirmishers; the 16th of September, glorious anniversary of our National Independence, was solemnly celebrated, an event that had been forgotten in this city for the last six years; our spies had again confirmed the news we already had, that neither in Goliad, nor Copano nor Corpus Christi was there any enemy force to be seen. Our mission was completed.*[188]

Unfortunately, the scouts that Woll sent out along the road leading from San Antonio toward Seguin did not do their duty. They reported that there was no news as far as the Cibolo. But soon there was be much more news than Woll anticipated.

As word of the Mexican incursion spread, the Manuel Flores Ranch at Seguin again became the rally point for volunteers. Matthew Caldwell, Jack Coffee Hays, James Bird and James Callahan quickly assembled a force of Rangers, scouts and volunteers. Callahan would serve as a lieutenant in Captain Bird's company.

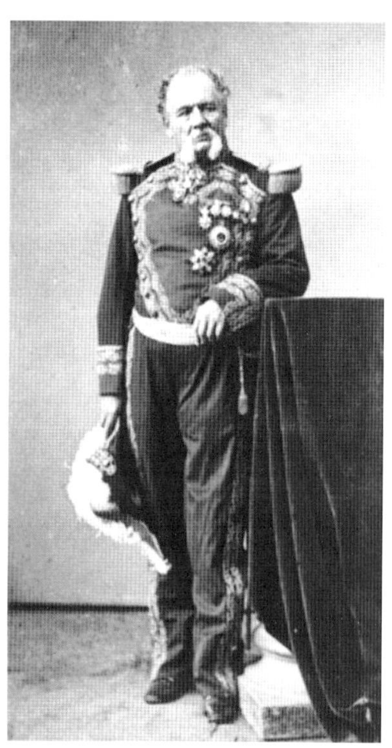

General Adrián Woll. *Texas State Library and Archives Commission.*

Callahan and the other Texans were well armed. "They belted on sometimes two, three or even four pistols, a large Bowie knife and shouldered their rifles," wrote Joseph Milton Nance.[189] The pistols were .36-caliber Colt Paterson revolvers. The Rangers also carried a variety of long arms, the most popular being the model 1840 flintlock musket. Other Rangers toted shotguns.

Sixty men alone came from Seguin and Gonzales. They united with Captain Hays's fourteen-man Ranger company that had been driven from the city with Woll's approach.

The Texans moved out on September 13 and rode to within twenty miles of San Antonio. That night, Callahan and the other Rangers slept beside the Cibolo. On September 17, after Woll had occupied San Antonio for a week, the Texans marched overland to Salado Creek,[190] about six miles east of San Antonio. Caldwell sent Hays forward to locate a likely place to confront Woll's command. Captain Hays selected a crossing on the Salado, about two miles above where Sunset Road crosses.[191]

Favorable terrain having been chosen, Caldwell marched his troops in the bright moonlight to the Salado and took up an advantageous position on the east bank, quietly posting guards and pickets.

As James Ramsay later wrote:

> *About midnight we took up the line of march, keeping away from the road. We came in sight of the enemy about daylight. We heard the rattle of Jack Hays' musketry. He had already engaged the enemy. Capt. Caldwell ordered the horses tied in the bottom, and the men formed in line of battle. Jack Hays had joined us by this time. The Mexicans appeared in front. There was a skirmish at a distance of about 600 yards.*[192]

Realizing he was outnumbered, Caldwell decided on an action that called for some of his Rangers to lure the Mexicans out of the Alamo and onto the prairie around Salado Creek. Meanwhile, Caldwell's main force of Texans would remain positioned within the creek bed where they had good cover.

Only thirty-eight horses were fit for duty among the Texan camp. Hays, with his fourteen Rangers, were assigned the mission along with Henry E. McCulloch, William A.A. "Big Foot" Wallace, Robert Addison Gillespie and sixteen others. The thirty-eight men rode from the Salado to San Antonio on the morning of September 17; they arrived outside the city at dawn.

The Rangers dismounted and prepared an ambush. Hays and McCulloch then remounted and, taking six men with them, boldly hazarded to within half a mile of the Alamo, taunting the Mexican cavalry to come out and fight. Hays had hoped to be pursued by about forty or fifty Mexicans.

Instead, Hays's gambit resulted in a charge of more than four hundred Mexican cavalrymen from the Alamo. Soon the soldiers rode in hot pursuit as Hays and his men galloped toward the Salado.

Woll had just completed preparations to move against Caldwell, and when Hays and McCulloch made their appearance, Woll's whole force of cavalry was already in the saddle. The general said he "would go in person and drive the Texian wolves from the bushes." Augmented by a large number of the Mexican residents of Béxar, the general moved to attack Caldwell's position.

The Rangers continued their hurried retreat across the mesquite-covered prairie toward Caldwell's location, where their comrades were camped among the cottonwoods, cedars and live oaks of the creek bottom. For the first four miles, the Texans kept out of reach of the Mexican cavalry without much difficulty. Too soon, however, fresh horses captured by Woll the day he took San Antonio began to gain on the exhausted mounts of the Rangers.

As the Mexicans gained ground, the Texans threw off blankets, hats and raincoats in an attempt to lighten their horses' loads. McCulloch, commanding the rear guard of ten picked men, pressed close on the heels of the foremost Rangers. "The race," wrote Reverend Z.N. Morrell, "was an earnest one."[193]

The Mexicans made a desperate effort to cut off Hays by passing his right flank. McCulloch kept between the Ranger captain and the Mexicans, sending couriers every half mile or so urging Hays to head for the timber. Finally, when the timber was reached, McCulloch had only one man with him, Creed Taylor. And Taylor was wounded in the hand. Much chagrined by his ill fortune, he managed to fasten his bridle rein above his elbow and with pistol in the other hand continued to ride.[194]

Some distance out on his horse, Captain Augustus H. Jones of Gonzales, a close friend of Hays, began to falter relative to the main force. Hays put the entire company behind Jones with his slower mount leading the way. The contingent led the Mexican force across the Salado to a point a half mile above the main Texan force.[195]

Callahan and the other Texans in camp had slaughtered a beef that morning and were busy cooking and eating when Hays's men scurried in, closely pursued by Mexican cavalry. The Texans' ruse, however, had its desired effect. The battle was joined on terrain favorable to the Texans.

Woll had pursued Hays with 1,200 regulars in addition to 200 or 300 *rancheros*, Indians and indigenous Mexicans. Hays and McCulloch, with their detachments, had aggravated Woll's advance with continued skirmishes.

General Woll reported:

> *I ordered Col. Sebastain Moro del Moral to take charge of the post with half of his Battalion, while I marched ahead with 200 Infantry, 100 dragoons of the Santa Anna squadrons, and two Artillery pieces; meantime the Bejar and Rio Grande Defenders had joined the Perez unit, so that added to the Capt. Francisco Castaneda*[196] *detachment, they counted 130 men whom I ordered to follow the enemy and keep him under fire without leaving him time to organize, while sending me continual reports; all this*

> *was executed with great precision, until reaching the Salado creek at a distance of 3 leagues—12 miles—from the city, the Texans suddenly veered off into the woods, and I learned that they had assembled a strength of about 300 men under Col. Caldwell, who had the intention of setting himself up during the day in the inextricable position at a water hole close to the city, there to await the numerous parties he had notified to join up with him from all directions, and then to attack us.*[197]

The Mexican force crossed the creek and took up a position on the hillside east of Caldwell's position. There it planted a battery and opened an ineffectual fire on the Texans. Caldwell's men were deployed and protected by the creek bank. The only danger Callahan had to guard against was the falling tree limbs the cannon shots tore from the large pecans over their heads.[198]

Miles Bennett reported: "The Enemy crossed the Salado above our position, and with bands of martial music formed on the beautiful open prairie four hundred yards east of us cutting us off from our Settlements and preventing all reinforcements from joining us."[199]

About 10:00 a.m., Woll's entire command formed and maintained continual fire, recalled N.B. Burkett, but "on account of the distance we did not pay a great deal of attention to them."[200]

Caldwell sent out a confident call for help. "The enemy are around me on every side, but I fear them not," he wrote to the men of the nearby settlements. Vowing to hold his position until reinforced, "Old Paint" invited the Texans to join in the sport. "It is the most favorable opportunity I have seen," he assured his neighbors. "I can whip them on any ground, without help, but cannot take prisoners. Why don't you come? Hurra for Texas."[201]

Throughout the day of September 19, Caldwell's men continued to vary their positions, scurrying about and making themselves obvious so that their forces might appear to be greater in number to the enemy.

To deceive the enemy, Caldwell had his troops casually march over some of the knolls in enemy view on the left. Then, descending into the hollow out of sight, they ran back at a double-quick time, falling again into ranks in the rear. By this ruse, the Texans kept up a continuous line although showing the same men two or three times. Throughout the day, Caldwell's men continued to circle the Mexican positions.[202]

Callahan was shocked to learn that among the Mexican forces was his old friend Juan N. Seguín, who now commanded the Mexican Bejar Defenders. Seguín, for whom the town is named, had become embroiled in local politics as mayor of San Antonio. Incriminated in playing a role in General Rafael Vásquez's invasion of San Antonio in March 1842, Seguín had resigned as mayor on April 18, 1842. Shortly thereafter, he fled to Mexico with his family. While living in Mexico, he participated—under duress, according to him—in Woll's invasion of Texas.

With good cover behind the embankment, on the right center of the Texas line, Callahan and the other Texans had a clear field of fire into a wide, grassy prairie that rose gently from the creek to a low ridge nearly eight hundred yards away. The other companies occupied the ground to the left.

From this vantage, Callahan had a good opportunity to judge the size of the Mexican detachment under his old nemesis Colonel Vicente Córdova. He also saw some eighty-five Cherokee Indians and renegade Nacogdoches Mexicans from Córdova's insurgents crawling into the hollow on the Texans' right. Anticipating an attempt to capture the Texans' horses, Callahan made a detail of fifteen men guard against surprise in that quarter.[203]

In preparing for the battle on the Salado, Caldwell told his men that the test had come. With his sleeves rolled up and a red handkerchief tied around his head, he stopped in front of the men and gave them a short speech: "Boys, I have longed to see the day when I would have a chance to fight these rascals, ever since I spent some time in a Mexican prison, now boys, the time has come, and I do not want you to shoot until you can see the whites of their eyes. If every one of you will pick your men and make a sure shot, we will whip hell out of them before they know it."[204]

A soldier of fortune, General Woll was an experienced field commander. He had been a defender of Paris with Napoleon, a U.S. Army field adjutant with General Winfield Scott and on the Mexican general staff with Xavier Mina. During the invasion, he served as a general officer under Santa Anna.

Responding to bugle and drum signals, the Mexican infantry formed up in four long lines of battle facing the creek. Woll positioned a thin line of skirmishers well to the front and held his dragoons in the rear to act as a reserve. Cavalry served as a screen for each flank.[205]

The Mexican cannons opened fire at point-blank range. When the artillery fire was lifted, bugles sounded and drums again rolled as the Mexicans charged. They first assaulted the Texans' center and left wing and then stormed down the hollow on the right. Woll sent four hundred soldiers, including forty Cherokees under General Vicente Córdova, in the first charge. About 1:00 p.m., the general led nearly five hundred more soldiers to the battlefield.

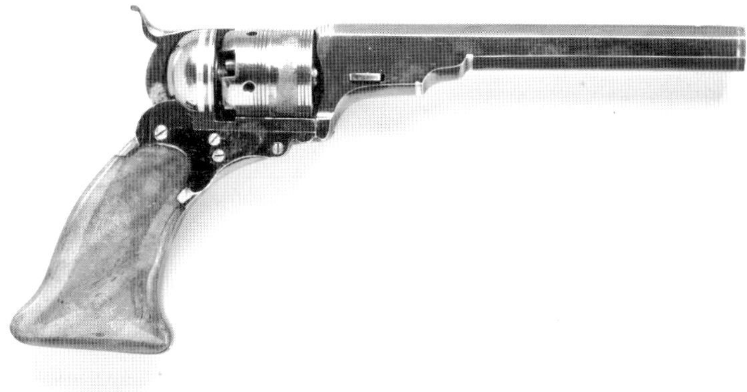

A Colt Paterson revolver. *http://www.imfdb.org/wiki/Colt_Paterson_1836.*

Jeffrey Robenalt wrote:

> *The Mexicans marched forward to the beat of their drums as if on parade, bayonets glistening in the late afternoon sun, and the Texas marksmen, concealed behind the cover of the earthen embankment, delivered volley after volley of devastatingly accurate rifle fire into the enemy's massed ranks. Mexican soldiers fell by the score, most of them hit in the head or center-punched in the chest.*[206]

Captain Bird's order to his men was "Lie low, boys, and be ready for the charge." As the enemy approached, he sprang up, shouting, "Now, boys, let them have it."[207]

Parson Carroll, an old Methodist preacher, stepped up on the bank and fired, shouting, "God take your souls!"[208] Callahan began a careful routine of firing and reloading and firing again. Due to his training and experience, he could maintain a firing rate of two to three rounds per minute. His Springfield model 1840 flintlock musket featured a forty-two-inch smooth-bore barrel. A sharp shooter, he sent the .69-caliber balls toward the enemy with good accuracy.

The firing became "at will," compelling the Mexican soldiers to fall back to their cannon. The ground became cluttered with their dead and wounded. For Callahan, this scene was like a flashback to 1836 at the Battle of Refugio. It was raining, and once again he was fighting the Mexican army he so despised. Rage colored Callahan's visage.

Caldwell formed his men under the banks in two ranks. Miles S. Bennett reported: "One ran[k] would advance and fire while the other loaded."[209]

Caldwell gave orders for half his men to reserve their fire. Those in front were to step back after a discharge and reload, while those with loaded rifles were to step up on the bank and fire. The Mexicans had to advance very close before they could see the Texans and then fell back from the deadly rifle fire. A loud, keen yell went up from the Texans as the Mexicans broke and dashed back out of range in disordered squads, leaving quite a number killed and wounded on the field.

Newly promoted, General Córdova had taken refuge behind a small mesquite in the retreat and was killed when he attempted to step out.

Bennet described the action:

> *I heard a general advance and I went under the bank and leaned against a little pecan tree. The tree I first picked out to protect me was shot entirely off by a cannon shot. The Mexicans came up within forty yards of our lines, cavalry, infantry and artillery. Our boys stood firm. One column under Old Córdova advanced upon us along a ravine that intersected the creek. Willis Randall shot and killed Old Córdova.…We killed and wounded a great many of the enemy when they made the general advance. The Mexicans fell back.*[210]

After this, according to Thomas Jefferson Green, Woll "used every persuasion to make his men charge the Texians, but to no purpose. The Texan rifle, when directed by steady nerves…was awfully destructive." As night came on and the firing ceased, Woll retired from the field.

During this time, Nicholas M. Dawson's command was marching to join Caldwell. Only a mile and a half away, these men were cut off and surrounded by Mexican troops. The Texans fought back a cavalry charge, inflicting a number of casualties on the enemy. The Mexicans then pulled back out of rifle range and opened fire on the Texans with their artillery. After a vigorous but futile resistance, the severely wounded Dawson sought to surrender. The Mexicans continued to fire, however, striking Dawson several more times. Seeing surrender to be impossible, he gasped out his dying words, "Let victory be purchased with blood." But the shattered Texans raised a white flag and laid down their arms. Ignoring pleas for mercy, the Mexican troops moved in and bayoneted the wounded and many of the others. By 5:00 p.m., what came to be called the Dawson Massacre was over.[211] Thirty-six Texans had died on the field, fifteen were taken prisoner and only two escaped.[212]

In the day's fighting on the Salado, Woll reportedly lost 104 men killed and many more wounded while only 1 Texan was killed and 9 to 12 were wounded.

Robert Hall later wrote:

> *Our commander, Old Paint Caldwell, was equal to a thousand men. No man who ever stood on Texas soil was his equal in battle. As soon as the bullets began to whistle he seemed to grow taller and look grander. I don't think it ever occurred to him that he might be hit. He rode over a battlefield as unconcerned as if he had been out cornshucking. His nerves must have been made of iron; nothing disturbed him.*[213]

Woll reassembled his battered troops and ordered a retreat to San Antonio. The Mexicans left 60 bodies on the battlefield and filled their wagons with another 44 dead and 150 wounded.

Rather than risk another engagement, Woll subsequently abandoned San Antonio on September 20. The procession included a herd of five hundred cattle and whatever wagons and carts on which they could lay their hands, piled high with plunder. Two hundred Mexican families seeking protection from the town's enraged Anglo citizens also accompanied the column as it headed back to the Rio Grande.[214]

On the Texas side, Caldwell ordered a council of war. Thanks to the insistence of Hays, the Texas officers decided to pursue the Mexicans and engage them again. Crossing the Medina River and moving toward present-day Castroville, Caldwell's forces began to close the distance.

Hays and his company led the pursuit, catching up with the Mexican rear guard near the Arroyo Hondo in midafternoon on September 22.

Just before four o'clock in the afternoon on September 21, 1842, the Mexican army was sighted on the east bank of Arroyo Hondo.[215] Convinced that an assault was imminent, Woll attempted to assume a defensive position on the Arroyo Hondo at a point where it makes a sharp bend to the west. He placed a four-pound field piece supported by infantry there. As his main army crossed the arroyo, the Mexican soldiers re-formed on the flats to the west, where a second four-pound field piece was placed facing eastward and commanding the approach to the crossing and the battery on the opposite bank.[216]

Caldwell gave Hays permission to assault the Mexican guns and promised to support the attack with his infantry. Led by Hays, the Rangers then made a courageous cavalry charge into the face of the Mexican cannons. The yelling Texans killed all five artillerymen as they overran the Mexican position.

Inexplicably, Caldwell's promised infantry support did not materialize. A dogged advance by the Mexican infantry forced Hays's Rangers to spike the cannons and retire.

Hays had his horse shot out from under him in the mêlée. Four of his Rangers suffered wounds, including Samuel Luckie.[217]

Observing that the Rangers were not supported by infantry or artillery, General Woll rallied and recaptured the battery.

A pause ensued. The two armies camped in sight of each other for two days, and the Texans did not attack. Being outnumbered and underprovisioned and facing fierce cannon fire, the Texan leaders were unable to rally consensus for an offensive action. The usually aggressive Caldwell held a council of war, and more time was lost in discussing the situation.

For Callahan, it was like a recurring nightmare. Once again, he was plagued by bickering among his commanders. Among the Texan officers, however, a heated difference of opinion arose as to the practicability of successfully attacking the enemy. McCulloch came to the front and called for volunteers to advance, and Judge John Hemphill urged the importance of an immediate attack.

According to Miles S. Bennet, "Lethargy had fallen upon the command that effectually retarded further progress." As night approached on the twenty-second, the Texans stood in their ranks, "suffering for water and tantalized almost to madness by the delay and want of harmony among our leaders."[218]

Following the battle, the Texans disbanded, and the Mexican forces continued their trek southwestward, back to Mexico. At three o'clock the next morning, Woll hustled his troops across the Arroyo Hondo and force-marched them toward the Rio Grande. The Texans skirmished with his rear guard, but no major clashes occurred.

Joining in Woll's retreat were two hundred *béxareño* families. In fact, Woll's departure almost reduced by half the number of *tejanos* at San Antonio. Prominent among these *tejanos* was Juan N. Seguín.[219]

Hays and his Rangers continued nipping at the rear of Woll's retreating army, giving him no respite. On one attack, Hays led his company into the Mexican encampment. Had he been supported, Woll's army could have been destroyed.[220]

Despite his lack of success in reclaiming Texas for Mexico, Woll was a wiley commander. He broke his force into separate commands to withdraw across the Rio Grande. Caldwell's force had returned to San Antonio by September 24.

There, welcome news awaited Caldwell's troops. Finally yielding to the growing tide of political pressure, President Houston had ordered General Alexander Somervell to organize an expedition to patrol in force along the Rio Grande, with authority to cross the border if he deemed it necessary. At long last, the Rangers would have an opportunity to take the fight to Mexico.[221]

9

THE SOMERVELL EXPEDITION

Soon after they arrived at the Salado on March 25, 1843, our men received the melancholy intelligence that they were to be decimated, and each tenth man shot. It was now too late to resist the horrible order. Our men were closely ironed and drawn up in front of all their guards, with arms in readiness to fire. Could they have known it previously, they would have again charged their guards, and made them dearly pay for this last perfidious breach of national faith. It was now too late! A manly gloom and a proud defiance pervaded all countenances. They had but one alternative, and that was to invoke their country's vengeance upon their murderers, consign their souls to God, and die like men.

—General Thomas J. Green, journal, 1845

On September 25, in front of the Alamo and before a crowd of 1,200, General Edward Burleson set into motion what would become known as the Somervell Expedition. Arousing the crowds' emotions, he outlined his plan: The Texas troops were to return home, obtain fresh mounts and supplies and be back in San Antonio in one month. From there, Somervell would lead them to Mexico.

Now a gritty combat veteran, Callahan rode with the Somervell Expedition, along with John Coffee Hays, Samuel Walker and Big Foot Wallace.

Houston had ordered two regiments of militia into service. In addition, he called for eleven volunteer companies. One of these companies was captained by Hays and seconded by First Lieutenant Henry E. McCulloch. Ephraim McLean served as second lieutenant.

On November 22, the final muster was held at San Antonio's Mission Concepción, and the expedition left for Mexico. Somervell's force included seven hundred men, two hundred pack mules and three hundred beeves for the use of the troops. The command included several preachers, many church members and many young farm boys from East Texas. Flaco, the Lipan chief, and a few of his tribe also accompanied the expedition.[222]

The expedition moved westward across the Medina River and then south in the direction of the Laredo Road. The weather turned cold, rainy and blustery. Many of the men were green, unused to the hardships of military campaigning. The harsh conditions affected the men's morale quickly.

Mules and horses oftentimes sank to their bellies in the saturated sandy loam soil. After three days of traveling from west to south, the Texan force finally made it to the Laredo Road. At last, there was firm ground to support the men and their livestock.[223]

Still, the strong northers continued. The Nueces River, the stream that Mexico claimed as the boundary of Texas and Mexico, was flooded. Led by Hays, the expedition crossed the fast-moving river with no loss of life. But during the night of November 25–26, the northers took their toll on the livestock. About midnight, the animals stampeded and were not rounded up until shortly after daybreak.

In hindsight, the Somervell Expedition was ill fated from the start. First, Jesse Lindsay McCrocklin's regiment initially balked at going on the expedition.[224] Second, the wet, bitter weather took its toll on man and beast. Third, while on a scouting party after crossing the Nueces, Hays captured two Mexican spies, one of whom escaped and undoubtedly told his superiors of the approaching Texans.[225]

The Ranger blamed for this escape was William Wirt Alsbury, the husband of Sarah Medissa Day of Gonzales. Due to Alsbury's negligence, the Rangers had to make an unsuccessful forced march toward Laredo in a futile effort to recapture the escapee. Events began to domino, and as Cicero Rufus Perry said, "You ought to have heard the Mexican women laughing at us. I told the boys when I heard the laughing, that the jig was up and the birds had flown."[226]

On December 8, the Texan expedition encamped at the mouth of Chacon Creek at its confluence with the Rio Grande, immediately south of Laredo.[227] The troops were tired, their horses were spent, food was scarce and their blankets and clothes were torn. Despite the less-than-ideal conditions, the following day a large number of the Texan volunteers rode into Laredo, searched and sacked the defenseless town.[228]

At Camp Chacon, General Somervell appeared to be indecisive. He moved from one location to another, not explaining why to his men. Although this posturing may have been confusing to the Mexican soldiers, the Texans were spoiling for a fight and in no mood to play a game of cat and mouse. Morale sank lower.

Houston's instructions to Somervell were to continue the invasion only if circumstances ensured a reasonable chance for success. Because almost one-third of the participants returned home soon after the capture of Laredo, Somervell determined that the remaining force was neither strong enough nor adequately outfitted to sustain further penetration into Mexico. He therefore ordered his men to disband and return to Texas. On December 19, Callahan and some two hundred other Texans rode home.

A large number of the Texans, however, felt betrayed by the order. Thus, over three hundred of the men elected to continue the raids in what came to be known as the Mier Expedition. Many men from Seguin remained on expedition.[229] Among the troops marching to Mier was William Wirt Alsbury of Seguin.

Captain William S. Fisher volunteered to lead this desperate band of men, and they at once elected him their general. Embarking in boats, they floated down the Rio Grande to the Mexican town of Mier.

General Pedro de Ampudia, commanding the garrison of Mier, arrived in the town with two hundred splendidly dressed soldiers. It was Christmas Day 1842.

The Texans discovered that Ampudia was in possession of Mier and prepared to give him battle immediately. Big Foot Wallace later said this was the hardest fought battle that he ever witnessed. The Texans forced a passage across the river in the face of a rainstorm of musket balls and a torrential shower of grape and canister.[230]

The Battle of Mier was fierce, lasting seventeen hours. By 2:00 p.m. on December 26, the Texans were spent. By one account, Mexican blood let by the sharpshooting Texans filled the town's gutters. In the battle, more than six hundred Mexicans were killed. Even so, the Mexican army eventually forced the Texans to surrender.[231]

Two hundred forty-two Texans prisoners were taken on the road to Mexico City. In Saltillo, the new commander, Colonel Domingo Huerta, moved the prisoners to El Rancho Salado. Diplomatic efforts led Santa Anna to a compromise: only one in ten would be put to death. In response, Colonel Huerta staged the infamous "Black Bean Incident." Huerta had 159 white beans and 17 black beans placed in a clay pot. The Texans were

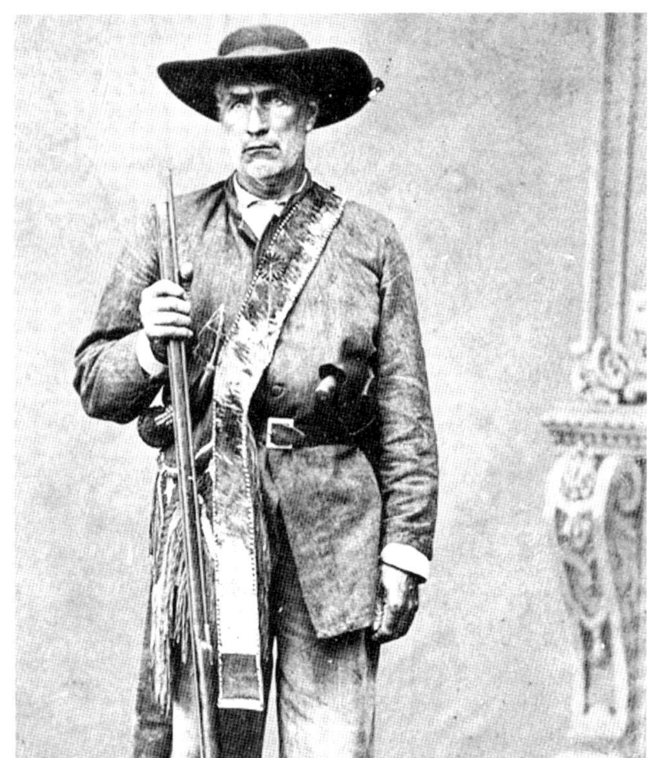

Right: Big Foot Wallace. *Texas State Library and Archives Commission.*

Below: *The Drawing of the Black Bean. Frederic Remington.*

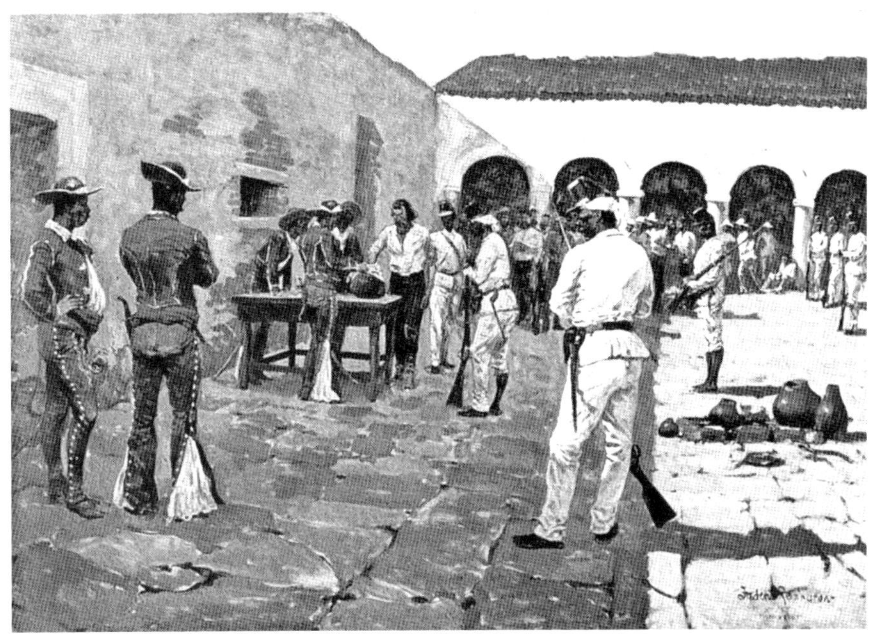

blindfolded and ordered to draw beans. Officers and then enlisted men, in alphabetical order, took their turns. The seventeen men who drew black beans were allowed to write letters home and then awaited their fate.

It is said that Big Foot Wallace drew a gray bean. The Mexican officer arbitrarily decided it was a winning white bean, and Wallace was spared.[232]

The white bean survivors finished the march to Mexico City and were later imprisoned at Perote Prison in the state of Veracruz, along with the fifteen survivors from the Dawson Massacre and about thirty-five other men captured by Woll in San Antonio. Some of the Texans escaped from Perote or died there, but most remained captive until they were released, by order of Santa Anna, on September 16, 1844. Among those men heading home to Seguin was Alsbury, who returned to this wife, Sarah.

10

SEGUIN RANGER STATION

Men talked hopefully of the future; children reveled in the novelty of the present; but the women—ah, there was where the situation bore heaviest. As one old lady remarked, "Texas is heaven for men and dogs, but a hell for women and oxen." They—the women—talked sadly of the old homes and friends left behind, so very far behind it seemed then, of the hardships and bitter privations they were undergoing and the dangers that surrounded them.
—Noah Smithwick

In Seguin, Sarah Medissa Day petitioned for divorce from William Wirt Alsbury on December 14, 1842, after four years of marriage and no children. Just prior to this time, Alsbury was involved with the Santa Fe Expedition, which had marched from Kenney's Fort near Austin on June 19, 1841. Alsbury remained a captive in Mexico until June 1842.

Sarah must have had grounds for divorce. In 1841, the Texas Congress defined the causes justifying divorce as "adultery, abandonment, cruel treatment, and outrages from one toward the other such as render their living together insupportable."[233]

Just three months after her divorce, Sarah Medissa Day Alsbury married James Hughes Callahan on March 25, 1843.

Their home was on the very edge of the savage wilderness. Sarah Day was a pioneer woman. Adele Lubbock Briscoe Looscan wrote in 1898:

> *While men are animated by love of adventure, desire for wealth or fame, which convert every obstacle overcome into a glorious triumph, female pioneers are sustained alone by the strength of their devotion to others, and weak hands learn to perform labors, and tender hearts to bear trials, unendurable by the sterner sex, and which in less perilous times would have been impossible, even themselves.*[234]

As if describing the situation on the Texas frontier, Looscan goes on to say, "It requires far less strength of character to face visible danger than to dwell calmly where it is known to be near, but keeps partially veiled."

The Callahans operated a 350-acre farm at Prairie Lea in what became Caldwell County.[235] This new county was created in 1848 from Bastrop and Gonzales Counties. Prairie Lea is near the San Marcos River and about ten miles southwest of Lockhart, the county seat. The first store was opened in Prairie Lea by Callahan in 1849. He became the postmaster on August 23, 1851. He also continued his services as a member of the local militia and a Texas Ranger. But for a time, he chose to be in the home guard and apparently did not participate in the war with Mexico in 1848.

A happy couple, James and Sarah became the parents of six children: Wesley Hughes Callahan, born about 1843; James Sanford Callahan, born about 1844; John A. Callahan, born about 1847; Catherine Callahan, born about 1849; Carolina Callahan, born about 1850; and William Milford Callahan, born 1852.

The general store and cattle became the primary economic base of the Callahan family. As their children grew, they began to take over chores and learn the business of cattle raising and farming. The farm was mostly subsistence crops. Sarah supervised the gardening and working the cultivator. She and the children also managed the chickens, hogs and goats. It was pastoral, but it was still the wild and hostile frontier of Texas.

Not all was quiet on the frontier. Callahan lived on the edge of peril. At Prairie Lea, he had to be ever vigilant to defend his family and neighbors from raids by Indians and outlaws. As T.R. Fehrenbach writes, "Some two hundred Texans were killed by Indians or carried off into captivity in the year 1849 alone."[236] Callahan slept with his handgun.

Richard Kruger wrote about how America grew:

> *Comanche, Apache, and other tribal warriors had been punishing Spanish, Mexican, and American intruders into their stark homeland for three centuries and been given no incentive to let up their murderous*

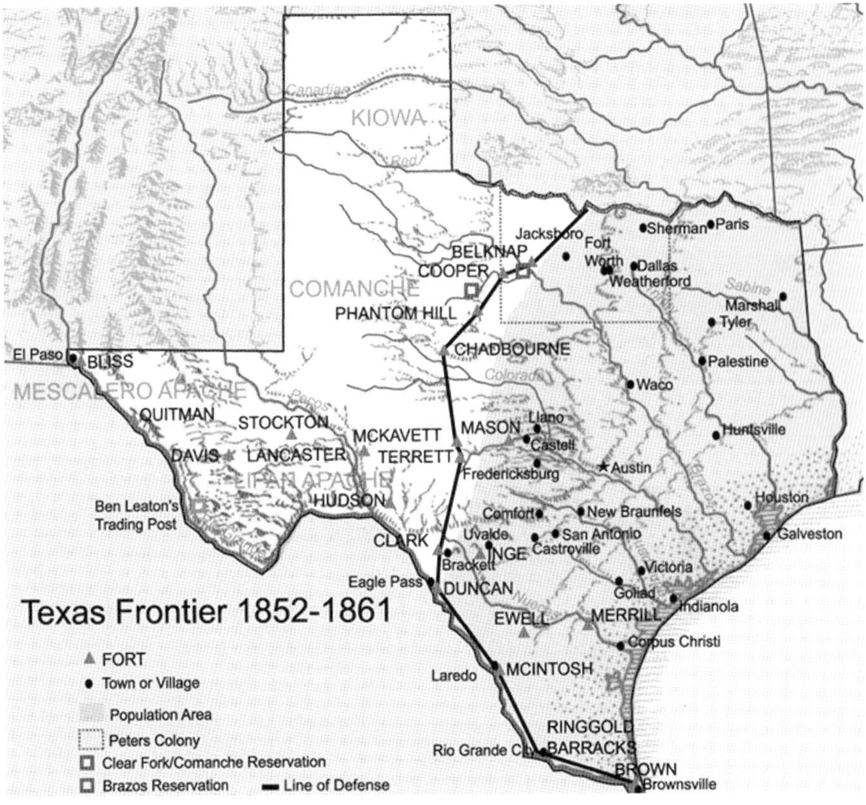

The Texas frontier in 1849–52. *Courtesy of Texas Beyond History.*

> *marauding and pillaging, horse stealing in particular. The U.S. Army had posted nearly 8,000 of its total of 11,000 soldiers along the southwestern boundary, but they could not halt the 75,000 or so native nomads in the region from attacking swiftly and taking refuge among the hills, buttes, and arroyos in a landscape where one's enemies could be spotted twenty or thirty miles away.*[237]

U.S. president John Tyler restarted negotiations with the Republic of Texas in 1844. His efforts culminated on April 12 in a Treaty of Annexation, an event that caused Mexico to sever diplomatic relations with the United States.[238] Tyler, however, lacked the votes in the Senate to ratify the treaty, and it was defeated by a wide margin in June. Shortly before he left office, Tyler tried again, this time through a joint resolution of both houses of Congress. With the support of President-elect Polk, Tyler managed to get

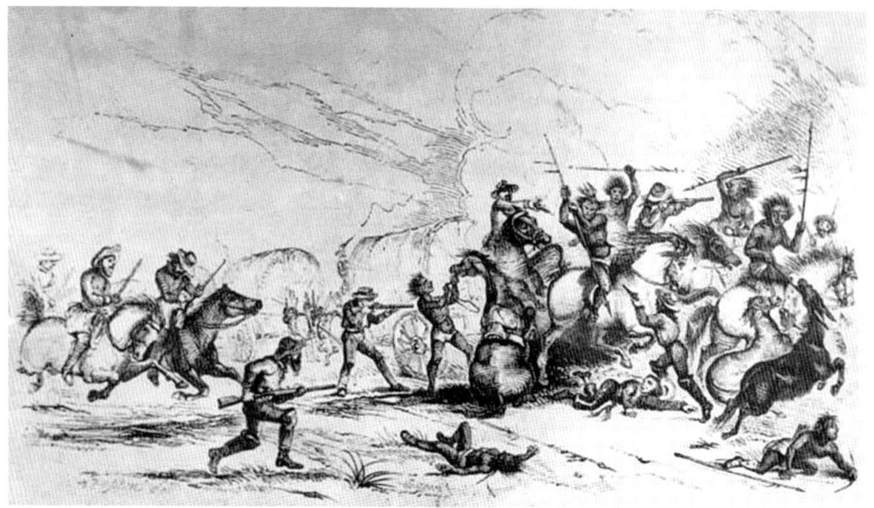

Apache Indians attack a wagon train. *Texas State Library and Archives Commission.*

the joint resolution passed on March 1, 1845, and Texas was admitted into the United States on December 29. American president James K. Polk attempted to secure Mexican agreement to setting the boundary at the Rio Grande and to the sale of Northern California. What Polk failed to realize was that no Mexican politician could agree to the alienation of any territory, including Texas.

Callahan's friend Robert Hall said, "I was opposed to annexation, and voted first, last, and all the time for the Lone Star. About the time General Taylor entered Texas at the head of a United States army, orders came for us to form a company and locate at San Marcos."[239] The Republic of Texas ratified the annexation treaty with popular approval. The bill was signed by U.S. president Polk on December 29, 1845, accepting Texas as the twenty-eighth state of the Union.

That year, 1845, Texas disbanded its army. The problem of frontier defense was relegated to the federal government. In a monumental blunder, the U.S. Army fielded the First Infantry to combat the Indians. Military posts, such as Fort Martin Scott, hopelessly tried to match swift raiders such as the Comanches by pursuing them after an attack with wagons of heavy infantry or worse, infantry troops consisting of farm boys mounted on plodding draft animals.[240]

Frustrated by the Mexican refusal to negotiate, President Polk, on January 13, 1846, directed General Zachary Taylor's army at Corpus Christi to advance to the Rio Grande. The Mexican government viewed that as an act of war. On April 25, the Mexican troops at Matamoros crossed the river and ambushed an American patrol. Polk seized on the incident to secure a declaration of war on May 13 on the basis of the shedding of "American blood upon American soil."

About this time, Ben McCulloch received orders from General Taylor to raise a picked company of about thirty mounted men for service as spies and scouts in Mexico. He raised a company of Rangers that became Company A of Colonel Hays's First Regiment of Texas Mounted Volunteers. McCulloch was fluent in Spanish and his woodsman's skills enabled him to slip back and forth across the lines undetected—more than once penetrating to within a mile of Santa Anna's own tent.[241]

Robert Hall wrote of the war with Mexico:

> *I joined this company, but furnishing a substitute for my old company. We marched to San Antonio and stayed a short time. There I bought the finest bowie knife I ever saw. It cost me twenty-five dollars. I carried it in my bosom during the whole war. I knew the Mexican soldiery well, and was familiar with the peculiar tactics of their scouts in throwing a lasso over the heads of their enemies. Many of our men in Mexico were captured and dragged to death in this way.*[242]

Many Rangers from the Seguin Station were active in the Mexican War. Unfortunately, there are no extant muster rosters of Texas enlisted men who fought in this war and, therefore, no record of Callahan serving in this war. But it appears likely he continued to serve as local home guard in the Seguin area.

At the close of the Mexican War in 1848, troops of the United States were withdrawn from Mexico and assembled in Texas. Under the provisions of the Treaty of Guadalupe Hidalgo, the United States was duty-bound to keep Indian raiders out of Mexico, a part of the agreement that the Comanches did not respect because they had not been consulted.

The War Department reorganized the army and its military geography to protect the newly acquired western frontier. This new land was a vast territory, increasing the domain of the United States by one third. The Department of Texas under the command of Colonel and Brevet Major General William Jenkins Worth was assigned 14 percent of the regular army. Twenty-two companies of the U.S. Army were assigned to prevent raids against the Mexican nation and Texan settlers.[243]

Suddenly, Callahan had the U.S. Army in his locality. The first frontier fort was built at Fredericksburg: Fort Martin Scott. Originally a Ranger station named Camp Houston, this army post was established by the First U.S. Infantry on December 5, 1848.[244]

Callahan was most familiar with Fort Martin Scott. In 1849, wagon trails bound for California arrived in Fredericksburg to obtain provisions for organize for their trek westward. Not only was the gold rush of the Forty-Niners a catalyst for this increase in traffic on the old Pinta Trail, but the opening of lands in west also created much traffic. Many had an escort of Texas Rangers like James Callahan. Unescorted travelers arriving in Fredericksburg sought a military escort from Fort Martin Scott to accompany them through the hostile lands to the west. These perils included the Comanche, Apache, Kiowa, Tonkawa, Kickapoo and Wichita bands, as well as banditti and brigands.

Callahan first visited the Blanco River area in 1841 while on McCulloch's Expedition. He was apparently impressed with the land along the river and so returned in 1853 with his friend, Eli Clement Hinds. An adept businessman, in 1854, Callahan joined with the operators of the Pittsburgh Land Company to purchase the league (4,428.4 acres) granted to Horace Eggleston by the government of Coahuila and Texas in 1835. The company was owned by General John D. Pitts, A.M. Lindsey, F.W. Chandler, William E. Jones and Callahan. They laid out the town of Pittsburgh, named for General Pitts, across the river from the site of future Blanco.

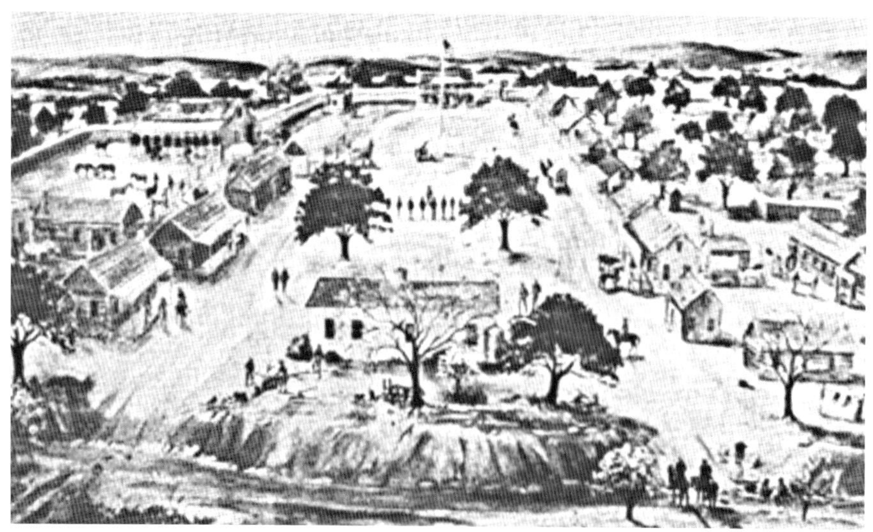

Fort Martin Scott. *Gotthold G. H. Lentz.*

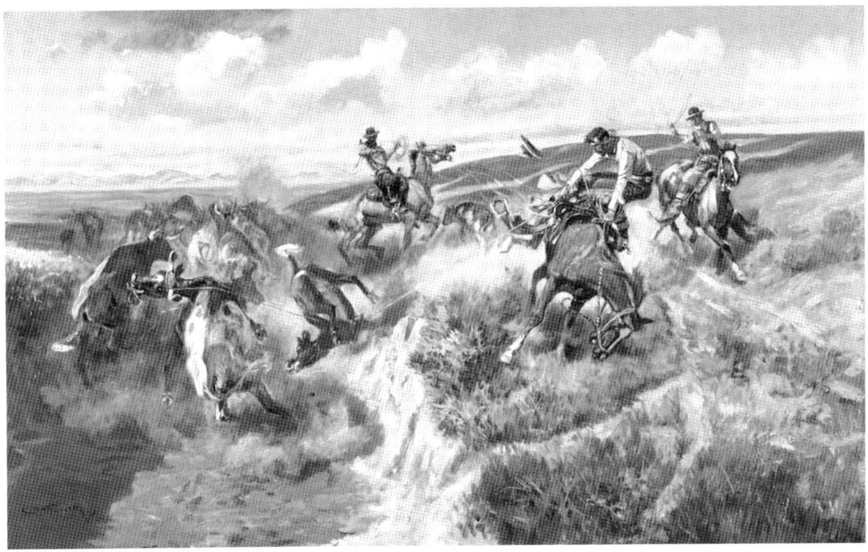

A Tight Dally and a Loose Latigo. Charles M. Russell.

The Callahans built their home on the Blanco River in 1854, thus becoming the first white settlers in what is now Blanco County. His homestead was a farm on the south bank of the Blanco River (originally called Martin's Fork of the Rio Blanco), about one and a half miles west of today's Blanco.[245]

James Callahan soon was employed as commander of a company of gunmen to guard a cattle drive from Seguin to California. Michael H. Erskine, cattleman and diarist, moved to Texas in 1839 and in 1840 to Gonzales County, where he purchased the José de la Baume Ranch[246] on the Guadalupe River near the Capote Hills, twelve miles southeast of Seguin. He took an active part in the development of early Seguin. When Guadalupe County was organized, he was elected chief justice. Erskine prospered in the cattle industry and from his Capote Ranch in 1854 drove a herd of 1,054 head of cattle to the gold fields of California.[247]

On the drive, he had the protection of an armed escort under the command of Callahan. Erskine kept a detailed diary of his experiences on this drive.[248]

The country west of San Antonio at that time was all frontier and completely controlled by hostile Indians and would require a strong escort to pass safely through. The escort consisted of thirty-five men and was commanded by Captain Callahan for a consideration of $1,500 for the trip. Only twelve men of this guard would be paid. The rest of the men were working their way to California and the gold fields.

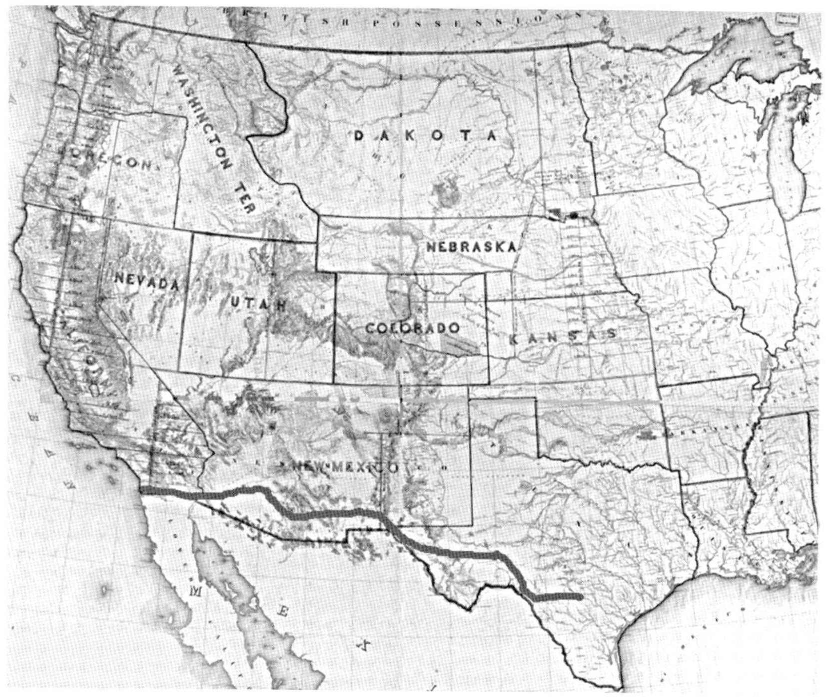

Callahan's route. *San Antonio to San Diego. 1858 War Department map in the collection of the Library of Congress).*

Erskine's cattle drive took them out to Quihi and Sabinal, across the Nueces to Elm Creek, Fort Clark and on out the California Trail. Along the trek to California, Callahan and his men defended the herd against Indian attacks in Comanche and Apache country. Erskine noted his diary that Callahan was very vigilant, keeping a "close watch and strong guard."[249]

Frederick Law Olmsted in 1856 saw herds of cattle being gathered near San Antonio for the drive to California. He examined one herd closely and found it amounted to four hundred animals escorted by twenty-five cowboys, mounted on mules. "Each man was armed with a rifle and a Colt revolver. These drovers knew how to use their weapons. When Indians on the Limpia River in 1854 stole three oxen from Michael Erskine's herd. Callahan fought ten of the Indians, killed five of them, recovered their stock and captured the Indians' ponies."[250]

On September 5, near Santa Cruz, Arizona, Callahan and his guards were confronted by forty Indians. The guards killed all but nine Indians, with the loss of one dead and five wounded. Callahan reached Los Angeles on November 23, 1854.

11

CALLAHAN'S EXPEDITION

If you prick us do we not bleed? If you tickle us, do we not laugh? If you poison us, do we not die? And if you wrong us, shall we not revenge?
—William Shakespeare

Jouette Fletcher McGee lay dead, a Lipan lance skewering his body from right shoulder to left hip. The lance had pinned him to the ground, though his body sat upright as if in defiance.

On that Friday morning, August 31, 1855, young McGee, aged fourteen years and eleven days, was slain by the Indians near Seguin. Surrounded by Lipan Apaches, he tried to get his small Mexican mule to make a run for it. The pigheaded mule refused to budge, leaving the defenseless McGee to the enthusiasms of the Indians. Crying and screaming, he kicked that mule, which simply would not move. The Lipans threw a lasso around the teenager and yanked him to the ground. Once and then again, he escaped the loop, running some three hundred yards up a hill to the place where he was speared and scalped.

The Reverend John McGee, father of Jouette, wrote an impassioned letter to the editor of the *Texas Christian Advocate*:

> *There is an awful responsibility resting some place with our governmental affairs. Here we have a Gen. and Staff, Depots of Ordnance and Subsistence, hundreds of government horses, forts, stations, and soldiers, agents with tens of thousands of dollars to feed the poor Indians, hundreds of thousands of dollars spent annually by our government for the defense of the frontier; and*

> *yet, from the Gaudaloupe* [sic] *to the Rio Grande, the country is overrun with murderous bands of thieving savages, and no security of either life or property....Things are in a worse condition now than when Texas stood alone. Who is to blame? People and press of Texas, speak, and speak boldly; who is to blame? Where and with whom does this blood rest?*[251]

Where was the U.S. Army? In the summer of 1855, three thousand U.S. troops, including the Second Dragoons, were transferred to Kansas to do battle in the First Sioux War following the Grattan Massacre.[252]

Settlers in Texas were left unguarded and virtually defenseless. Indian raiders responded accordingly with terrifying thefts and murders. As it turned out, the dragoons were not directly involved in the major engagement with the Sioux.[253]

By June 20, 1855, Texas governor E.M. Pease had heard enough grievances against the depredations by the Indians and, lacking U.S. Army resources, called on General Persifor F. Smith, who commanded the Department of Texas, to send a "company of mounted men into the neighborhood for its protection, to remain there as long as the public service will permit."[254]

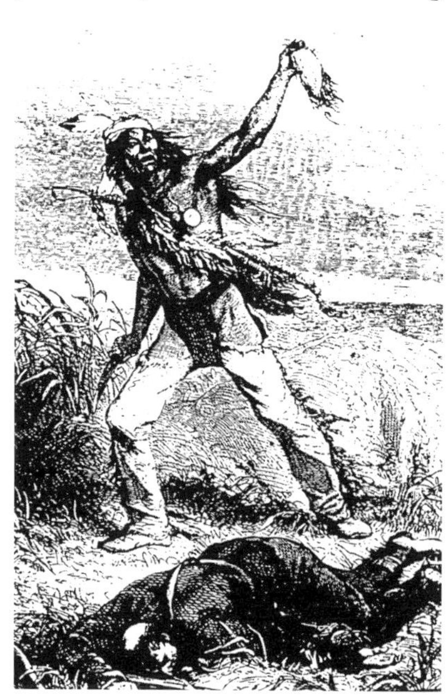

Native American Holding Up the Scalp of His Enemy. Illustration for La Nouvelle-France *by Eugene Guenin (New York: Hachette, 1900).*

General Smith had written to Pease promising that a "party of mounted riflemen would be sent to the neighborhood where recent depredations have been committed."

Camp Davant, in Bandera Pass, was created by the U.S. Mounted Rifles in 1855. Camp Verde, in Kerr County, would be established close at hand by the U.S. First Infantry on July 8, 1856.[255]

Texas had a response. Governor Pease sent Texas Ranger captain Callahan to sort this out. Callahan was now on a mission to seek out and "chastise" the Lipan Apaches. He was skilled as a soldier and Indian fighter, having fought with many legendary Texas heroes. These Texas Rangers had become known as "Los Diablos Tejanos"—the Texas Devils.

General Zachary Taylor described them thus:

> *One species of mounted force, peculiar to the western frontier of the United States is…efficient. The inhabitants of that frontier, from their vicinity to hostile Indians, are well practiced in partisan warfare, and although they will not easily submit to discipline, yet take the field in rough, uncouth habiliments, and, following some leader chosen for his talent and bravery, perform partisan duties in a manner hardly to be surpassed.*[256]

Most of the Ranger force was disbanded during the years following the end of the Mexican-American War on February 2, 1848, since the protection of the frontiers was now an official duty of the U.S. Army. At this same time, the Indian agent Robert S. Neighbors was working to relocate the Lipan Apaches to the upper Guadalupe River in 1848.[257] Neighbors reported:

> *The Lipans were very strong at this time. It was said that they could put 500 warriors in the field any day. There had been rumors that this powerful tribe wanted to make peace with us, but we did not believe it. One day I looked from the door of my house and saw not less than a thousand mounted warriors not a mile away. They were mounted on gaily-caparisoned horses, and their bodies were painted as if ready for battle.*[258]

Euro-American settlers continued to move up the Guadalupe River. Fredericksburg was settled in 1846, Curry's Creek in 1847, Sisterdale in 1848, Boerne in 1849, Kerrville in 1852 and Comfort in 1854. As more settlers sought to establish homesteads in lands traditionally occupied by Indians, the skirmishes with the native peoples became a major political issue. The Lipan Apaches had been raiding in this part of Texas all summer and into the fall of 1855 and then retreating across the border into Mexico near Piedras Negras.[259]

Public outcry was remarkable. Citizens complained and implored government officials for help. Jefferson Davis, then secretary of war, received complaints from J.E. Doss, William G. Thomas and Charles A. Campbell of Fredericksburg. Responding to them in a letter on May 12, 1855, Secretary Davis noted that he had communicated this concern to General Smith for "such action on is part as will afford you all the protection he can give, consistently with the wants of other sections of the country and the interests of the public service."[260]

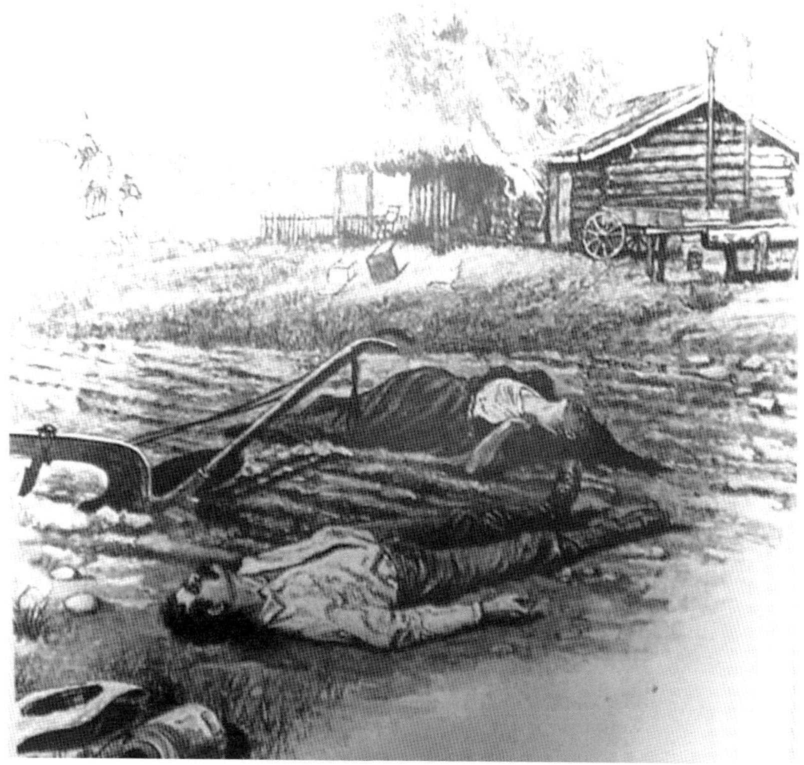

The aftermath of an Indian attack. *From* Harper's *80 (1890): 731.*

General Smith reported:

> *Drove after drove of horses were stolen and taken at once across the Rio Grande, where they were protected from pursuit by Mexican minor civil authorities.…Party after party of Lipan Indians, living under the protection of the Mexican authorities behind Laredo and near San Fernando de Rosas, came into the settlements singly and joining here in parties of five to thirteen, stole horses from all the ranches on the Medina, San Antonio and Cibolo Rivers, murdered several persons, and escaped by rapid flight across the Rio Grande, with much of their plunder.*[261]

On July 5, 1855, an exasperated Governor Pease wrote to Callahan directing him to form a company of Texas Rangers (without provision of supplies) and pursue Indians who were terrorizing the settlers in the Hill Country, "to follow them up and chastise them wherever they may be found."

Callahan's company of Rangers was ordered by the governor to serve three months unless sooner discharged—from July 20 to October 19, 1855. This was their "term of enlistment." Pease also ordered that Callahan's company not exceed in number a mounted company of the U.S. Army, which was composed of one captain, one first lieutenant, one second lieutenant, four sergeants, four corporals, one farrier, two buglers and seventy-five privates. The men were to supply their own equipment, firearms, ammunition, horses and forage.[262]

Governor Pease ordered Captain Callahan to divide his company:

> *Send a portion of it to such a point as will afford protection of the settlements in Medina and Bexar Counties, west and south of the point where it was first intended your entire company should be stationed. I therefore desire that you should divide your company and station one portion on the Guadalupe where the recent depredations were committed, and the other portion at such point as will afford protection to those settlements in Medina and Bexar Counties that have been recently visited by the Indians.*[263]

When Callahan received his orders, he began formulating a plan of action. Based on his combat experience, Callahan worked to develop intelligence about his enemy—the Lipan Apaches. To this end, Callahan sent one of his Rangers, August Schmidt, to spy on the Lipan village on the Sabinas River in Coahuila, Mexico.

John W. Sansom recorded this event: "Schmidt found abundant proof to satisfy any reasonable man....As additional evidence, he brought back to Texas from Mexico two horses that he bought from the tribe which, on being seen, were identified by a settler on the Guadalupe, a Mr. Slidel, as being his property."[264]

Callahan now had the information he needed to formulate a plan of action against those very same Lipans who had been raiding in his district. This plan he kept close to his vest.

Sansom noted in his memoir, "Governor Pease authorized Callahan to raise and organize another company of State troops to be under his command, the unexpressed but well-understood reason for this increase of force being to put enough men in the field to follow depredating bands into Mexico, up to their headquarters, and there to chastise them."[265]

The Lipan main encampment was at San Fernando de Rosas (modern Zaragoza) in Coahuila, Mexico.[266] Originally called the Villa of San Fernando de Austria, it became a Lipan village in 1751 when Chief Bigotes left Texas for Coahuila.[267]

12

A TANGLED WEB

Oh, what a tangled web we weave
When first we practice to deceive.
—*Walter Scott,* Marmion

Callahan had his orders to seek out and "chastise" the Lipan Apaches. What appeared to be a simple, direct command from the governor was complicated by externalities beyond Callahan's control. The captain rapidly became entangled in treacherous socio-political quagmire beyond his control. These external influences would have a profound effect on what came to be called the Callahan Expedition.

In the years immediately following the Mexican War, troubles arose in Texas that would agonize everyone: Indian raids, Mexican banditos, Texas outlaws, runaway slaves and filibustering expeditions.[268] This plague of woes became a catalyst for lawlessness, which not only impeded the progress of the region but also threatened to interrupt friendly relations between the Mexico and the United States.[269]

Texas, at that time, was described by Mexican officials as

> *the refuge for criminals flying from justice in Mexico; adventurers from the United States, who sought a fortune, unscrupulous of the means of procuring it; and vagrants from all parts of the State of Texas, hoping, in the shadow of existing disorganization and lawlessness, to escape punishment for their crimes.*[270]

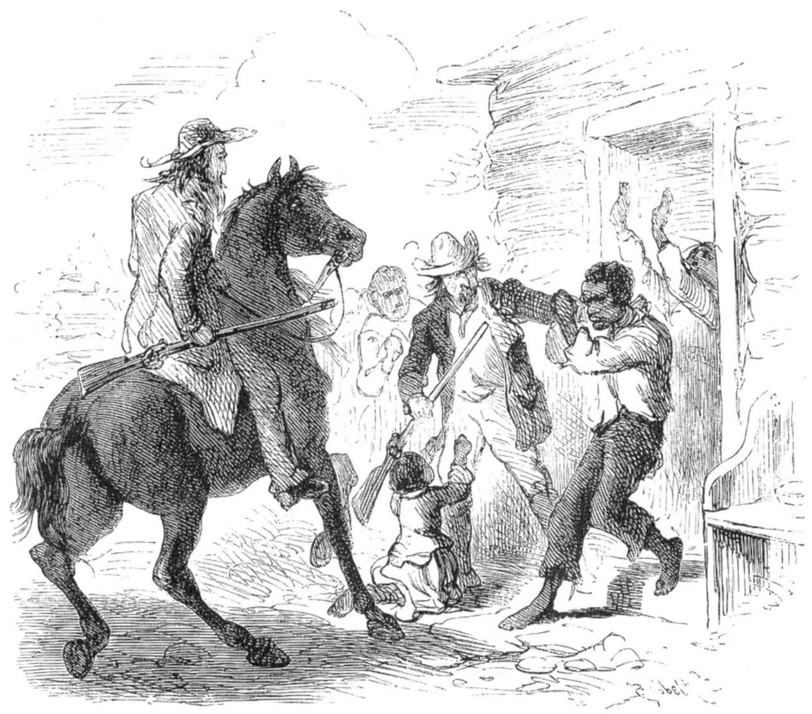

"Operations of the Fugitive-Slave Law." *Benson J. Lossing, http://www.crossroadsofwar.org/galleries/slavery-before-the-war.*

Section nine of the general provisions of the constitution of the Republic of Texas, ratified in 1836, made slavery legal in Texas. In early 1846, Texas was formally admitted to the Union as a slave state. According to the first official Texas state census in 1847, the state population counted 38,753 slaves and 102,961 whites.

In 1848, the Texas legislature passed a law aimed at punishing those who might assist escaping slaves. Anyone helping slaves plan a rebellion would be punished with death. Ship captains giving passage to runaways would receive from two to ten years in the penitentiary. Anyone who stole or enticed a slave from his or her owner would receive three to fifteen years of hard labor. Free persons of color who aided a slave in escaping would receive from three to five years in prison.[271]

By 1850, the slave population in Texas had increased to 58,161.[272] An unanticipated consequence of the fast-growing number of slaves in the state was the matter of runaway slaves. In 1850, an estimated three thousand slaves had successfully escaped to Mexico, and an additional one thousand crossed into Mexico between 1851 and 1855. Ninety percent of the runaways were men, most between ages twenty and forty, because they had the endurance to deal with the long, difficult journey. All ages were represented, however, from five months to sixty years.[273]

In the 1850s, prominent Texas citizens and businessmen became distressed about the number of runaway slaves in Mexico. Meetings were held throughout southern Texas in 1854 and 1855. It was resolved that the black Seminole presence in Nacimiento (a town in Coahuila, Mexico) was chiefly responsible. They raised $20,000 for an expedition to go after the runaways at Nacimiento.[274]

Texans had been willing to pay up to a $600 reward for the return of runaway slaves found living in Mexico. John S. Ford advocated the capture and return of these runaway slaves to Texas. He claimed that slaves worth a total of $3.2 million could be found in Mexico. This would put the number of those who traveled the pathway of freedom into Mexico in the range of four thousand.[275]

By 1855, slaveholders became so alarmed at this trend that they requested help from the federal military. Roughly one-fifth of the standing U.S. Army was subsequently deployed at garrisons along the Texas-Mexico border in a vain effort to restrict the flood of runaway slaves. One of those posts was Fort Duncan at Eagle Pass.[276]

On August 25, 1855, slave owners of San Antonio sent a letter to Colonel Emil Langberg, military commander of Coahuila, inquiring about "the conditions under which the Colonel would deliver up the Negros who had taken up refugee in Mexico." An offer was made to provide money in exchange for the return of runaway slaves "delivered to the river."[277]

The slave owners of San Antonio also made a veiled threat, hinting that a force of two hundred men stood ready to enter Mexico and apprehend the fugitives under the pretext of pursing Lipan Apaches who committed depredations in Texas. Aware then of these provisions, Langberg expressed interest, but only if the slaves were exchanged for runaway Mexican "peons" living in Texas.[278]

Colonel Langberg then took up the matter with Nuevo León officials. The government of that state responded that, although it was mindful of the losses suffered by both countries in this respect, it could only take the matter up with the governor of Texas, not with private individuals. The communication then answered the threat of the citizens of San Antonio in the following words:

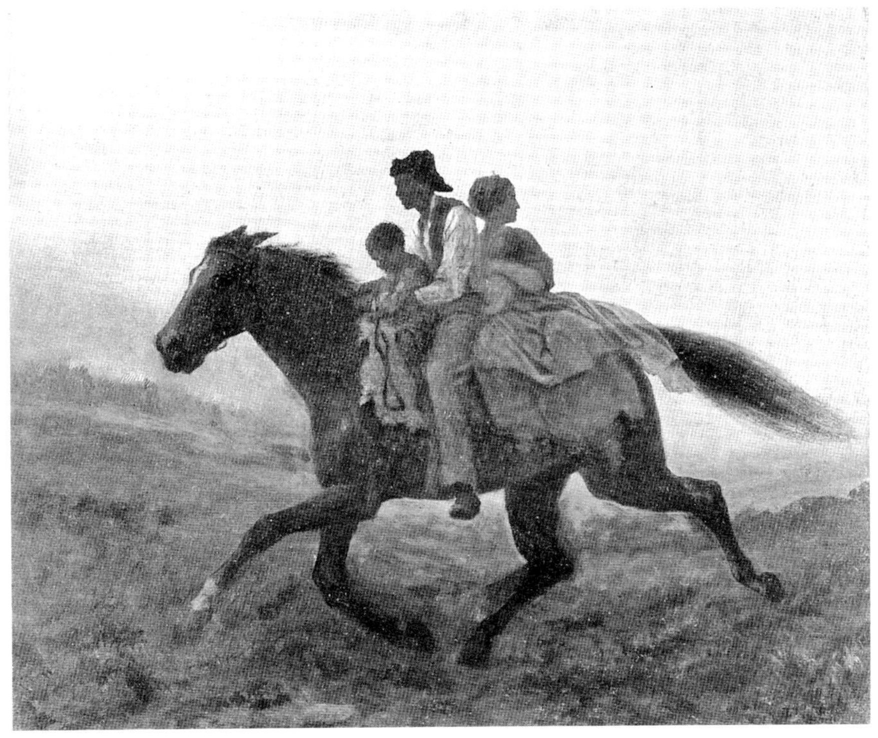

A Ride for Liberty, 1862. *Scanned from* Eastman Johnson: Painting America, *figure 74, page 137.*

> *If notwithstanding the foregoing* [namely, the willingness to come to an agreement with the State of Texas regarding the recovery of the fugitives] *the people of "Béjar" who have addressed you* [Col. Langberg], *decide to invade our frontier with a view to recovering their runaway Negroes and stolen horses, in this case you will be compelled to resist force with force.*[279]

During that summer of 1855, many Texas newspapers openly advocated a military "filibustering" expedition into northern Mexico, which was experiencing insurrectionist violence.[280]

At that time, the word *filibuster* had a nefarious meaning. The term is derived from the Dutch word *vrijbuiter*, which translates as "freebooter." The Spanish corrupted the term, and from their *filibustero* came the English version, which meant plunderer or pirate. In the words of a former filibusterer, it came to mean "adventurers who, during the decade preceding

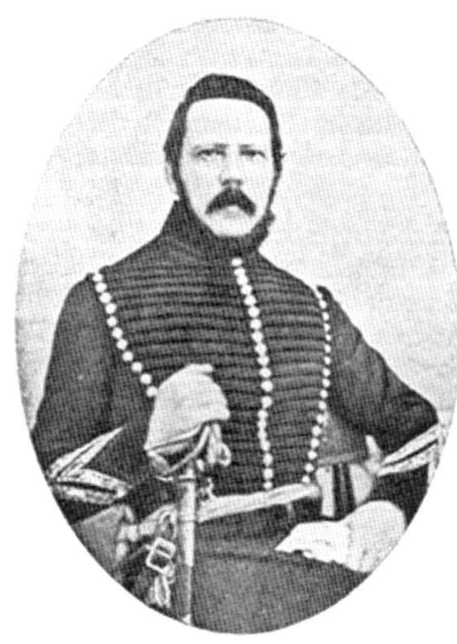

Colonel Emil Langberg. *Photograph from* P.S. Vig, Danske i kamp i og for Amerika, *Museum of Danish America, http://www.danishmuseum.org/explore/danish-american-culture/viewed-through-the-lens/edward-emil-langberg.*

the Civil War, were engaged in fitting out and conducting under private initiative armed expeditions from the United States against other nations with which this country was at peace."[281]

William Robertson Henry, a grandson of Patrick Henry, was a notorious filibusterer, adventurer and Texas Ranger. In July 1855, Captain Henry organized, with due public notice in the newspapers, a company of volunteers to intervene in Mexico and establish a government that would not threaten Texas interests.[282]

Henry was a version of the iconic Byronic hero—dark, handsome, brilliant but cynical and self-destructive.[283] He was mad, bad and dangerous to know, "a man proud, moody, cynical, with defiance on his brow, and misery in his heart, a scorner of his kind, implacable in revenge, yet capable of deep and strong affection."[284]

In letters to General Santiago Vidaurri, the governor of Nuevo León and one of the most powerful men of northern Mexico, Henry volunteered his services to support Vidaurri. The general was in a state of quasi-revolution against the supreme government of Mexico and had taken control of Nuevo León. Henry and others presumed that Vidaurri wanted to secede from Mexico and seek admission into the United States for the Republic of the Sierra Madre.[285]

While Captain Callahan was mustering his company, Henry published in several newspapers a proclamation to the people of Texas, announcing the preparation of an expedition that would join the revolution in Mexico. Vidaurri declined the offer.[286]

This well-publicized planned expedition to Mexico alerted the Mexican forces.

13
BANDERA

No gaudy trappings, no gay equipments, had any place in the necessary outfit of a Ranger, and no fifes nor drums, no brass bands, and no silken banners nor fluttering pennons accompanied these stern men on their swift and silent rides on the trail of the foe.
—Wilburn H. King

Concerned about Indian depredations in the Hill Country, Governor Pease wrote to General Smith stating that there were no U.S. troops stationed in the vicinity and no actions had been taken against the Indians in the last eighteen months. Pease went on to speculate that another raid by the Indians "would enrage the citizens so that they may arm themselves and do such violence to the Indians that a Gen. war would result." He requested that Smith station troops on the upper Guadalupe.[287]

General Smith responded to the governor, promising that a "party of mounted riflemen would be sent to the neighborhood where recent depredations have been committed." The result was the establishment of a little-known military outpost in Bandera Pass in 1855 by one company of Mounted Rifles under command of Lieutenant J.H. Edson.[288] Edson's commander was Captain John G. Walker. This unit was one of Smith's elite forces on the Texas frontier.[289]

In obedience to his orders, Callahan mustered eighty-eight men into Ranger service in San Antonio on July 20, 1855.[290] The mustering officer was J.D. Pitts, an associate and friend from Blanco. Most of Callahan's men were from the Prairie Lea and Seguin area. A few were from San Marcos

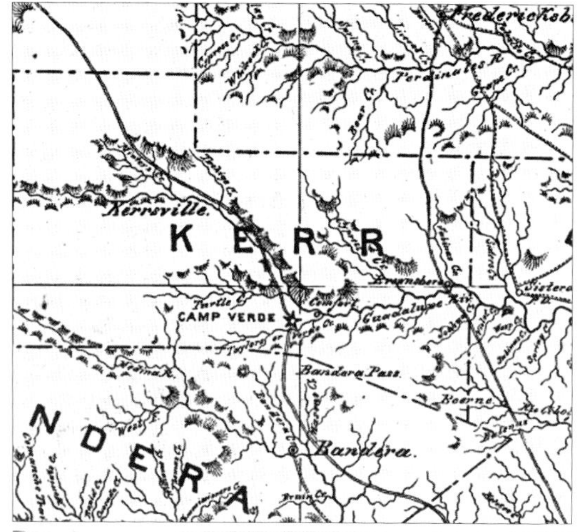

Left: Map of Bandera Pass. *Courtesy of Perry-Castañeda Library Map Collection.*

Below: Bandera Pass. *Photograph by Starr Bryden.*

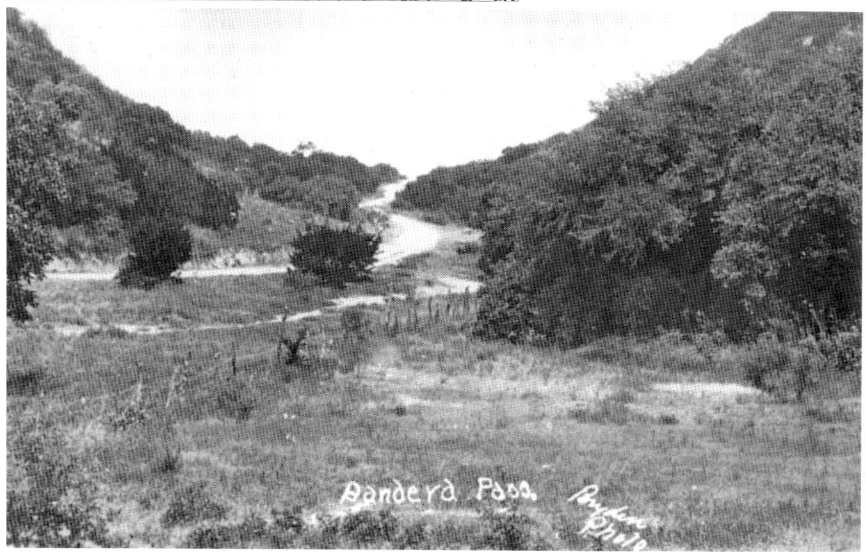

and the Austin area. Ages ranged from sixteen to forty-four. Callahan was forty years old.[291]

Callahan's company set up camp in strategic Bandera Pass at the boundary between Kerr and Bandera Counties. The men bivouacked in the southeast end of the canyon, beside Bandera Creek.[292] Nearby were the graves of five Rangers killed in John Coffee Hay's battle with the Comanche in Bandera Pass, around 1840–1843.[293]

Bandera Pass is a narrow, V-shaped natural erosion cut in the long limestone ridge separating the Medina and Guadalupe Valleys just south of the Bandera-Kerr County line. The Spanish named these hills Lomería Grande.[294] The Spanish captain José de Urrutia "discovered" the pass in 1739 while campaigning against the Apaches. By that time, the pass had been well known to Native Americans for some twelve thousand years.[295]

The Rangers were typically armed with the 1851 Colt Navy .36-caliber revolver, a derringer or small backup handgun (such as the .31-caliber Colt model 1849 pocket revolver) and, perhaps, shotguns of 10 or 12 gauge. Most carried Bowie knives. All of these weapons were for close-quarter combat. A Ranger armed with a Colt revolver and an extra cylinder could fire ten rounds in forty seconds, and Rangers frequently carried two pistols and spare cylinders.

Lighter than the Colt Walker of .44 caliber, the Colt Navy revolver could be worn on the belt instead of in a saddle holster. Famous Navy users included John Coffee "Jack" Hays, "Bigfoot" Wallace, Ben McCulloch, Addison Gillespie, John "RIP" Ford, "Sul" Ross and most Texas Rangers prior to the Civil War.[296]

As their long arm, Callahan's men most likely carried the .52-caliber Sharps model 1851 carbines. This was due mainly to the higher rate of fire (eight to ten shots per minute) of the breech-loading mechanism and superior quality of manufacture. Some say the Sharps rifle was one of the finest rifles ever built. The Sharps made a superior sniper weapon of greater accuracy than the more commonly issued muzzle-loading rifled muskets. The military versions of Sharps rifles were known as Sharps shooters, later condensed to "sharpshooters."[297]

The Sharps rifle was not a repeater, as it held only one shot. It used a falling-block action, which used a metal breach lock that slides up and down in grooves cut into the breech, controlled by a lever. Typically, a soldier could fire between eight and ten shots per minute, depending on his skill. The carbine was a shorter version of the regular rifle and was used primarily by cavalry troops.

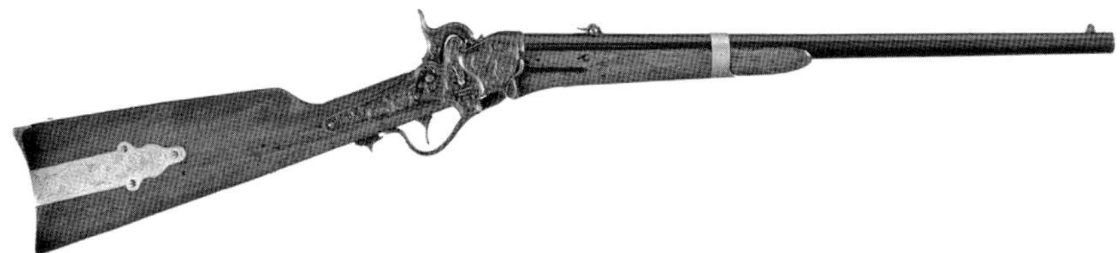

Sharps carbine, model 1851. *http://hi-luxoptics.com/blog/2016/02/17/the-rebirth-of-old-reliable-the-sharps-rifle-part-1/.*

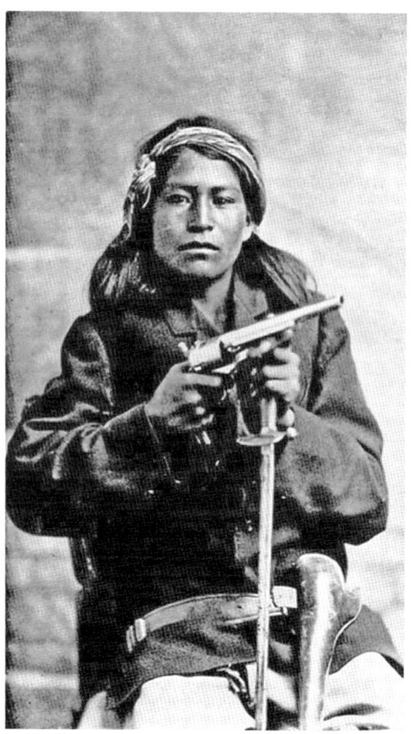

An Apache with a Colt Revolver. *https://www.pinterest.com/thefillies/wild-west-weapons/.*

The Ranger outfitted with a Sharps loaded his weapon from the breech, a comparatively simple job either from the back of a horse or from a prone and protected position on the ground. He opened the action, loaded a paper- or linen-encased powder and conical (Minié ball) cartridge, closed the action (trimming the paper or linen and exposing the powder), cocked the hammer, pulled the trigger and fired his weapon.[298]

Callahan's Rangers also brought shotguns from home. These were 10 or 12 gauges cut down to eighteen inches as a coach gun. These were well suited for close combat. Typically, these appeared in service as a double-barreled shotgun.

Each man was outfitted in the traditional Texas Ranger regalia: a small provisions wallet generally holding *panola* (parched corn), tobacco and ammunition. They all carried knives on their belts; it was their weapon of last resort. Many wore the traditional Mexican serapes. Their horses were fitted with Mexican saddles, hair rope *cabristas* (halters) and rawhide Mexican *riatas* (lariats).[299]

Callahan's company was actively engaged in pursuing Indians in the Hill Country northwest of San Antonio. On August 28, 1855, they were in Llano County at Camp Crabapple, and on August 30 and 31, the Rangers were at Camp Enchanted Rock.[300] Through the months of July, August and into September, Callahan's company remained busy in the Hill Country. Darren L. Ivey wrote that Callahan's company had several confrontations with Indians.[301]

Callahan's Rangers fought a battle in Bandera County in August and again on September 7, 1855. It was a harbinger of the future, as the combat is said to have been with Wild Cat (Coacoochee) and his Seminoles. In 1849, the Seminole war chief led his followers along with some southern Kickapoo warriors from the Arkansas reservation through Eagle Pass to Mexico. He and his cohorts were welcomed by the State of Coahuila, where they were placed on military reservations with supplies to defend the area against the forays of other hostile Indians.[302]

By mid-September, half of Callahan's men were reported in Gillespie County at Fort Martin Scott near Fredericksburg.[303] The remainder was along the Guadalupe River.[304]

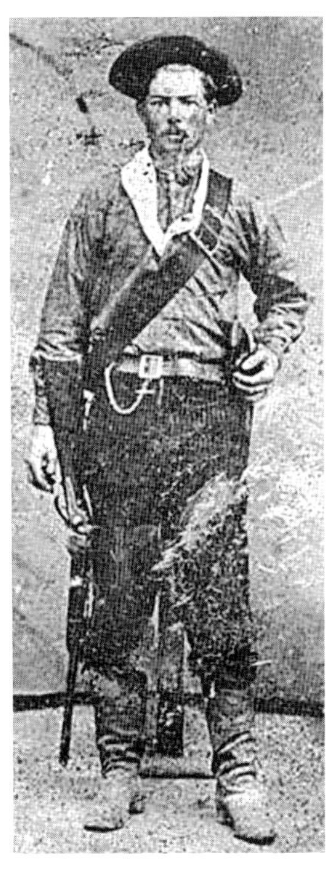

A Ranger with a Sharps carbine. *https://en.wikipedia.org/wiki/History_of_the_Texas_Ranger_Division.*

Acting on August Schmidt's secret reconnaissance of the Lipan Apaches at San Fernando, Callahan made preparations to seek out and "chastise" these raiders. On August 1, Callahan issued Special Order No. 1, instructing Lieutenant Ed Burleson Jr. to go to either Austin or San Antonio and contract for supplies.[305] In Austin, the governor endorsed the order, and supplies apparently were obtained in San Antonio. Callahan's company stored these supplies in the town of Bandera, where John Riley rented two small houses to the Rangers, one for a commissary and the other for a hospital.[306]

Callahan wrote another letter to Burleson on August 15. The letter contained important information regarding the forthcoming expedition. In this communication, Callahan explained to his quartermaster the means by which he would recompense his Rangers—assuming that the Texas legislature would be unable to compensate the volunteers.

> *I want every man to understand that if he goes with me to the Devil's River or any place I wish to go and if anything, is taken…it belongs to those that go and will be divided accordingly. I wish to inform the men under your command that if any property is taken from the Indians by any of the scout, it belongs to the men that take it. If those in camp receive no share in such…this will induce the boys to go on scouts.*[307]

On August 31, Callahan again wrote to Burleson: "I am bound to go to the Rio Grande if nothing happens.…I believe some of the boys have found out about the arrangement so I wrote to you as though my

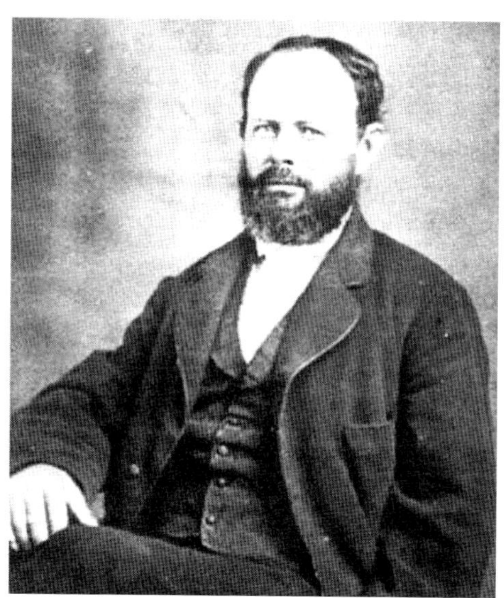

Right: Edward Burleson Jr. *Texas State Historical Association.*

Below: *A Pack Mule. Frederic Remington.*

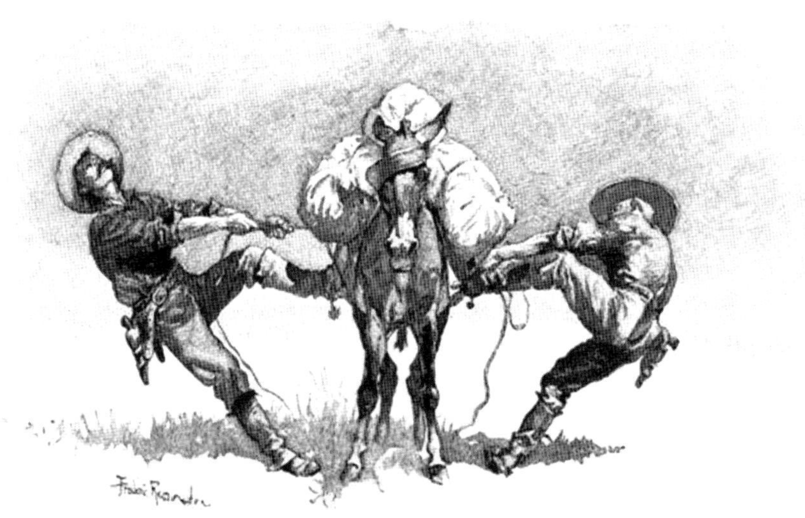

intention was to go to the upper country…to keep the matter as much of a secret as possible."[308]

Callahan's company departed the village of Bandera on September 18, 1855. Riding as if on the parade ground, Callahan's Rangers passed in review through town. In a column of fours, the Rangers trotted past the crowd. Dogs barked, men nodded and ladies and children waved as the Rangers moved out.

An ordinary day's ride for cavalry is about thirty miles, but on a forced march, mounted troops can cover fifty miles within twenty-four hours. A single horseman, or a small detachment, can easily exceed this distance. Callahan's company had miles to go; they rode hard.

The Rangers headed west for Encina on the Leona River. This small village—today's Uvalde—lay close by the U.S. Army post at Fort Inge and Leona Springs.[309]

Callahan led his men on the old military road from Bandera to Fort Lincoln on the west bank of Seco Creek.[310] Slowly descending through the rugged Hill Country, the Rangers emerged at the fort on old Woll's Road.[311]

Fort Lincoln had been built in 1849 and staffed by Companies E and G of the Eighth U.S. Infantry, commanded by Major James Longstreet. Fort Lincoln was abandoned on July 20, 1852, after the frontier line had advanced westward. The buildings remained intact for some time, and the Texas Rangers established a headquarters at the site.

The old fort was an important post at a major intersection with Woll's Road. The Texas Ranger camp there continued to provide protection for the settlers of the area and the wayfarers on the road between San Antonio and the Rio Grande.

Woll Road was actually the "Smugglers' Trail" used since the 1740s by merchants from Coahuila, Texas and Louisiana. After the Texas Revolution and during the decade of the Republic of Texas, commerce between the towns and villages in northern Coahuila and those in southern Texas was forbidden by Mexican authorities. A clandestine trade did continue, however, between San Antonio and the Mexican settlements, particularly those near the Rio Grande. Replacing the guarded main crossing sites near Presidio del Río Grande at Guerrero was a smuggler's trail that followed a more direct, though northerly, course to San Antonio over which trade caravans moved. The trail left San Fernando de Rosas (modern Zaragoza) and crossed the Rio Grande at a ford near the mouth of the Rio Escondido, thirty miles upriver from the old Presidio San Juan Bautista at Guerrero.[312]

This was the same trail used to surprise San Antonio by Spanish colonel Ignacio Elizondo in 1813, General Santa Anna and the Vanguard Brigade in 1836 and General Rafael Vasquez in 1841. General Woll followed this trail when he raided San Antonio in 1842.[313] In 1846, U.S. general John E. Wool ordered U.S troops from San Antonio on an expedition into Mexico. Wool ordered a detachment of 1,300 troops under Colonel William S. Harney to examine and explore the old smuggler's trail. Wool backtracked Woll's 1842 route.[314]

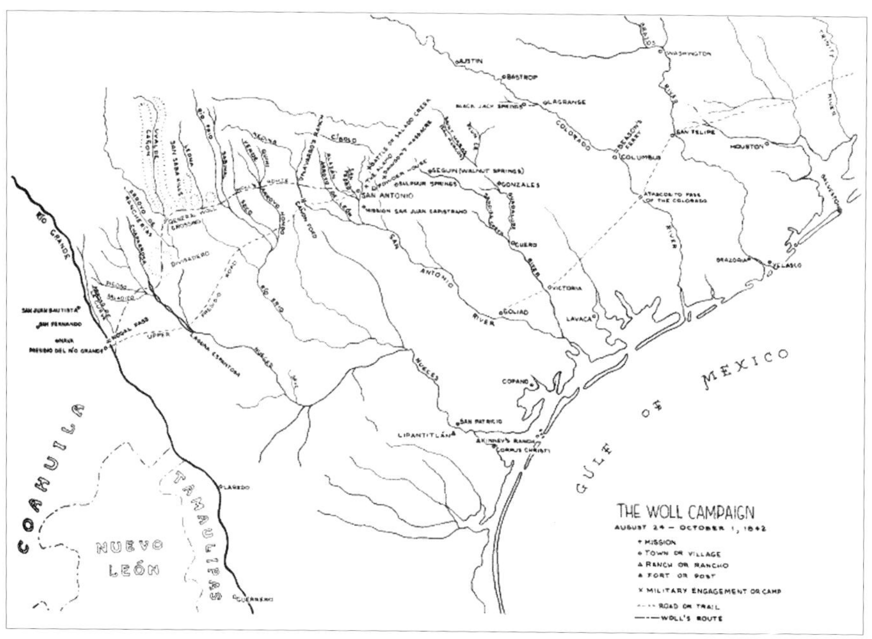

A map of Woll's Road. *Republic of Texas map by John Arrowsmith.*

Callahan and his lieutenants made a decision to follow Woll's Road, which went straight to their destination at the Lipan village at San Fernando de Rosas. This route would avoid the heavily traveled El Camino Real and enable the Rangers to march on their objective with some measure of discretion.[315]

Woll's route traversed present-day Medina, Uvalde, Zavala and Maverick Counties before the Rio Grande. The distance from San Antonio to the west bank of the Rio Grande over the route was 164 miles.[316] This region was called the Despoblado (unpopulated abandoned place), a vast, forbidding wilderness of sparse vegetation, stretching in a funnel shape from a broad area in the Central Plains southward across the Rio Grande and deep into Mexico.

Many in Callahan's command knew this old road well.[317] These veteran Rangers had fought battles with the Indians and Mexicans all along the route. Many had participated in the engagement with Woll and the following Somervell Expedition. Others had fought in the Mexican War.[318]

Soon the Rangers traversed the coastal plains. The old trail to the Leona River crossed what must have seemed to be perpetual prairie. For anyone approaching from the east, a traveler can soon see the location of Encina (now Uvalde) as small isolated mountains begin to appear on the horizon. They rise two to four hundred feet above the plains. These are the extinct volcanoes of Uvalde County. One of these volcanic cones marked the location for Fort Inge.[319]

On September 25, Callahan's company camped at the village of Uvalde on the Leona River.[320] Woll's army had camped here on September 6, 1842. The Leona Springs were the justification for this place. Leona (or Mountain Lioness) Springs is actually four groups of springs on the Leona River in Uvalde County. The springs rise under artesian pressure from the limestone of the Edwards aquifer, recharged by the Nueces River and streams to the northwest.

Surrounding Uvalde was the unending savanna, an ocean of undulating grassland, in the immensity of which occasional stands of live oaks and post oaks seem utterly lost.

14

RENDEZVOUS AT UVALDE

Then mount and away! Give fleet steed the rein—
The Ranger's at home on the prairies again;
Spur! Spur in the chase, dash on to the fight,
Cry vengeance for Texas! And God speed the right.
—Old Texas Rangers song

Just south of Uvalde stood the U.S. Army post of Fort Inge.[321] While encamped at Woll's Crossing on the Leona River, the Rangers could see the flag of the United States that waved atop the singular peak of the igneous hill that rises sharply above the army post. This isolated basalt cone was named "Pilot Knob" but later renamed Mount Inge. Army units and officers of the post included the U.S. Mounted Rifle Regiment, under Captain John G. Walker. The major road west from San Antonio forked in the area of this fort. One road went toward Fort Clark in what is now Kinney County and El Paso, the other to the Rio Grande at Eagle Pass. Travelers heading west "strapped on their guns" in this region, as this was the start of hostile Indian country. Troops from Fort Inge guarded against hostiles, including Indians, bandidos from Mexico and Texas desperadoes.

John W. Sansom wrote of the Callahan Expedition, "We proceeded to Uvalde where there was both an organization of the new company and a reorganization of the old one, and more shifting about of the men from one company to another." Sansom says that the men were at this business for four days.[322]

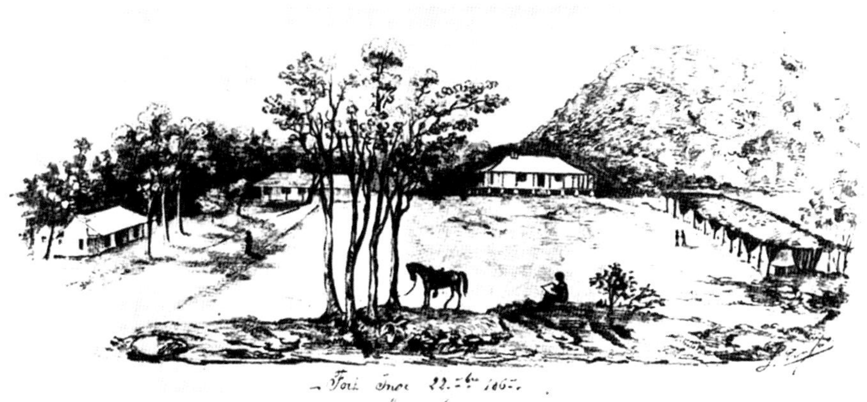

Fort Inge. *National Archives.*

In July 1855, William R. Henry attempted to organize an army of volunteers to intervene in Mexico. Captain Henry led his expedition of twenty men across the Rio Grande to offer their services to the revolutionaries. "Their services were refused and they were advised to cross back to Texas, which they did."[323]

Again, in August 1855, Henry's company was arrested by the Mexican army for a slave-hunting expedition into Mexico. Jailed until September, Henry's thirty-five men were released and rode from Mexico to the Leona River, where they allied with the Callahan Expedition on September 25.[324]

The arrival of Henry's company at Uvalde quickly became a confounding complication in Callahan's situation. It was easily apparent that despite having been arrested once, Henry still had an ambition to return to Coahuila to capture runaway slaves for bounty.

Henry was supremely confident and fearless, but his boldness often bordered on folly. John Salmon "RIP" Ford said that Henry "had rather exalted notions, and was difficult to control. He was brave, and possessed merit, but had the credit of interfering with his superior officers. He was not always in the wrong."[325] Henry's schemes were often grandiose, reflecting that fervor so common at the time that the United States, and especially Texas, indeed enjoyed a hemispheric Manifest Destiny.[326]

Henry offered considerable experience and skill as a military officer. He served in the Mexican War as a member of the U.S. Second Dragoons and saw action in Vera Cruz, Puebla and Cerro Gordo. Callahan knew Henry as a captain of Company C Texas Mounted Volunteers stationed in San

Antonio from December 1854. In March 1855, Henry's company ranged from the Rio Grande to the head of the Guadalupe River above Kerrville.

There was a quarrel during the election of officers. Henry and Callahan had a dustup about who was going to command Callahan's expedition. J.S. McDowell described the action as "sparring."[327] The audacious Henry, brash as usual, openly challenged Callahan for the leadership of the Texas Ranger expedition. Apparently, others that day were not so certain of Henry's exalted opinion of himself.

Callahan was unanimously elected as overall commander of the new battalion, but several members of the command expressed anger with the election of Henry as a company captain. Because of his reputation, Henry gained the position by only a small majority. Those who did not wish to serve under Henry formed a third company under Captain Nathaniel Benton.[328]

Benton had just caught up with Callahan's company on the Leona. He brought more Rangers from Seguin, including his son Benjamin Eustace Benton. Benton was married to Harriet McCulloch, the sister of Callahan's fellow Rangers and Indian fighters Ben and Henry Eustace McCulloch.[329]

Now comprising three companies of Texas Rangers, the newly formed battalion with Callahan as its commander included these officers:

J.H. Callahan, captain; Ed Burleson, first lieutenant; William Kyle, second lieutenant; eighty-eight men; mustered in July 20, 1885; mustered out October 19, 1855.

Nat Benton, captain; H.B. King, first lieutenant; Charles A. Read, second lieutenant; twenty-six men; mustered in September 15, 1855; mustered out October 15, 1855.

William R. Henry, captain; Tom Houston, first lieutenant; thirty-six men; mustered in September 15, 1855; mustered out October 15, 1855.

About this time, J.S. McDowell began a journal of this expedition. McDowell's notes were published by the *Texas State Times* on September 15, 1866. Excerpts were printed in the *Galveston Daily News* on January 8, 1893.

John Sansom wrote, "We were not long in agreeing upon nicknames for our respective companies. Those of us who had originally enlisted under Callahan came to be known by the name of 'Regulars,' while Henry's men were called 'Esquimaux' and Benton's 'Mohawks.'"[330]

After the organization of companies, Callahan assembled the newly formed battalion and—for the first time—revealed his strategy to attack the Lipan Apaches at San Fernando de Rosas. He told his men how he earlier had sent August Schmidt as a spy into northern Mexico to find the encampment of these Indians. Schmidt located the Lipan encampment at San Fernando de Rosas. When Schmidt brought back word and proof that these Lipan Apaches were the guilty parties, Callahan planned his expedition to ride into Coahuila, crossing the Rio Grande near Eagle Pass to attack the Lipans in their mountain stronghold. He kept this information a secret to avoid compromising their mission.

Callahan told the assembled battalion that their orders came from Governor Pease and he expected to obey them to the letter. The veteran captain stressed that if it became necessary to cross the Rio Grande into Mexico they would do so for the sole purpose of chastising the Indians. He made no mention of pursuing and capturing runaway slaves.[331] Callahan told his men that if the Rangers crossed the Rio Grande, they would do so only to chase and punish the Indians. They were not to harm any Mexican citizens or take their property: "If any man expected to act otherwise, he should leave or face punishments."[332]

While encamped on the Leona, Callahan's battalion spent time training, hunting and amusing themselves. Scouts who had been sent out returned to Fort Inge, reporting fresh Indian signs and a trail that headed in the direction of the mouth of Las Moras Creek on the Rio Grande. Callahan vowed to hound the Lipans.[333]

Sansom noted in his memoir, "During this time Charles A. Patton was accidently shot, fifteen buckshot penetrating the upper third of the thigh. To even up matters, Jim Derby and I engaged in a wrestling match and in the tussle his left leg was broken just above the ankle. These mishaps put both Patton and Darby on the invalid list."[334]

Twenty-six Rangers were sent home to central Texas to defend the frontier. Callahan's company was now reduced to 60 men. The battalion of three companies totaled 111 men.[335]

The Callahan Expedition rode out of Encina (Uvalde) headed for the mouth of Las Moras Creek on the Rio Grande some seventy miles away. Callahan's men were classic light cavalry. They rode in a column of twos. To prevent surprise attack, some riders were always posted in front, on the flanks and in rear of the column. They were denominated from their position: advanced guard, flankers and rear guard.

From the moment the Callahan Expedition left the Leona River, the Rangers came under the immediate threat of attack by Lipans, Seminoles, Kickapoos and Comanches. Every man rode vigilantly, their weapons at hand. The men of the Callahan Expedition knew full well the nature of the enemy that they would face.

For those Rangers who had not fought Indians before, the evening campfire stories provided vivid images of the barbaric nature of these warriors. The Mexicans called these Indians *Los Indios Bárbaros del Norte*.[336]

The Callahan Expedition now faced a severe trial. The road before it crossed the mesquite-acacia savanna of the Rio Grande plains. It was not an easy trek. Woll's Road led across a wide expanse of thorn brush called the Brasada.[337] The Spanish word *brasada* refers to something burned or burning, such as embers or hot coals. It was commonly used in the nineteenth century to refer to the dense south Texas thorn scrub, perhaps because of the burning heat of the ground in that area in summer, noted in several early travelers' journals.

Now a battalion, the three companies of the expedition left Uvalde on September 26 headed for the mouth of Las Moras Creek, a tributary of the Rio Grande. As Sansom recorded, "There our commander had planned to cross into Mexico, make direct for the Lipan villages on the Rio Sabinas and, surprising its people and punishing them for their thievery and atrocities."[338] There was a ford on the river named Paso de las Piedras Negras near Quemado, eighteen miles northwest of Eagle Pass.[339]

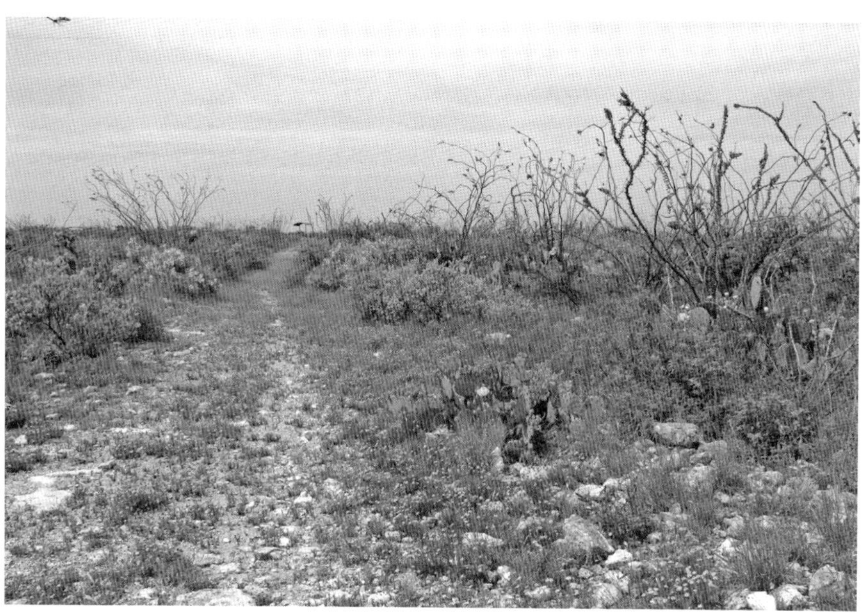

Trail through La Brasada. *Photograph by Jack Johnson.*

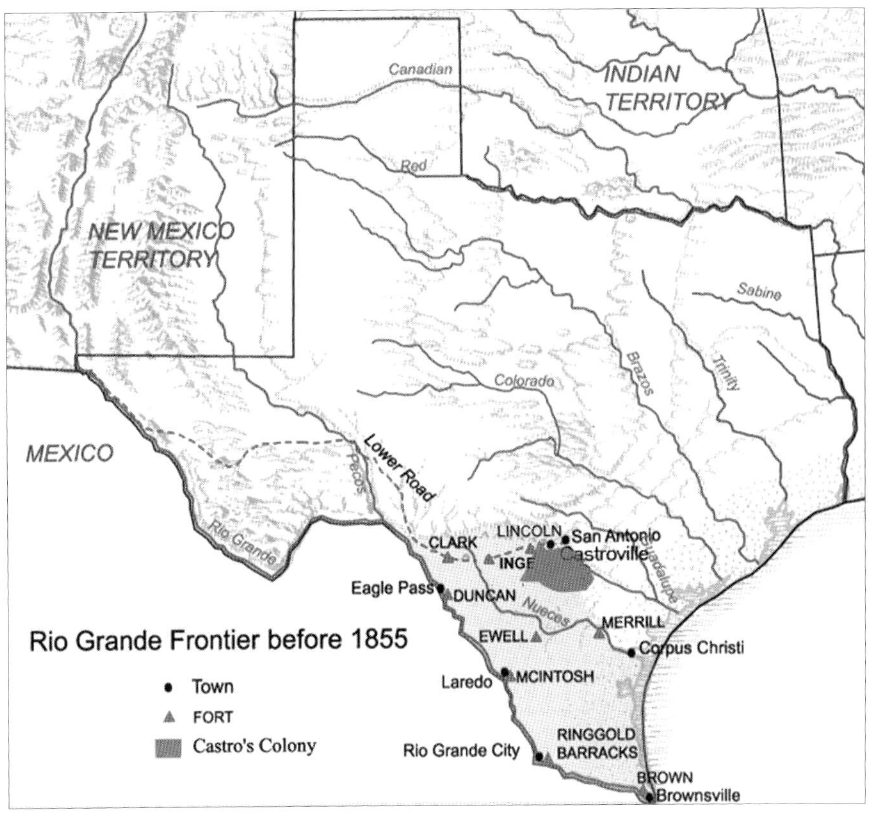

A map of Nueces Strip. *Courtesy of Texas Beyond History.*

The Texas Rangers rode into the infamous Nueces Strip. Many of them had crossed this stretch before. The Nueces Strip encompasses the area between the Rio Grande and the Nueces where the two rivers flow parallel to each other before the Nueces makes a bend to the east. It is a region in which settlers were attacked by Indians from all directions.

Until the mid-1850s, most of the U.S. Army's energies in Texas were directed at constructing new forts and pacifying the brush country south of the Nueces River. In 1850, ten companies of the army's Second Dragoons and First Infantry, commanded by Captain William J. Hardee, assisted by Rangers under William "Bigfoot" Wallace, conducted a sweep of the Nueces Strip that produced four engagements with hostile Indians.[340]

Leaving the Leona River at Uvalde, the Rangers came to the crossing on the Nueces River after about ten miles. Here Callahan's scouts found fresh

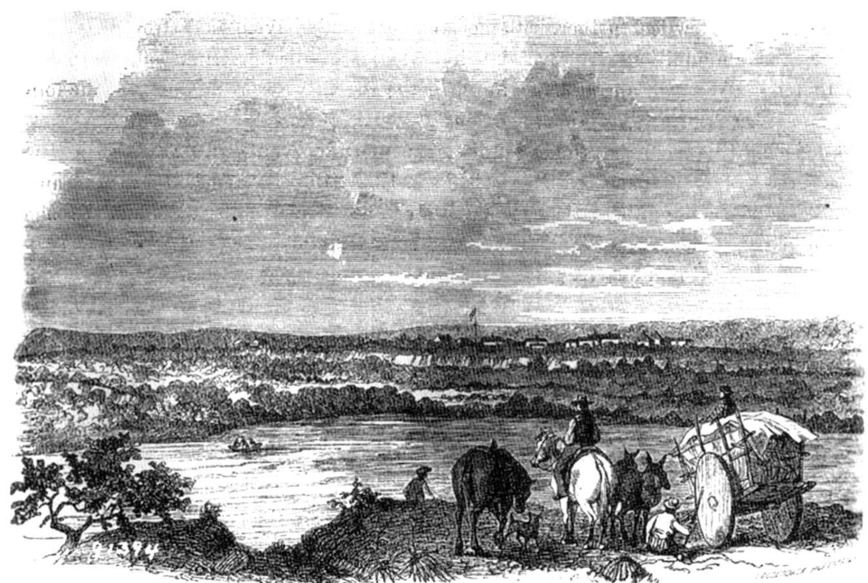

View of Fort Duncan, near Eagle Pass.

A view of Fort Duncan. *Engraving prepared for William H. Emory's* Report on the United States and Mexican Boundary Survey, Made Under the Direction of the Secretary of the Interior *(1857); University of Texas–Austin.*

tracks, indicating a large force of Indians. The hoof prints appeared to lead to the Rio Grande. At this point, the Callahan Expedition left Woll's Road and headed for the village of Quemado on the Rio Grande.[341]

Arriving at the mouth of Las Moras Creek on the Rio Grande on September 29, 1855, Callahan's battalion was unable to cross over to Mexico due to high and swift water. The Rangers experimented with makeshift rafts, but the effort was soon abandoned. A.J. Sowell wrote that the Rangers stayed encamped at the mouth of Las Moras Creek for several days waiting for the floodwaters of the Rio Grande to fall. Sowell noted that besides the three captains, other Rangers at Las Moras included Eustace Benton (son of Captain Benton), Henry King, Hughes Tom, Ben Paton, John W. Sansom, Fabian Hicks, James McCormick, Hal Holland, Willis Jones, Wesley Harris, Wall, Clopton, Bassham, Smith, Gregor and many others.[342]

At sundown, on September 30, the battalion of Rangers left Las Moras Creek and moved down the Rio Grande to find a more suitable crossing. As John W. Sansom reported, "We found the Rio Grande at that point with a two-foot rise in it, the result of heavy rains above, and at once made our way down stream to a point thirty miles below, and opposite the little Mexican town of Piedras Negras."[343]

Callahan and the others rode all night. On the evening of the next day, they halted four miles north of Fort Duncan. They camped on Elm Creek, a tributary of the Rio Grande that has its mouth at its conjunction with that river, 1.1 miles upriver from Eagle Pass. The three captains—Callahan, Benton and Henry—went into Eagle Pass. When they returned to the Ranger camp, they reported that they had obtained some boats for crossing.[344]

15

FORT DUNCAN

So during all the period I lived at Fort Duncan [1854–55] *and its sub-camps, nearly sixteen months, fresh vegetables were practically unobtainable. To prevent scurvy, we used the juice of the maguey* [agave] *plant, called pulque.*[345]*…At reveille roll-call every morning this fermented liquor was dealt out to the company, and as it was my duty, in my capacity of subaltern, to attend these roll-calls and see that the men took their ration of pulque.*

—*Philip Henry Sheridan,* Personal Memoirs of P.H. Sheridan, General, United States Army

Fort Duncan was a thorn in Callahan's side throughout the expedition into Mexico. Because the U.S. Army had strict orders to prevent raids into Mexico and to protect the Indians, Callahan went to extraordinary efforts to avoid contact with the garrison at Eagle Pass.

Lieutenant Colonel William Grigsby Freeman's report of July 27, 1853, described the post's housing in plain terms: "The quarters for the men are wretched hovels not fit for occupancy."[346] The most distant of the line of Rio Grande posts, Fort Duncan stood across a deep ravine from Eagle Pass, a village comprising "eight or 10 tolerably good buildings and the same number of mud hovels occupied by the lower order of Mexicans." There also were "three or four stores for sale of goods principally adapted to the Mexican market." Freeman reported there were two ferries available near the post and the river was fordable half a mile above.[347]

Fort Duncan caused a rudimentary settlement to spring up at the crossing below the post. Almost immediately after the establishment of Fort Duncan, emigrant groups bound for California by way of Mexico began arriving at the Paso del Águila (Eagle Pass) ford.

Frederick Law Olmsted visited Eagle Pass in 1854 and noted the many slave hunters and runaway slaves residing in Piedras Negras, as well as the many saloons and gambling houses that catered to Fort Duncan's soldiers and other unsavory characters. Olmsted wrote:

> *First, as we rode up the hill, there were half a dozen tottering shanties, mere confused piles of poles, brushwood, and rushes, with hides hung over the apertures for doors; broken cart wheels, yokes, and other rubbish lay about them; fowls had their nests in the loose thatch, and swine were sleeping in holes they had rooted out on the shady side…there were two or three adobe houses, looking like long, two story sepulchers, which Jack Woodland* [Olmstead's guide] *said were stores: and then.as we rode over the brow of the hill and there appeared only a few low huts beyond….I asked our guide where was the town. This is it is what he said.*[348]

The early history of Eagle Pass was often characterized by violence. The settlement and adjoining fort were frequently attacked by the Lipan Apache and Comanche Indians. Piedras Negras became a haven for fugitive slaves, and both banks of the river were infested with outlaws.[349]

On June 15, 1850, a group of thirty-four men commanded by Andrés Zapata, Gaspar Salazar and Antonio Ramírez met with Colonel Juan Manuel Maldonado to give the news that they had created a pass point at Piedras Negras, to the right of the Rio Grande, south of Fort Duncan. They named it Nueva Villa de Herrera, but it later became Villa de Piedras Negras. In Otto Schober's history of Piedras Negras, the local historian points out that the thirty-four men were repatriates (Mexican Americans) who arrived on June 15, 1850, in what was then called "Colonia Militar de Guerrero en Piedras Negras."[350] In Spanish, *piedras negras* translates to "black stones"—a reference to coal deposits in the area.

The U.S. Army garrison at Fort Duncan had received explicit orders to stop all armed incursions into Mexico. Callahan was unsure about the reaction of the post's commander, Captain Sidney Burbank, to his border crossing. The Rangers rode wide around of the cantonment.

Callahan decided to cross into Mexico at the old river ford, Paso Del Águila. This ford was at the mouth of the Rio Escondido (Little River) where it enters the Rio Grande, three miles downriver from Piedras Negras, Coahuila, and Eagle Pass, Texas. The Escondido led straight to the Indian encampments at San Fernando de Rosas.

On the morning of October 1, 1855, twelve men under the command of Captain Henry stole two small boats (skiffs) on the Fort Duncan side of the border. They rowed these boats three miles downstream to where the Rangers were encamped at the old Paso de los Adjuntos del Río Escondido (Paso Del Águila). As Henry's detachment neared the crossing, the men called out a warning to Callahan that the Mexicans had followed him downriver and were threatening an attack on the Mexican side.[351]

Consequently, the initial crossing was made by Henry's company in the dark. Despite the flooding waters, twenty-nine men rowed across and set up a defense perimeter on the Mexican shore.[352] They were at the mouth of Rio Escondido.[353] Henry's company held this position for a few hours. With no sign of an enemy, Henry ordered half of his men to remain while the others returned to Texas. This pattern of rotation continued through the night.[354]

A delegation from Piedras Negras appeared on the morning of October 1, confronting the Rangers from the Mexican side of the border. They demanded to know the Rangers' intentions. Satisfied with assurance that the Rangers were interested only in the pursuit of the Indians who had raided into Texas, the Mexican delegation from Piedras Negras offered its help in making the crossing and in fighting the Indians.[355]

John W. Sansom wrote:

> *Capt. Callahan, with his interpreter, rode into Piedras Negras and called upon the Alcalde of that place. To this officer he stated he had not brought the forces under his command into Mexico for the purpose of making war on or doing injury of any kind to its people, but that his sole object and aim was to punish the Lipans for their many crimes committed on Texas soil, and that all he asked of the Alcalde was his moral support. Pleased and flattered, apparently, by Callahan's visit and request, the Alcalde was not slow in promising his moral support with every appearance of good faith."*[356]

J.S. McDowell recorded that the *alcalde* offered aid in crossing and, more remarkable, offered volunteers for Callahan's campaign. The first offer was accepted, and the second was declined with thanks. "No protests were made from any quarter."[357]

Callahan reported that while in the act of crossing, a paper, written in Spanish, was brought to him by Colonel Langberg informing the U.S. officers at Eagle Pass that Captain Callahan was permitted to pass into Mexico in pursuit of the Indians.

Callahan also reported that he crossed in the presence of U.S. officers and "with the full understanding, on my part, that it was entirely agreeable to the authorities on both sides of the river, that I should cross over."[358] Callahan reported that his efforts were well known to the authorities on both sides.[359] The presence of the U.S. Army during this crossing is verified by the official report that Second Lieutenant William M. Davant was drowned during this activity.[360]

On crossing the Rio Grande, Callahan left 6 men guarding the horses on the Texas shore. His battalion then numbered 105 men.[361] Callahan resolutely pressed on directly to the Lipan Apache camp at San Fernando de Rosas.

With this singular publicly stated objective, Callahan crossed his battalion over the swollen Rio Grande on October 1. The passage took all day, with the men in the boats and swimming the horses and mules. The supplies were left in care of the six Rangers who remained on the Texas shore. There was no interference with the passage.[362]

At dawn on the morning of October 3, Callahan moved his forces away from the Rio Grande and toward their objective—the village of San Fernando de Rosas—thirty miles distant. They followed the Rio Escondido upstream. This river would lead them to the Apache encampment. The landscape was desolate and flayed, as if it were a part of the brasada, only worse.

The Lipan Apaches were at San Fernando de Rosas. The location was at the foot of the Sierra Santa Rosa, at the "5 *manantiales*" (five springs) region in northern Coahuila. The Lipan were themselves refugees, driven from the buffalo-rich high plains and Edwards Plateau of Texas by the even more formidable Comanches, the "Lords of the South Plains," and their allies or associates. In this respect, the Lipan's cattle-stealing expeditions, and their raiding in general, were desperate expedients to maintain the abundant way of life they had enjoyed on the buffalo plains.[363]

Mexican officials recruited Native Americans to defend their northern settlements and ranches in Coahuila and Nuevo León from Comanche and Kiowa raiders. Christopher Luntzel, a German who served as an interpreter for Indian agents in Texas, reported that the Lipan residing near San Fernando de Rosas had been invited there by the Mexican government.[364]

Callahan was well aware of the firearms of the Lipan Apaches. This bit of intelligence was revealed to the Texans by the contents of a wagon belonging

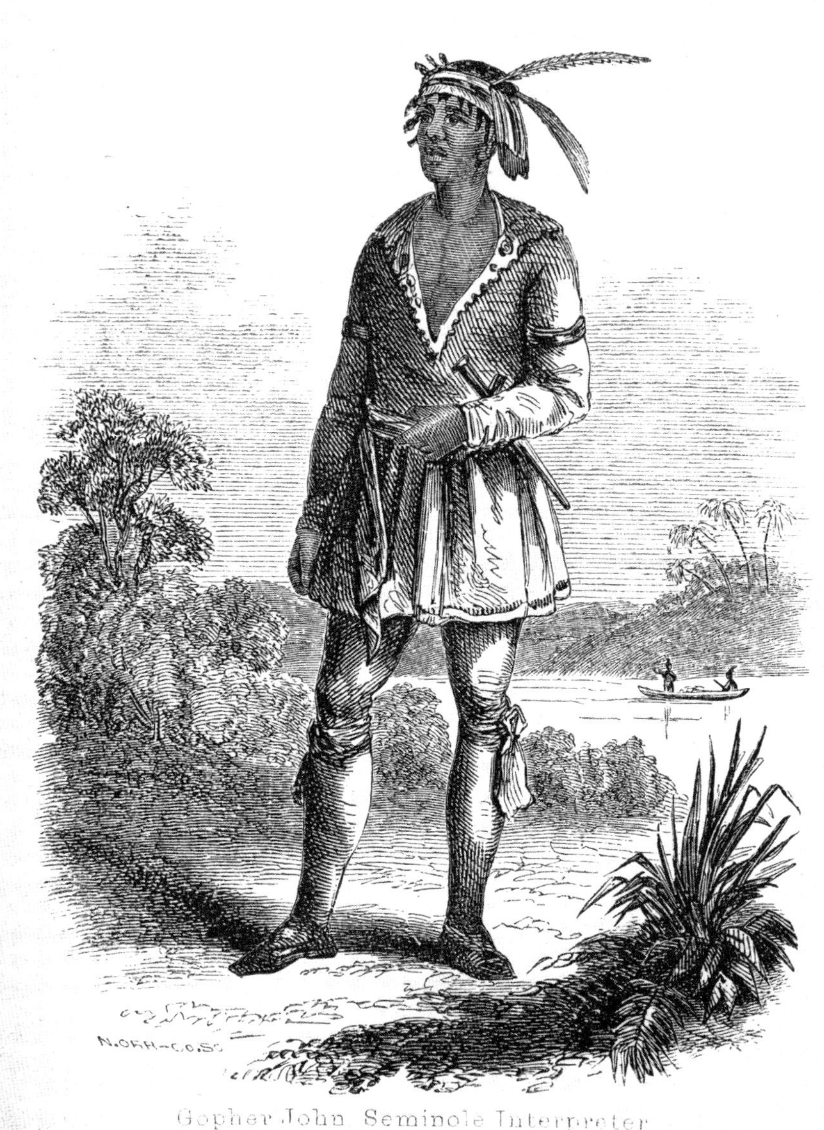

Gopher John, a black Seminole. *Engraving of John Horse, aka Gopher John, attributed to N. Orr of N. Orr & Richardson, S.C., N.Y., published in Joshua Reed Gidding,* The Exiles of Florida *(Columbus, OH: Follett, Foster and Co., 1858).*

to a Lipan chief in 1849. "The inside of the carriage was well supplied with Colt and Sharps rifles, Colt pistols, a double-barreled shot gun, lots of ammunition, a spyglass, and a number of small but useful tools."[365]

In the summer of 1855, the Lipan, accompanied by Seminoles, struck north out of Coahuila. These were the raids to which James Callahan's Rangers responded. Settlements along the Guadalupe, Blanco and Cibolo Rivers were hit hard. This was the heart of the Hill Country and Callahan's ranging territory.[366]

An unexpected foe that confronted Callahan's Expedition was the Seminole Indians. Well known for the Seminole War fought in Florida in 1816, the Seminoles were skilled warriors.[367]

Under the leadership of Wild Cat and John Horse, the Seminoles left the reservation for Mexico in 1850. The Mexican government provided the Seminoles with a home in exchange for protection of the border from marauders.[368]

In July 1850, the Seminoles, allied blacks and Kickapoos were admitted to Mexico and temporarily settled at San Fernando de Rosas (now Zaragoza, Coahuila), at La Navaja, near Presidio Monclova Viejo and at the Colonia Militar de Guerro.[369] In Mexico, the new settlers faced a different set of hardships, but for the first time, the black Seminoles were truly free. They were still subject to raids from slavers, such as William R. Henry, but the slavers had to come across the border to get at them and were seldom successful. As early as 1854, irate slaveholders formed militia groups to cross into Mexico to retrieve runaway slaves at Nacimiento.

Reports of Indian raids and sightings of blacks in Texas fueled the tensions with the U.S. Army and led to a flurry of accusations against Wild Cat's band.[370] The Seminole chief elected to attack settlers on the Medina River with the help of the Lipans and Tonkawas and in August 1855 attacked Callahan's Texas Rangers near Bandera.[371]

16

BATTLE OF RIO ESCONDIDO

But when the blast of war blows in our ears,
Then imitate the action of the tiger;
Stiffen the sinews, summon up the blood,
Disguise fair nature with hard-favour'd rage;
—Shakespeare, Henry V, *Act 3, Scene 1*

Following a brisk ride of some eight miles on the road to Santa Rosa, Callahan was met by a Mexican rider warning of an ambush ahead. The Rangers were disbelieving of the man and continued riding southeast down the road to San Fernando de Rosas. They eagerly looked forward to the coming combat with the Lipan Apaches.

After all the assurances of the *alcalde* and alliances made with the Mexican army at the Rio Grande, Callahan dismissed this warning out of hand. The Rangers had no indications of any trouble. Surely, they would not be attacked by the Apaches, especially at this distance from their encampment.[372]

Callahan gave the command to move out. When the column of Rangers reached a point fourteen miles from Piedras Negras, Callahan stopped in his tracks. They were at a place called La Maroma,[373] where the Rio San Antonio intersected the Rio Escondido. Sansom described this as "nothing more than a big creek." The precipitous banks rose ten feet above the surface of the water. Not a structure was to be seen, but large ditches ran from the river to farms four miles or more away. The road to Santa Rosa passed at a distance of five hundred yards from the stream over a flat, featureless plain.[374]

The column of Rangers had ridden only a short distance up the road when four Indians suddenly appeared on the on the same side of the riverbank. They galloped toward the middle of the column of Rangers. Two halted at about three hundred yards, but the other two charged, firing arrows. Thus confronted, the Rangers dismounted, and Zack Bugg and Brent Shiller brought their shotguns to bear, wounding one of the Indians' horses.

Hearing these shots, Callahan rode back to the middle of the column with his interpreter. Assuming the confrontation was with the Mexicans, he rode out toward them for the purpose of explaining the Rangers' presence in the interior of Mexico. As Callahan advanced, the Indians withdrew without speaking.

Callahan formed his column into a battle line facing the Rio Escondido. To his surprise, six or seven hundred Mexican soldiers and Indians climbed up the riverbank and formed a battle array parallel with the stream. Proud, trained, experienced and, in splendid uniforms, the Mexican troops had been waiting for the Rangers for several days. The Rangers found themselves confronted by four times their number.

The scene of massed soldiers, well disciplined and in splendid professional uniforms, was not the enemy Callahan had anticipated. He was instantly confronted by the nightmares of battles fought so long ago and still intruding into his thoughts every day. This memory was the recurring bad dream of Callahan's life, haunting him even at the Rio Escondido.

The three companies of the Mexican army that unexpectedly appeared on the battlefield at Rio Escondido consisted of the commander of the Northern Coahuila Section, Lieutenant Colonel Manuel Menchaca; the Morelos Company, commanded by Captain Miguel Patino; and Evaristo Madero, captain of the Guerrero Company. These companies were named for the geographical location in which the unit was originally raised.

A great angry growling arose among the ranks of the Rangers. The Mexicans had hoodwinked Los Diablos Tejanos. These Rangers were men of courage, for each man came up on the line despite being possessed by fear of being killed and, even worse, fear of being horribly wounded.

With a well-executed maneuver, half of the Mexican troops moved to the left, and the other half moved to the right. Their line of battle outstretched that of the Rangers and threatened their flank, as well as their rear. The Rangers found themselves well within the angle of a V-shaped formation. Captain Henry observed, "These men are being handled by a man trained on the battlefield, and we are almost surrounded."[375]

Callahan, Benton and Henry weighed their options. It was Henry who offered that there was but one best way, and that was to charge their right wing, drive it on their center and then turn on their left, fighting hand to hand, if need be, until the battle was done.[376]

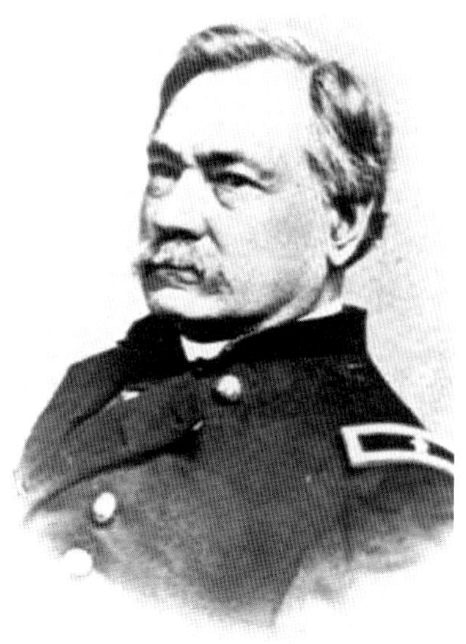

Captain Sidney Burbank. *Courtesy of Fold3.*

This strategy seemed to suit Callahan. He ordered Captains Henry and Benton to lead their companies in the attack. Callahan then addressed his own company, calling on them to "remember the barbarities committed by Indians and Mexicans on our people."[377]

Callahan cantered up and down his battle line, telling his men to make a desperate fight and at his command to charge the enemy. Taking his place at the front of the battle line, Callahan stood up in his stirrups and cried out, "Now, boys, remember the bloody son of McGee and charge!"[378]

Instantly, the Texas Rangers yelled their battle cry, a high-pitched, quavering roar. In truth, it was a spontaneous release of the huge surge of adrenaline that these men were experiencing.

The Rangers slammed into the Mexican line. It was a mêlée. Sowell described the charge as a "desperate fight....Pistols, rifles, and shotguns rang out on every side, mingled with the yell of the Texans, the war whoop on the Indians, and the loud imprecations of the Mexicans."[379]

William Kyle, a veteran of that charge, called the four-hour battle at Rio Escondido "one of the hardest Indian fights ever fought."[380]

When they charged, the Rangers did not see an irrigation ditch until it was too late. In jumping the ditch, four of the Texan horses fell, dismounting their riders. Those Rangers rose, fighting hand to hand until they were slain. For a moment, there was only the beseeching cries of the wounded horses.

All the rest of the party continued the charge, passing clear through the Mexican line and forming between the Mexicans and the creek, the Rio Escondido.[381] There the men took a strong position and awaited the enemy to act.[382]

The Texans had casualties from this charge. Willis Jones, Hal Holland, H.K. Clopton and Augustus Smith were killed. Eustace Benton, Henry King, Nathaniel Benton and a man named John Gregory were wounded.

Young Eustace Benton had fallen, wounded, from his horse and was lying in an exposed position. A musket ball had struck him over the left eye and remained in his head. Wesley Harris, of Seguin, risked his life to retrieve Benton and carry him to safety.[383]

As the Rangers were dismounting and taking defensive positions in the creek, some two hundred Mexican infantry appeared. These troops had been hiding in the thicket within gunshot but had not until this moment revealed themselves. The infantry brought heavy fire to bear on the Texans. The bodies of dead Rangers lay on the battlefield and fell into the hands of the enemy. Some said that these bodies were taken by the Indians and later mutilated.[384]

The Rangers reloaded their Colts and fired again and again. With the Sharps carbines, the Texans were much more deliberate and accurate in their fire. It became a sniper's war. The remaining horses and mules were held in the creek bed. Many of them were badly wounded.

The gunfire continued until sundown. Both sides ran out of ammunition. With the Texans well protected by the riverbank, the Mexican and Indian forces began to slip away in the direction of San Fernando de Rosas to the south.

According to Sansom, the lack of ammunition made rapid movement imperative. Callahan refused to advance, saying that if he continued on to the Lipan village he would "only greatly deepen the offense already committed against the peace and dignity of Mexico." Callahan is reported to have been convinced that his men "would be followed and overtaken and captured by overwhelming numbers and himself and men, much as survived, be subjected to a long and terrible imprisonment, if not massacred in cold blood."[385] Memories of the Goliad Massacre plagued him.

If, however, Callahan led his men to Piedras Negras, he would likely get across to the American side before a sufficient force could be assembled to make escape impossible. As Sansom wrote, "Callahan thought hard and fast, as, under the unfavorable circumstances surrounding his little forces it behooves him to do—the result of his thinking being shown by an order that we obeyed with surprising alacrity: it would be foolish to attempt just then to reach the Lipan villages, and as he could not stay there, his only recourse was to retreat."[386]

The Rangers painfully made their way toward Piedras Negras. The wounded Rangers were successfully taken away. Eustace Benton was carried for that long distance by Captain William A. Pitts, of Austin, who placed the wounded and unconscious boy in his saddle and rode behind him on the same horse, tenderly holding his little friend in his arms. Benton's father, Captain Benton, was wrought almost into frenzy by what he considered the death wound of his only child. The Rangers left five dead on the ground, in addition to many horses and about thirty pistols, guns or rifles, which were picked up by the Indians.[387]

Callahan had been defeated once again by the Mexican army. His campaign to chastise the Indians had failed. His expedition was close to being lost.

17

BATTLE OF PIEDRAS NEGRAS

I soon discovered that the place contained a considerable number of armed men, concealed in houses, and that preparations had evidently been made to attack.
—James H. Callahan

Colonel Menchaca found that the Texan *aventureros* had fled the Rio Escondido. At eight o'clock on the morning of October 6, he followed them to Piedras Negras, where they were "*bien fortificados en el muelle de Piedras Negras* [well fortified at the Piedras Negras dock]." The Mexican forces had been "detained awaiting ammunition."[388]

The Mexican army, local citizens and the Indians eagerly anticipated another chance to deal with the hated Texas Rangers. Like a storm, their fury rose in thunder and lightning.

Piedras Negras had some 1,500 inhabitants. Callahan expected the worst, as the countryside was in pandemonium.[389] Callahan "demanded the *alcalde* surrender the town....In case of refusal, he proposed sacking it forthwith."[390]

A citizens' delegation met with Callahan and accepted the unconditional terms of surrender. The battle-weary Rangers then paraded in military formation into the heart of Piedras Negras.

The *alcalde*'s residence stood adjacent to an old stone fort that Callahan seized as his headquarters. The *alcalde* then gave his keys and authority to Callahan. As the Rangers set up in the aged fortification, they found it something of a military museum.[391] The *alcalde* had promised to have all arms and ammunition delivered to the new headquarters—an action promptly undertaken.[392]

With the Texans camped around the old fortification, Callahan arranged with the *alcalde* for rations and forage for men and horses. Some Rangers wanted to cross over to Texas immediately, and a few deserted. Pride, however, forbade any hurried departure, and only a few weak-kneed men considered it.[393]

Piedras Negras is situated on a terrace above the Rio Grande, with a sharp escarpment dropping to an extensive floodplain. The Rangers dug in below this embankment and on the south bank of the Rio Grande, some two hundred yards below the town. An officer from Fort Duncan came to the river's edge and yelled across to the Rangers, asking if they needed help crossing the fast-moving river, then on a fifteen-foot rise. Callahan's men answered in the affirmative, and the blue-tunicked officer told them that they would have assistance.[394]

Callahan is said to have crossed the Rio Grande to confer with Captain Sidney Burbank at the federal garrison. "Burbank," in his official role, "told him to get out of Piedras Negras as he, Callahan, had not business there, and that while he was getting out he would protect him."[395]

In a surprising letter to people of Texas—written on October 4, 1855—Callahan pleaded, "Men of the frontier, come then and help us. Let none come but those who will and can fight. If you come, come quickly; and come well prepared." This letter, with a detailed account of the expedition, was later published in full in the *New York Times*.[396]

Having issued an appeal to Texans for help and expecting reinforcements, Callahan chose to stay in Piedras Negras and spurned Captain Burbank's offer of assistance. One of the enduring mysteries regarding the Callahan Expedition is the decision to remain in Mexico at this time and the call for help to the American people.

Callahan did have his wounded taken by boat to Fort Duncan on October 4. Later that evening, Callahan visited them and spent the night at the fort. The next morning, back in Mexico, Callahan received word that the Mexican army was forming outside Piedras Negras. That information apparently caused Callahan to lose his enthusiasm for a fight. He hurriedly sent a note to Burbank requesting covering fire for the transfer of his men across the border. Burbank, evidently miffed at Callahan's previous rebuff, refused to provide cover.[397]

Callahan had not found it suspicious that the *alcalde* seemed so friendly and supportive of Callahan's mission to punish the Lipans. After all, he had eagerly promised to furnish all the forage the Rangers needed. The *alcalde* told Callahan that the Battle of Rio Escondido had been brought on by a mistake—that the object of his expedition was not rightly understood by the Mexican military. "He was given to understand that if we wished to pursue the Indians, he could do so unmolested. This lie was told merely to decoy Callahan east of Piedras Negras, so that the Mexicans could carry out their previous design of massacring his command."[398]

Callahan, once again, had been tricked. Badly mistaken in his reading of the *alcalde*, Callahan discovered that the Mexican official had only been trying to hold the Rangers in Piedras Negras until the Mexican military, along with local militia and friendly Indians, arrived.[399]

The captain and his officers informed the *alcalde* they did not wish to have any further difficulty with the Mexicans and would not injure their property or persons. But the Texan captain made it equally clear that if they attacked the Rangers while they occupied Piedras Negras, he would do everything necessary for the protection and safety of his command, even to the point of destroying the place.[400]

The Mexican army had marched to the Villa Fuente on the Rio Escondido and encamped. Colonel Manchaca sent a note to Burbank at Fort Duncan in which he said, "Sir, take your American dogs out of Piedras Negras or I'll march in there and kill every one of them."[401]

At this point, Captain Burbank, insulted, tore up the note and ordered artillery trained on the town. Four cannons were aimed across the river. Burbank said, "If you attack my countrymen while they are crossing the river, I shall pour shot and shell into your ranks."[402]

Learning of the proximity of the Mexican army, Callahan once again decided to ask aid of the garrison at Fort Duncan. Writing to Burbank, he entrusted the letter to Aaron Burleson. Burleson was an excellent swimmer. Stripping, he tied his clothes to the top of his head and, entering the water, struck boldly out for Texas. Landing safely, he delivered the letter. Receiving a written reply to it, he again swam the river and delivered the dispatch to Callahan.

As Sansom wryly pointed out, "Whatever the excellence of West Point as an educational institution, and however it taught 'rading and rithmetic' the majority of the three r's, it had signally failed in any attempt made to teach the commander at Fort Duncan the art of 'riting' legibly. At any rate, neither Callahan nor his lieutenants could decipher the communication."[403]

Fortunately, Judge X.B. Saunders came to aid of the officers, saying, "He could read anything in the English language that a United States officer could write." The communication said, in essence, that Callahan's troops could look for no assistance from Fort Duncan because they had entered

Mexico without authorization of the U.S. government. The communication went on to say, according to Sansom, "if we did not get away from where we were, the garrison battery would turn its guns on us and force us away."[404]

On the third day, Sansom and Cole McRae were sent to scout the eastern approaches to Piedras Negras. They discovered that Langberg was advancing on Piedras Negras with a force of 1,200 men. The Mexican army came within view of the village at 4:00 p.m.

Trapped at the flooded river and encircled by the Mexican army, the Rangers had thoughts about their possible capture. They remembered stories they heard of the sufferings and humiliations of the Goliad and Mier prisoners and "resolved, each man of them, that if they must die then they would die as gamely as ever Texans had died."[405]

Callahan, in particular, could not shake the vision of the massacre at Goliad in which 357 of his unarmed comrades had been mercilessly butchered after surrendering. Above all else, the Ranger captain swore to never again make the mistake of surrendering to the Mexican forces.

The Rangers seized the *alcalde*'s cannons and moved them into a defensive position at the riverbank. Most likely, the Mexican artillery was the light four-pounder that fired both iron and copper solid shot and anti-personnel rounds. The latter was essentially grapeshot encased in cloth or rawhide shrunk tightly around its contents.[406]

As Sansom wrote, "We seized the three pieces of artillery, two of which were mounted upon the same pair of wheels and were known among our boys as the 'Double Flirt,' and the other, which lay flat upon the ground, was called by us 'The Ground Hog'. Putting the 'Ground Hog' on the fore wheels of a wagon, and fastening it in place with chains, we carried the three guns along with ammunition at a place where it could do the best work."[407]

Concerned about his field of fire, Callahan named a detail whose duty it would be, if the emergency demanded it, to torch nearby houses that might afford shelter to the enemy or obstruct the Rangers' fire.[408]

In Piedras Negras, the residents, becoming alarmed, started to evacuate the town. Some of the Texas Rangers pursued them and took arms and munitions from the Mexicans.[409]

The latest news was that the approaching enemy forces now numbered as many as one thousand soldiers, led by Langberg himself. The forces consisted of six hundred regular troops and four hundred volunteers.

"They're coming," Jesse Sumpter heard a Mexican say.[410] Climbing up on the house he'd been sleeping in, Sumpter raised his glasses. "[I] could see the Mexicans coming over the hill from the Little River [Rio Escondido]," he

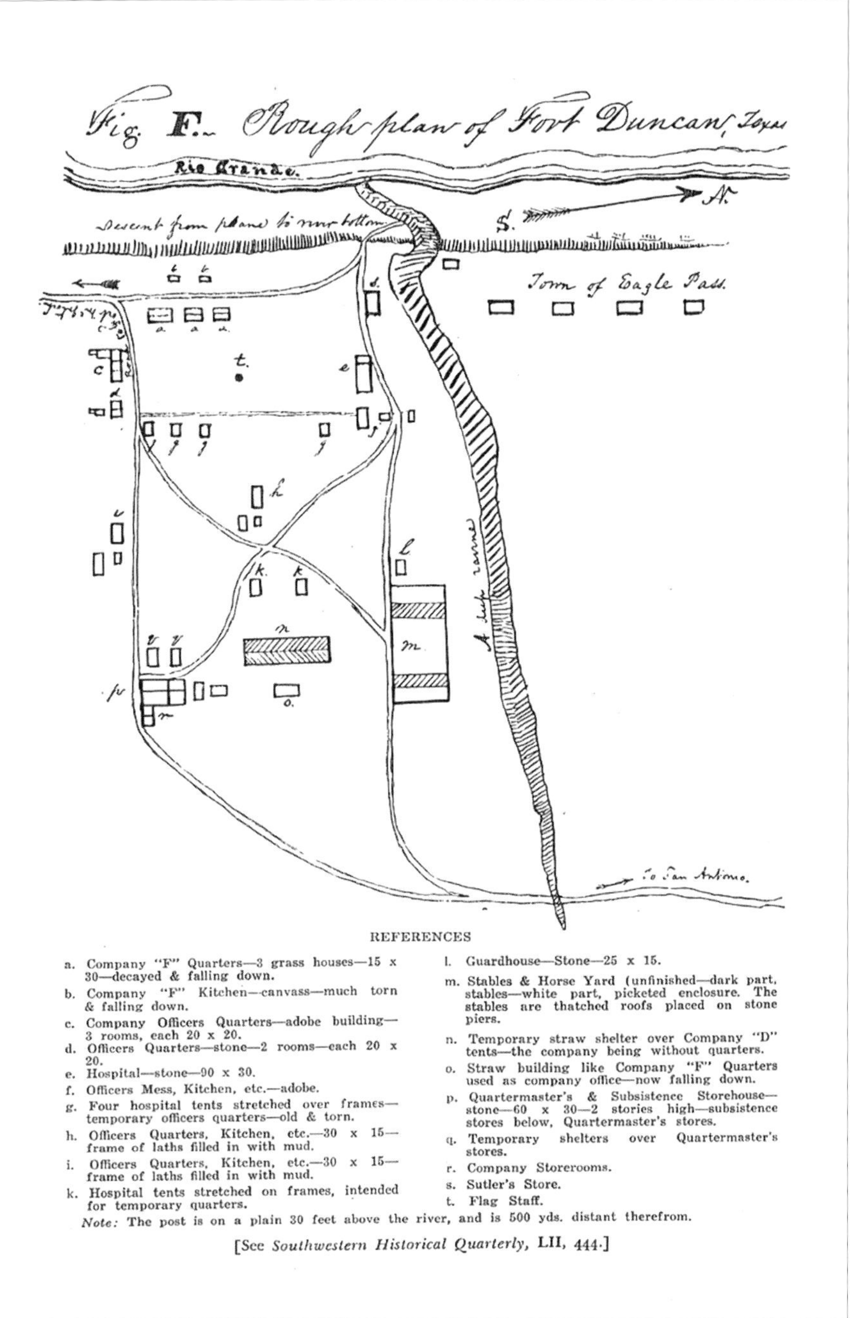

A rough plan of Fort Duncan. *From* Southwest Historical Quarterly *52, no. 4 (April 1949): 444.*

later recalled. "They marched on until they got they got to what is known as the Laguna, just beyond Piedras Negras."[411]

Langberg formed his troops into a battle line, with his center in front of the town, his flanks extending to the river above and below the Rangers. This movement closed the Texans in a trap from which they had no escape except across the turbulent Rio Grande, swollen even more by heavy rains above. The treacherous *alcalde* had instructed that the ferry be set adrift, and other small boats had been concealed.[412]

The Mexican army divided its force, sending a large party downriver from the Texans and forming another group in front of the Rangers, about 360 yards off. When the Rangers opened fire on the Mexican forces with their captured cannons—firing grapeshot—the enemy's advance became confused and stalled.

Callahan waited until dark and then burned Piedras Negras to cover his retreat across the river. His men provided heavy covering fire while others ran through the town torching everything that would burn. It is said that Hughes Tom applied the first torch. Most of the houses were *jacales*—crude huts of pole-and-thatch construction. Such structures could be set on fire almost as a fast as man could gallop by on a horse. Flames raced through the village, destroying most of the town. Captain Burbank reported that "the countryside for miles around was lit up as bright as day by the burning town."[413]

The scene as viewed from Fort Duncan was quite dramatic. Across the Rio Grande, the night sky was aflame as the village of Piedras Negras burned. Against this backdrop, the silhouettes of the Rangers could be seen as they struggled to escape with their lives. In a near suicide ride, men raced their horses down the steep escarpment to the river. Scrambling into boats, the Rangers fired back into the village, their muzzle flashes providing brief glimpses of the ensuing struggle.

Captain Burbank received a written message from Callahan and Henry asking for the protection of the United States flag to empower them to cross the river. Burbank discerned Callahan's desperation, noting the fact that some men were deserting and that the Texas contingent was then reduced to about seventy men. The desertion of his Rangers in the face of fire only deepened Callahan's despair. The situation was on the verge of a rout.

Captain John G. Walker of the United States Mounted Rifle Regiment appeared out of the crowd of spectators. He was dressed in civilian clothes and offered to help to ferry the Rangers across. Walker's troops came to the aid of the Callahan Expedition.[414]

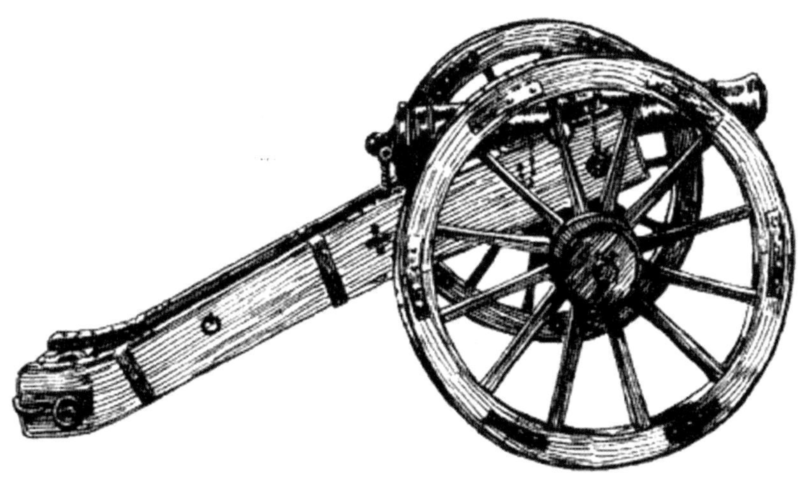

A six-pound cannon. *https://www.tamu.edu/faculty/ccbn/dewitt/adp/history/1836/the_battle/the_weapons/cannon.html.*

J.S. McDowell reported that, with the help of Walker, the fleeing men had collected a small fleet of boats, barges, rafts, skiffs and a rope ferry to make their escape.[415] At 7:00 p.m., Callahan ordered his men into the boats. The men pulled hard for the American side. Halfway across, one of the small boats tied to the barge broke loose and drifted a half mile downstream before managing to land on the Texas shore.

Callahan's wounded men were ferried over by boat.[416] Of these, Captain Benton had his arm shattered from wrist to elbow; Lieutenant Burleson was wounded in the shoulder; John Gregory, in the breast and lung; Ben F. Patton, through the neck; and young Eustace Benton had been shot in the head, the bullet shattering his skull. These men were taken to the hospital at Fort Duncan and attended by Dr. John Gaston Barbee, the Rangers' surgeon.[417]

After two-thirds of the Rangers had recrossed the Rio Grande on October 7, a large Mexican force pinned down the remaining twenty-five Texans on the Mexico side of the river. Under spotty fire, the Rangers retreated to the ferry, under the bluff, and commenced crossing the floodwaters. While the boat, loaded with twelve or fifteen men and their baggage, was underway, the rope connecting the boat to the cable broke, and the ferry went swiftly down the strait but fortuitously beached on the American side several hundred yards below. It was hauled back and landed on the Mexican side again.

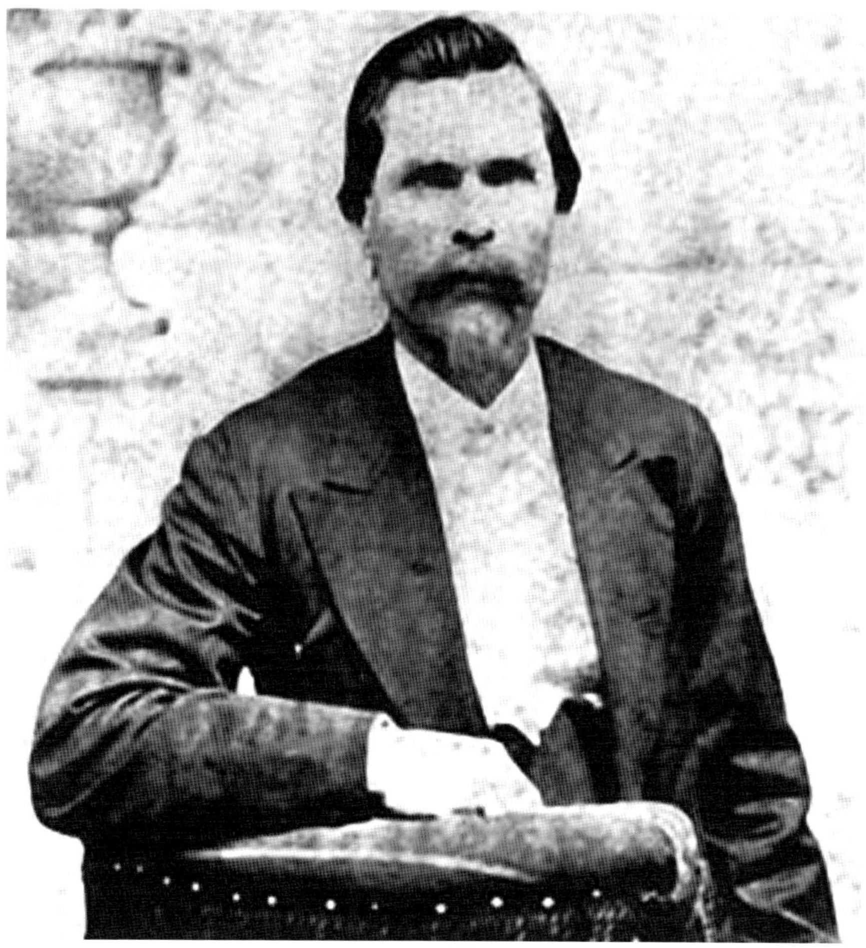

Dr. John Gaston Barbee. *Barbee family history; crossroads.barbees.org/DNA/Members.htm.*

The Texas Rangers were able to cross the raging waters but had to abandon thirty horses on the Mexican side of the Rio Grande. Callahan later reported these horses as captured. Seventeen pack mules, belonging to private individuals, were also lost in Mexico.[418]

In full view of civil and military authorities, Callahan's troops carried with them the "spoils of war" that they plundered in Piedras Negras, as was the custom. The townspeople had fought against the Rangers and were then considered as combatants and their goods deemed spoils of war. When Callahan organized the expedition, he explained to his quartermaster, Burleson, the means by which he would recompense

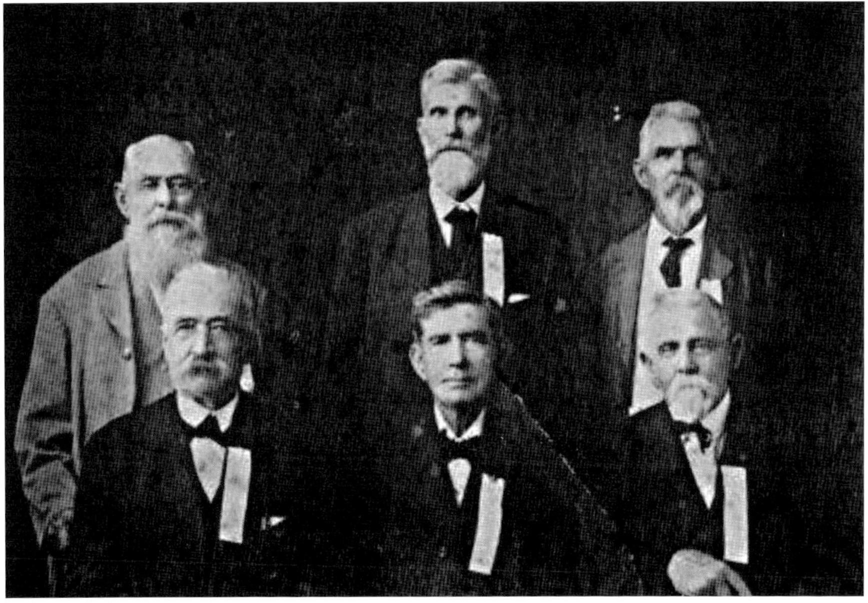

Captain J.H. Callahan's Expedition survivors' San Antonio reunion: (*left to right, first row*) D.C. Burleson, Dave Wattin and Simple Tom; (*second row*) Bill Pitts, John Campbell and John Samson. *Courtesy of Portal to Texas History.*

his Rangers, assuming that the Texas legislature would be unable to compensate the volunteers.

Jesse Sumpter, living in Eagle Pass, reported, "There were a good many men riding about the town of Eagle Pass and everyone I saw had…jewelry displayed about his neck and breast, such as gold necklaces, chains, ear-rings, finger-rings, watches and other articles…which they seemed to take delight in displaying."[419]

By 2:00 a.m. on October 7, the remnants of the Callahan Expedition were back in Texas and encamped three miles south of Fort Duncan. The Rangers made fortifications of the looted sacks of corn, sugar and flour. From these bastions, the Rangers exchanged fire with the Mexican forces with rifles and cannons.

Eustace Benton, the young son of Captain Benton, did not show any signs of life for three days from the time he was shot. The only way that the attendants could tell he was breathing was by holding a soft, downy feather close to his lips.

Suddenly, on the third day, young Benton opened his eyes as if waking from a sleep. Seeing Rangers standing around him, he asked for his gun, thinking the battle still raged. Benton remembered the musket ball hitting him in the face but nothing else of the incident. That musket ball was never extracted from his head.

The bodies of some of the dead Rangers were also taken back to Texas. These included Willis Jones, W.H. Clopton, August Schmidt and William Holloway. These Texas Rangers were buried at Fort Duncan under the direction of Lieutenant Charles Reid.[420]

Callahan gathered his men for the long ride home. Now beaten and ragged, these Rangers found in one another a bond that exists only in combat, among brothers. They were brave and strong and broken all at once. The die had been cast. The Callahan Expedition cantered away from their Rubicon—the Rio Grande.

18

THE RETURN

And now you'll be telling stories
of my coming back
and they won't be false, and they won't be true
but they'll be real.
—Mary Oliver, A Thousand Mornings

Captain Callahan mustered out his Ranger company with honorable discharges for all at Fort Martin Scott in Fredericksburg on October 20, 1855. This formality marked the end of their contracted term of service as originally set by Governor Pease. The simple paperwork done, the men scattered to reunite with family and friends.[421] The captain rode on southeast to his home in nearby Blanco County.

The Rangers had not accomplished their mission, and some of them had died or suffered debilitating wounds. But their return was met with enthusiasm and celebration. None was more delighted than Callahan's wife and family. Sarah rushed to him as he dismounted. Her husband was home, safe and sound. His children hugged his frayed pants as he strode into his cabin. The sun had never seemed brighter as Callahan remembered how good it felt to be home.

Callahan immediately defended his invasion of Mexico, claiming that he had received permission from the Mexican authorities to cross the river in pursuit of the Lipans. For his part, Governor Pease defended Callahan's burning of Piedras Negras, saying that it was justified because the Mexicans had deceived Callahan by leading him into an ambush.

Callahan's published letter of October 13 reads: "Before leaving Eagle Pass, I had abundant and conclusive evidence of a deep laid, preconceived plan, on the part of Mexican authorities and people, to induce me to march my command into the interior, and then to overwhelm us with numbers and then massacre the whole command."[422]

The *San Antonio Herald* of October 16, 1855, reported that after Callahan had fallen back on the town of Piedras Negras, the *alcalde* quailed beneath Callahan's glare. The battle had been a big mistake. "The *alcalde* was given to understand that if we wished to pursue the Indians, he could do so unmolested. This was merely to decoy him east of Piedras Negras so that the Mexicans could carry out their previous design of massacring his command," the San Antonio newspaper said.[423]

Callahan had this to say on October 20 about his actions:

> *I informed him again that I did not wish to have any further difficulty with the Mexicans and would not injure their property or persons, but if they attacked me while I occupied the place, I would do everything necessary for the protection and safety of my command, even to be destructive of the place itself. The Alcalde left and returned no more. I soon discovered that place contained a considerable number of armed men, concealed in houses and that preparations had evidently been made to attack such as the command as might escape slaughter in the fight. Forty or fifty were taken prisoners, disarmed and discharged, and perhaps as many more made their escape.*[424]

U.S. public opinion weighed heavily in favor of Callahan and his expedition. General Smith expressed doubt that the Ranger force would face prosecution, given that sentiment and fear ran high in the region. "They represent the whole affair as a brilliant and successful exploit," complained Smith, "and as such, no doubt, the newspapers throughout the country will represent it. They are upheld by, with very few exceptions, the whole population; and as the Indians who have committed the depredations here are undoubtedly upheld and encouraged by the Mexican authorities, it is hard to convince the Texans that retaliation on the innocent is not the way to correct the evil."[425]

The defeat of Callahan caused surprise and indignation in San Antonio. Shortly after the return of the Callahan Expedition, a public meeting was held, committees and officers were chosen and preparations were made for what was designed to be a larger expedition against Mexico. The express purpose of this meeting was to punish the Indians raiding out of Mexico.

On October 16, the following call to meeting was made through the *San Antonio Sentinel*:

> *To The People of Texas.*
>
> *At a meeting of the citizens of Bexar county, the undersigned were appointed a committee to appeal to you to take this matter into your own hands, as the Federal and State governments have been appealed to in vain. Your fellow-citizens have been cruelly and shamefully murdered almost within view of the capitol of your State and the headquarters of the army of the United States. Your women have been violated and your children carried into captivity. Frontier settlements have been broken up and their property carried into Mexico. Mexico has violated the letter and spirit of our treaties with her, by aiding and abetting the Indians in their robberies, harboring them within her borders, and fighting their battles when pursued to their camps. Texans, to the rescue and let no repose be taken until victory, complete and triumphant, shall be ours. On the Cibola near the mouth of the Santa Clara, will be the point of rendezvous, and the fifteenth day of November is designated as the day when the expedition will move.*
>
> *Respectfully,*
> *Wm. E. Jones*
> *J.H. Callahan*
> *J.A. Wilcox*
> *Jno. Sutherland*
> *Asa Mitchell*
> *S.A. Maverick*[426]

The initiative collapsed due to "lack of ardor" and a hostile attitude in Washington. Nothing more came of this. Henry did continue his adventures in Mexico, but Callahan never again ventured across the border.[427]

No matter the failure of his foray into Mexico, Callahan continued to serve as a Ranger captain in the Rio Blanco area. During this time, he was on the state payroll as late as April 1856.[428]

The undefeated Lipan Apaches of Mexico continued to raid into the Hill Country. On numerous occasions, Callahan and his comrades rode out to defend friends and family.

Callahan endeavored to continue a "normal" life at his place on the Blanco River. He was, after all, the ranking Ranger in his part of the state and leader of the local home guard. He ran a farm, raised cattle and horses and cultivated crops. He hired Calvin Blassingame, a neighbor's son, as a hand. Calvin's father was Woodson Blassingame, who rented an adjacent acreage from Callahan. Another son, Luther Blassingame, age twenty, had been a private in the Callahan Expedition.

On April 7, 1856, Callahan's close friend, William S. "Mallheel" Johnson, said that Blassingame was spreading malicious stories about Callahan. This allegation against Blassingame was buttressed by another friend, Eli Clement Hinds. Both men were trusted colleagues of Callahan.

Hearing this gossip, an infuriated Callahan decided to sort things out. He told young Calvin Blassingame to go tell his father that he wanted to meet with him to discuss this insult. While no gauntlet had been formally tossed, the implication was plain enough. A prideful man intended to defend his honor, one way or the other.

On April 7, 1856, Callahan, along with his associates Mallheel Johnson, William's son Thomas Johnson and Eli Hinds, went to talk to Woodson. The Blassingame farm was a mile west of Callahan's place.

Don Watson of San Antonio wrote, "Upon approaching the Blassingame cabin, Callahan yelled for Woodson to come out."[429] At that, gunfire broke out. Most accounts say the Blassingames fired first, from the cabin.

James Callahan took a shotgun blast squarely in the chest and died instantly. Mallheel Johnson also was killed. Thomas Johnson emptied his weapon before his horse bolted and fled the scene. The gunfire also spooked Eli Hinds's horse, but before it ran, Hinds was shot three times, with two shots piercing his throat.

None of the Blassingame family was injured.

Callahan's body was later retrieved by his friends. He was brought home to his wife, Sarah, who was beyond grief. His body was washed and his wounds covered. He was dressed in fresh clothes. Placed in a wooden coffin, Callahan lay in state on the porch of the house he had built on the southern bank of the Blanco River.

James Hughes Callahan was laid to rest at the old burying ground now known as the Blanco Cemetery, which was located on his land. [430] Still numb with shock, Sarah could only stand and watch as they bore his body, stiff and cold, in that wooden coffin to his burial place. Six Rangers served as his pallbearers. Callahan's daughters sang a hymn. Sarah wept. John Henry Brown spoke of Callahan as "this modest but gallant man."[431]

Despite his service to Texas and his status in the community, Callahan's grave was not marked, and neither was Johnson's. Callahan was buried next to his infant son, William Milford Callahan. The heartbroken Sarah would join them only a year later.

AFTERWORD

O lost,
And by the wind grieved,
Ghost,
Come back again.
—Thomas Wolfe

Shock exploded into rage, and more than fifty men mounted up to avenge the murder of their Captain Callahan.

A wide range of stories exist regarding the Blassingame incident and the events that immediately followed the assassination of Callahan and Johnson.[432]

One account was written in a letter by Calvin Blassingame on April 8, 1856. This message was widely distributed, seeking sympathy and support for the Blassingame family. It is posted on the Blassingame family Web page. "The Blassingames were immediately arrested, under guard of fourteen men each. Kemp's account[433] says the father, son and mother were all three arrested other accounts that only Calvin and Woodson were arrested, but Mary was with them in the Lange cabin when the mob arrived."[434]

Angered friends of Callahan and Johnson arrived at about midnight on Sunday, April 13, 1856. Vengeance reared its ugly head.

Neighbor John M. Watson described the action:

> *On April 14, 1855, a mob of men, reportedly as large as 100 strong, approached the Lange cabin and demanded the Blassingames be turned over to them. There is a great deal of confusion and differing reports of what happened*

> *next, but the cabin was overtaken. The two Blassingame men were drug out by their heels and told to run. They refused, claiming they had done nothing wrong, feeling they had acted in self-defense against Callahan. Mary Blassingame, meanwhile, escaped into the nearby woods. The two Blassingames were shot where they stood. One news account stated that Woodson had more than 50 bullet holes in him and that supposedly, young Thomas Johnson had emptied his gun into the body, although he was never indicted for any part in the killings. Lange turned out to be the "ring leader" of the lynch mob.*[435]

Woodson and Calvin Blassingame were not buried in the Blanco Cemetery, which at that time was on Callahan's farm. Instead, they were buried near their cabin in what is now known as the Sauer family cemetery, located about three miles west of present-day Blanco. This cemetery is very near the old Blassingame cabin that still stands today.[436]

In the aftermath of this event, at least twenty-two indictments were handed down for the murders of Woodson and Calvin Blassingame. The primary defendant in the case turned out to be none other than George Lange, the justice of the peace charged with ensuring a fair trial for these men. Five were acquitted, two had charges dismissed against them and a third had a hung jury and was held over for retrial.[437]

The Callahan Expedition immediately blossomed into an international incident. Mexico rejected the American justification that it was a legal campaign in "hot pursuit" of Lipan Apaches that had been raiding into the Texas Hill Country.

Mexico fiercely condemned the invasion and the burning and looting of Piedras Negras. Vidaurri, recently appointed commander of the northern frontier, and Langberg, the commander of the state of Coahuila, were both extravagantly outraged. They wrapped themselves in the cloth of self-righteousness

To employ a bit of a magical misdirection, the Mexicans propagated the claim that Callahan's Expedition was really a campaign to capture runaway slaves and the hot pursuit of the Lipan Apaches was but a thin disguise. A letter printed in the *Texas State Times* on November 11, 1855—apparently from a Mexican officer—claimed, "The invasion caused much indignation but the allegation that…[it] was perpetrated in order to recover runaway Negroes only makes it worse."[438]

Langberg stoked the flames with letters published in the Mexican newspapers.[439] Mexican public opinion ran so high that the U.S. legation under Ambassador James Gadsden suffered the vitriol of Mexican dailies.[440]

Gadsden made no apology, replying to the Mexican complaints that it was the United States, not Mexico, that had been wronged. Gadsden pointed out that the newspapers of Mexico City had published accounts of the incident "calculated to mislead" and that Callahan had been acting under the order of the governor of Texas for the purpose protecting the lives of citizens from "savages…known to be in the service of Mexico." Moreover, Gadsden asserted that because "Callahan had been invited into Mexico by the Mexicans, and then deceived; they were justified in destroying Piedras Negras to prevent annihilation."[441]

While Callahan was mustering his company in July 1855, William R. Henry of San Antonio published in several newspapers a proclamation to the people of Texas announcing the preparation of an expedition that would join the revolution in Mexico. Among these announcements was the one in the *National Intelligencer* that Almonte, Mexican minister to the United States, noticed that an invasion of Mexico was being prepared in August 1855. Almonte wrote to Marcy on August 15 to have the leader of the invasion band arrested.[442] The leader of that well-publicized invasion was Henry, not Callahan.

Marcy dithered, and the protest had no effect on Henry's ambitions. This diplomatic protest was, in fact, the advance notice that the Mexican government had received of an impending invasion. On August 25, 1855, some Americans from San Antonio sent a letter to Colonel Langberg, military commander of Coahuila, inquiring about "the conditions under which the Colonel would deliver up the Negros who had taken up refugee in Mexico." Langberg gave a favorable reply.[443]

A brief article in the *San Antonio Herald* dated August 14, 1855, notes that "Capt. Wm. Henry and forty or fifty others had crossed over into Mexico and had been arrested by Mexican authorities."[444]

Captain Henry did lead a company of men into Mexico at Piedras Negras in August and was detained until early September. Upon release, Henry's company met up with Callahan in Encina/Uvalde on September 25. Henry and his company did participate in Callahan's Expedition, reaching the Rio Grande on September 29, 1855.[445]

Henry eventually arrived at his reckoning when he was killed in a gunfight in downtown San Antonio in a squabble over a contested command of a Confederate army unit.

At this time, Mexico was politically percolating; Santa Anna was at the end of his reign, and Juan N. Álvarez became temporary president of Mexico on October 4—just in time for the Callahan Expedition to intrude

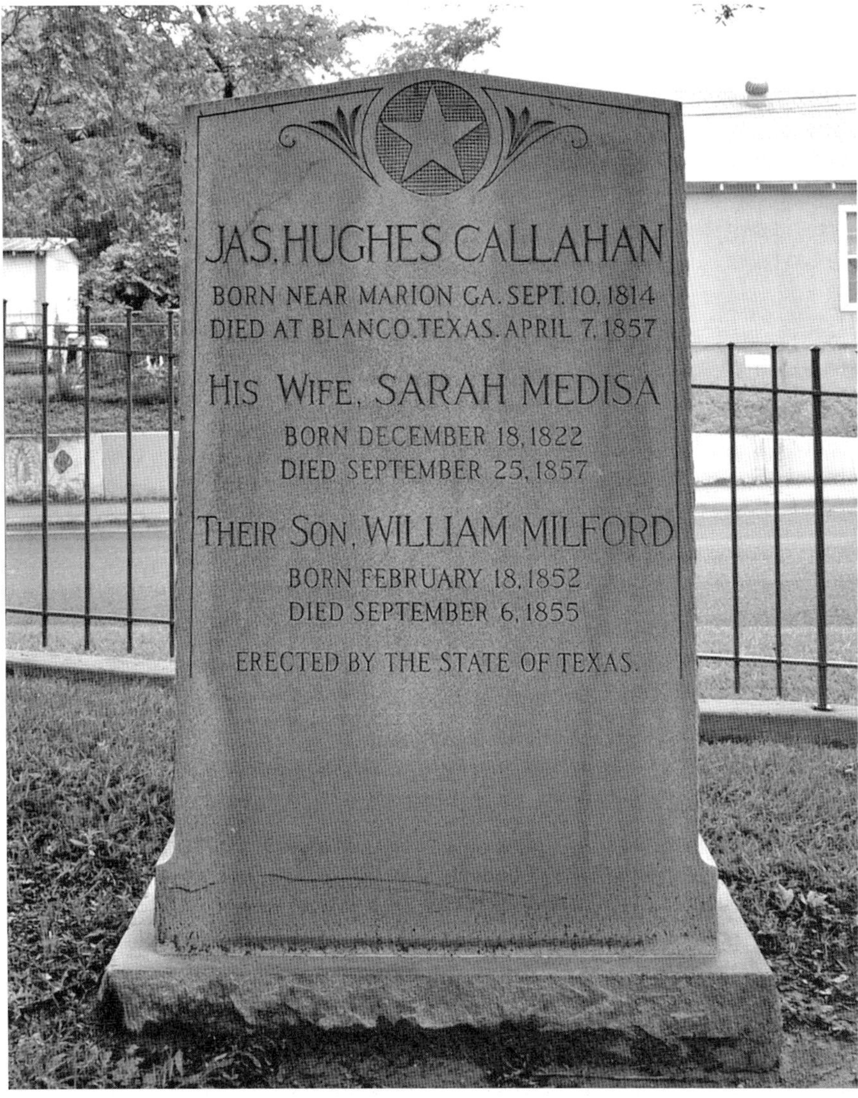

Callahan's head stone. *Texas State Cemetery, Austin.*

into his administration of that country. The Mexican protest of the Callahan Expedition was made under the aegis of the Álvarez government.

In the 1930s, during the run-up to the Texas centennial celebration, Callahan's burial site was identified by an old-timer. After the grave was identified, the state dug up the graves of Callahan, his wife and child and reinterred them in the Texas State Cemetery in Austin.

The graveside oration was delivered by Victor Gilbert, a state representative from Callahan County. The Texas legislature of 1857–58 named the county of Callahan as a tribute to his memory.[446]

Callahan came to Texas in 1835 as an idealistic young soldier in the Georgia Battalion fighting for the cause of Texas independence. He survived the Battle of Refugio and the Goliad Massacre. Over the next twenty-one years, Callahan fought to protect Texas settlers from Apaches, Seminoles, Comanches, Kickapoos, the Mexican army, outlaws, banditti and insurgents. From 1839 to 1841, he commanded a group of minutemen in Guadalupe County who chased and fought Indians and Mexicans accused of stealing horses. He also volunteered for more formal campaigns between 1840 and 1842. He served as a first lieutenant in Matthew Caldwell's company in 1840 and became a company commander during the incursion of Rafael Vásquez in 1841, in which he led a retreat from San Antonio. The next year, his sixty-man company helped expel Adrián Woll from Texas and saw action at the Battle of Salado Creek. Later that year, Callahan also served as a lieutenant in the Somervell Expedition.

His military activities then ceased until 1855, when he commanded the punitive expedition into Mexico that bears his name.

After all the campaigns, battles, narrow escapes and dodging hundreds of arrow and gunshots, Callahan was assassinated less than a mile from his home, by his next-door neighbor.

NOTES

Chapter 1

1. *Savannah Republican*, November 19, 1835.
2. Ibid.
3. Brown, *Hesitant Martyr*. Much remains unknown about Georgia volunteers in Texas because the muster rolls were destroyed. In the case of Ward's battalion, the muster rolls were destroyed with the burning of San Felipe.
4. Spellman, *Forgotten Texas Leader*.
5. Stout, *Slaughter at Goliad*.
6. "The Betsy Ross of Texas." In 1835, in response to an appeal for aid to the Texas cause, the Georgia Battalion, commanded by Colonel William Ward, traveled to Texas. Joanna Troutman designed and made a flag of white silk, bearing a five-pointed blue star and two inscriptions: "Liberty or Death" on the obverse and, in Latin, "Where Liberty dwells there is my country" on the reverse. She presented the flag to the battalion, and it was unfurled at Velasco on January 8, 1836, above the American Hotel. It was carried to Goliad, where James W. Fannin Jr. raised it as the national flag when he heard of the Texas Declaration of Independence. The flag was accidentally torn to shreds, however, and only its remnants flew above the battle. At the request of the Texas governor, Troutman's remains were transferred to the Texas State Cemetery in Austin in 1913. Her portrait hangs in one of the legislative chambers of the Texas capitol.
7. "Lone Star on Texas Flag Was Made by Georgia Girl," *San Antonio Express Newspaper*, September 12, 1934.

8. Haas, *Massacre*, 59.
9. *Macon Telegraph*, January 21, 1836.
10. 28°57'42.876"N 95°21'37.8"W. Old Velasco (encompassed by present-day Surfside Beach) on east side of the mouth of the Brazos River.
11. Hobart Huson, "Goliad Declaration of Independence," *Handbook of Texas Online*, http://www.tshaonline.org/handbook/online/articles/mhg01.

Chapter 2

12. Crockett, *Col. Crockett's Exploits and Adventures in Texas*. In 1836, a sensation was created by a new book titled *Col. Crockett's Exploits and Adventures in Texas: Wherein Is Contained a Full Account of His Journey from Tennessee to the Red River and Natchitoches, and Thence Across Texas to San Antonio; Including Many Hair-Breadth Escapes; Together with a Topographical, Historical, and Political View of Texas…Written by Himself*. It was published by "T.K. and P.G. Collins" (actually Carey and Hart, who had published some of Crockett's authentic, though heavily edited, writings). They claimed that it was Crockett's journal that had been taken from the Alamo by Mexican general Manuel Fernández Castrillón and later recovered at the Battle of San Jacinto, where the general was killed. It became a huge bestseller. For over a century, the book had a profound influence on the public's view of the Texas Revolution and Davy Crockett's career, despite the fact that the author's true identity had been revealed in 1884.
13. Bugbee, "Old Three Hundred," 108–17.
14. Encompassed by present-day Surfside Beach.
15. "Battle of Velasco," *Handbook of Texas Online*, http://www.tshaonline.org/handbook/online/articles/qfv01.
16. Herbert Fletcher, "Texian," *Handbook of Texas Online*, http://www.tshaonline.org/handbook/online/articles/pft05. The term Texan or Texian was generally used to apply to a citizen of the Anglo-American section of the province of Coahuila y Tejas or of the Republic of Texas. For consistency, "Texan" has been used throughout this book, except where "Texian" appeared in direct quotations.
17. Tucker, *Encyclopedia of the Mexican-American War*.
18. Stout, *Slaughter at Goliad*.
19. "Santa Anna 1794–1876," MexicanHistory.org, http://mexicanhistory.org/santaanna.htm.

20. Davenport, Notes from an Unfinished Study.
21. "Muster Roll. Capt James C. Winn's 3rd. Co. Georgia Battalion 1st Regiment Texas Volunteers from 31st. December to 29th. February 1836."
22. Reid, *Texan Army*; Robert P. Broadwater, "A Most Uncommon Rifle, The Model 1817 U.S. Flintlock," http://www.militarytrader.com/military-trader-news/model_1817_us_flintlock.
23. The Consultation grew out of a proposed meeting of Texas representatives to confer on the prerevolutionary quarrel with Mexico. This idea was first advocated by opponents of revolution in the early summer of 1835 in Mina Municipality. Moderate and radical elements endorsed the concept to present a unified front. A meeting in Columbia on August 15 first used the term *consultation*, perhaps to avoid the revolutionary connotations that the word *convention* implied in Mexican politics.
24. Collin McKinney (April 17, 1766–September 9, 1861) was a land surveyor, merchant, politician and lay preacher. He is best known as an important figure in the Texas Revolution, as one of the five individuals who drafted the Texas Declaration of Independence and the oldest person to sign it.
25. Todish, *Alamo Sourcebook, 1836.*
26. Haas, *Massacre*, 60.
27. Site of the Town of Copano, Texas State Historical Marker No. 4937. The marker reads, "Named for the Indians who lived here; Important Texas port, 1722-1870; The landing place of many colonists; Winter quarters of the Texas Revolution Army in 1835." This marker was moved from its original location on Copano Bay (five miles northeast of this site) in 1978.
28. Nuestra Señora del Refugio Mission, the last of the Spanish missions in Texas. Very little is left to see of the last Catholic mission in Texas except some foundation stones on the church grounds along U.S. 77; coordinates of riverbank, 28°18'21"N 97°16'29"W
29. Dunn, "Founding of Nuestra Señora del Refugio," 174–84.
30. Turner, "Mejía Expedition."
31. Houston also believed that the council had exceeded its authority in authorizing the Matamoros expeditions. In an effort to prevent what he feared would be a military disaster, Houston admonished Governor Smith to approach the council. He cited Neill's protests of Grant's actions, which had left the Bexar garrison, mostly sick and wounded men, virtually destitute. On January 10, enraged by Houston's report, Smith

attempted to dissolve the council, which retaliated on January 11 and 12 by impeaching the governor and recognizing Lieutenant Governor Robinson as the acting executive.

32. Stout, *Slaughter at Goliad*.
33. 28°38'48"N 97°26'52"W.
34. In September 1835, Cos was sent by Santa Anna to investigate the refusal of Texans at Anahuac to pay duties imposed after Santa Anna had established himself as president of Mexico with centralized powers. General Cos landed three hundred men at Matagorda Bay, established headquarters in San Antonio and declared his purpose of ending resistance in Texas. A force of Texans under Stephen F. Austin and Edward Burleson held the Mexican troops in the siege of Bexar until Cos surrendered after an attack led by Benjamin R. Milam in December 1835.
35. Stout, *Slaughter at Goliad*.
36. Garland Lively, "Colonel James Walker Fannin's Regiment at Goliad."

Chapter 3

37. "Antonio López de Santa Anna," Sons of Dewitt Colony Texas, http://www.tamu.edu/faculty/ccbn/dewitt/santaanna.htm.
38. Jennings, "Riding to Victory."
39. Ibid.
40. Ibid.
41. Weddle, *San Juan Bautista*.
42. Dimmick, *Sea of Mud*.
43. 28°38'48"N, 97°22'54"W.
44. Sheila M. Ohlendorf, "Urrea, José De," *Handbook of Texas Online*, http://www.tshaonline.org/handbook/online/articles/fur02. Enlisted from Cordoba, Jalapa and Orizaba, the Yucatán battalion became *el Batallón de Tres Villas*. Few of the Mayan Indians who made up the battalion understood their Spanish-speaking officers.
45. Robert C. Morris, quoted in Roell, *Matamoros and the Texas Revolution*.
46. Nofi, *Alamo and the Texas War for Independence*.
47. Stout, *Slaughter at Goliad*.
48. Fagan, *Little Ice Age*. The Little Ice Age was a period of cooling that occurred after the Medieval Warm Period. It has been conventionally defined as a period extending from about 1350 to about 1850.
49. Ibid.

50. Fort Lipantitlán (meaning "Lipan land") was conceived about 1825 by José M.J. Carbajal. The site, now in northwestern Nueces County, was camping grounds of the Lipan Apache Indians on the west bank of the Nueces River about three miles upstream from the old town of San Patricio, which is on the east side of the river.
51. Smith, "James W. Fannin," 79–90.
52. Letter from W.B. Travis and James Bowie to James W. Fannin, February 23, 1836, http://www.tamu.edu/faculty/ccbn/dewitt/adp/history/bios/travis/travtext.html.
53. O'Connor, *Presidio La Bahía del Espíritu Santo de Zúñiga*.
54. Roell, *Remember Goliad!*.
55. Talley, "Leadership Principles."
56. Roell, *Remember Goliad!*.
57. The Convention of 1836 was the meeting of elected delegates in Washington-on-the-Brazos, Texas, in March 1836. The Texas Declaration of Independence was the formal declaration of independence of the Republic of Texas from Mexico in the Texas Revolution. It was adopted on March 2, 1836, and formally signed the following day.
58. The Republic of Texas (in Spanish, *República de Texas*) was an independent sovereign country in North America that existed from March 2, 1836, to February 19, 1846.
59. 29°30'32"N 97°26'52"W.
60. *Degüello* is a Spanish noun from the verb *degollar*, to describe the action of throat cutting. More figuratively, it means "give no quarter." It "signifies the act of beheading or throat-cutting and in Spanish history became associated with the Battle music, which, in different versions, meant complete destruction of the enemy without mercy" (https://en.wikipedia.org/wiki/El_Deg%C3%BCello).
61. "The Convention of 1836," Washington on the Brazos, http://www.tamu.edu/faculty/ccbn/dewitt/adp/archives/documents/washingtononbrazos.html.
62. Brown, *Papers*.
63. Flanagan, *Sam Houston's Texas*.
64. Hardin, "Hard Lot."

Chapter 4

65. Stout, *Slaughter at Goliad*.

66. 28.17°N, 97.3°W.
67. DeShields, *Tall Men with Long Rifles*.
68. Roell, *Remember Goliad!*.
69. "Massacre at Goliad—Captain Jack Shackelford's Account," Sons of Dewitt Colony Texas http://www.tamu.edu/faculty/ccbn/dewitt/goliadshackelford.htm.
70. Brooks served in the United States Marine Corps eleven months before leaving New York for Texas on November 5, 1835, to volunteer for the Texas army. Chadwick was admitted to the United States Military Academy at West Point on July 1, 1829, but resigned on April 30, 1831. He was appointed sergeant major of William Ward's Georgia Battalion.
71. "With the Georgia Battalion—Samuel G. Hardaway's Account," Sons of Dewitt Colony Texas, http://www.tamu.edu/faculty/ccbn/dewitt/goliadsanpat2.htm#hardaway.
72. De La Peña, *With Santa Anna in Texas*.
73. Roell, *Remember Goliad!*.
74. "Diary of Col. Francisco Garay," Sons of Dewitt Colony Texas, http://www.tamu.edu/faculty/ccbn/dewitt/goliadurrea.htm.
75. General José Urrea, "Diary of the Military Operations of the Division Which Under the Command of General José Urrea Campaigned in Texas February to March 1836," Sons of DeWitt County, Texas, http://www.tamu.edu/faculty/ccbn/dewitt/goliadurrea.htm.
76. Dimmick, *Sea of Mud*.
77. Hardin, *Alamo 1836*.
78. Stout, *Slaughter at Goliad*.
79. Ibid.
80. Ibid.
81. "Diary of Col. Francisco Garay."
82. Baker, "Fannin's Massacre—Account of the Georgia Battalion," 245.
83. Ibid., 160
84. "Capture of King and Ward at Mission Refugio," Sons of Dewitt Colony Texas, http://www.tamu.edu/faculty/ccbn/dewitt/goliadsanpat2.htm.
85. *Savannah Republican*, June 15, 1836.
86. Stout. *Slaughter at Goliad*.
87. Foote, *Texas and the Texans*, 25.
88. "L.T. Pease Narrative on Ward's Battle at Mission Refugio," Sons of Dewitt Colony Texas, http://www.tamu.edu/faculty/ccbn/dewitt/goliadsanpat2.htm.
89. Ibid.

90. Ibid.
91. Sullivan, *Texas Revolution.*
92. Robertson, "Captain Amon B. King." In the public square across the street from the county courthouse in Refugio, the King Monument stands as an honor to Captain King and his men. In the early 1900s, the square was owned by the State of Texas and was named King's State Park.
93. Stout, *Slaughter at Goliad.*
94. Ibid.
95. Urrea, "Diary of the Military Operations."
96. "At Mission Refugio Related by Henry Scott," Sons of DeWitt Colony Texas, http://www.tamu.edu/faculty/ccbn/dewitt/goliadsanpat2.htm.
97. Joseph W. Andrews, "Account of Ward and King at Mission Refugio" Sons of DeWitt Colony Texas, http://www.tamu.edu/faculty/ccbn/dewitt/goliadsanpat2.htm.-
98. Stout, *Slaughter at Goliad.*
99. This is now in Refugio County but was then in the municipality of La Bahía.
100. The Battle of Coleto, the culmination of the Goliad Campaign of 1836, occurred near Coleto Creek in Goliad County on March 19 and 20, 1836. The Mexicans called the engagement La Batalla del Encinal del Perdido, or Battle of the Lost Woods. The Texans called it Fannin's Fight. It was one of the most important engagements of the Texas Revolution.
101. "Capture of King and Ward at Mission Refugio," Sons of Dewitt Colony Texas, http://www.tamu.edu/faculty/ccbn/dewitt/goliadsanpat2.htm.
102. Ibid.
103. *Savannah Republican*, June 15, 1836.
104. Davenport, "Men of Goliad," 1–41.

Chapter 5

105. Talley, "Leadership Principles."
106. Stout, *Slaughter at Goliad.*
107. "A Campaign in Texas," *Gonzales Inquirer*, 1853.
108. Stout, *Slaughter at Goliad.*
109. Ellenberger, "Illuminating the Lesser Lights."
110. "Fannin's Fight & the Massacre at La Bahia Goliad," Sons of Dewitt Colony Texas, http://www.tamu.edu/faculty/ccbn/dewitt/goliadframe.htm.

111. "Evacuation of Goliad, Battle of Coleto & Surrender of Fannin," Sons of DeWitt Colony Texas, http://www.tamu.edu/faculty/ccbn/dewitt/goliadcoletohuson.htm.
112. Stout, *Slaughter at Goliad.*
113. Moore, *Texas Rising*, 134.
114. Stout, *Slaughter at Goliad.*
115. "Surrender of Fannin," Sons of DeWitt Colony Texas, http://www.tamu.edu/faculty/ccbn/dewitt/goliadcoletohuson3.htm.
116. "Massacre at Goliad—Mexican Centralista Descriptions," Sons of the Dewitt Colony Texas, http://www.tamu.edu/faculty/ccbn/dewitt/goliadmex.htm.
117. Louis E. Brister, "Holzinger, Juan José," *Handbook of Texas Online*, http://www.tshaonline.org/handbook/online/articles/fhoaa.
118. Harbert Davenport and Craig H. Roell, "Goliad Massacre," *Handbook of Texas Online*, http://www.tshaonline.org/handbook/online/articles/qeg02.
119. Stout, *Slaughter at Goliad*; Carlos E. Casteñeda, trans., ""Surrender of the Force at Goliad Under the Command of James W. Fannin," Sons of DeWitt Colony of Texas, http://www.tamu.edu/faculty/ccbn/dewitt/goliadmex.htm.
120. "Massacre at Goliad—Captain Jack Shackelford's Account," Sons of DeWitt Colony of Texas, http://www.tamu.edu/faculty/ccbn/dewitt/goliadshackelford.htm.
121. Stout, *Slaughter at Goliad.*
122. Ibid.
123. Brown, *Hesitant Martyr*, 160.
124. Haley, *Sam Houston.*

Chapter 6

125. Johnson, *History of Texas and Texans*, 439.
126. Stout, *Slaughter at Goliad.*
127. Benjamin Franklin Hughes, as quoted in Harbert Davenport, "The Angel of Goliad," Sons of Dewitt Colony Texas, http://www.tamu.edu/faculty/ccbn/dewitt/goliadangel.htm.
128. John C. Duval, as quoted in Baker, "Fannin's Massacre—Account of the Georgia Battalion," 368.
129. "Massacre at Goliad—Captain Jack Shackelford's Account."
130. "Account of Capt. Benjamin Holland," Sons of DeWitt Colony Texas, http://www.tamu.edu/faculty/ccbn/dewitt/goliaddiverse3.htm.

131. Ibid.
132. "Extract from the Diary of Col. Nicolás de la Portilla," Sons of Dewitt Colony Texas, http://www.tamu.edu/faculty/ccbn/dewitt/goliadurrea.htm).
133. "Massacre at Goliad—Mexican Centralista Descriptions."
134. Stout, *Slaughter at Goliad.*
135. Baker, "Fannin's Massacre—Account of the Georgia Battalion," 245.
136. "Massacre at Goliad—Captain Jack Shackelford's Account."
137. Brady, *Border Fights & Fighters.*
138. Brown, *Hesitant Martyr.*
139. Joseph H. Spohn, "Account of Fannin's Death," Sons of Dewitt Colony Texas, http://www.tamu.edu/faculty/ccbn/dewitt/adp/archives/documents/fanninsdeath.html.
140. Ibid.
141. Stout, *Slaughter at Goliad.*
142. "Massacre at Goliad—Captain Jack Shackelford's Account."
143. Jenkins, *Recollections of Early Texas.*
144. "Santa Anna 1794–1876."

Chapter 7

145. Cutrer, *Ben McCullouch.*
146. Miller, *Life of Robert Hall.*
147. "Brazos," in Miller, *Life of Robert Hall*, 54.
148. Gesick, *Under the Live Oak Tree.*
149. Sowell, *Rangers and Pioneers of Texas.*
150. Gesick, *Under the Live Oak Tree.*
151. "Agreement of James Campbell, Arthur Swift, Matthew Caldwell."
152. Gesick, *Under the Live Oak Tree.*
153. Ivey, Assad, Roemer and Eaton, *Archaeological and Historical Survey.*
154. Moellering, "History of Guadalupe County."
155. Harold J. Weiss Jr., "Hays, John Coffee (1817–1883)," *Handbook of Texas Online*, https://www.tshaonline.org/handbook/online/articles/fhabq.
156. McDowell, *Now You Hear My Horn.*
157. Nance, *Attack and Counterattack.*
158. Jeanette H. Flachmeier, "Johnston, Albert Sidney," *Handbook of Texas Online*, http://www.tshaonline.org/handbook/online/articles/fjo32.
159. Nance, *Attack and Counterattack.*

160. Ivey, Assad, Roemer and Eaton, *Archaeological and Historical Survey*. Agatón Quiñones fought Hays's horsemen at Hondo Creek in 1842.
161. Nance, *Attack and Counterattack.*
162. Ibid.
163. Moore, *Savage Frontier.*
164. Ibid.
165. Ibid.
166. Turner and Hester, *Field Guide to Stone Artifacts.*
167. 29°18'33"N 100°25'17"W.
168. Luther, "Boneyard—An Ethno Archeology Project."
169. 30°13'N 100°29'W.
170. Texas Historical Marker No. 5171010096, 30°13.691'N 98°48.518'W.
171. Luther, *Fort Martin Scott.*
172. Brown, *Indian Wars and Pioneers of Texas*, 84.
173. Moore, *Savage Frontier*, 221.
174. 30°3'5220"N 99°11'23.2131"W.
175. Hindes, Wolf, Hall and Gilmore, *Rediscovery of Santa Cruz de San Sabá.*
176. "The Second Flying Company of Alamo de Parras," http://www.tamu.edu/faculty/ccbn/dewitt/adp/history/hispanic_period/parras.html. *La Segunda Compañía Volante de San Carlos de Parras*, a company of one hundred Spanish colonial mounted lancers. Their lasting legacy would be to give their name to the former Mission San Antonio de Valero that would become known as the Alamo because of their association.
177. Berlandier, *Indians of Texas in 1830.*
178. Luther, *Camp Verde.*
179. 30°10'29"N 99°22'49"W.
180. 30°30'N 99°41'W.
181. Moore, *Savage Frontier.*
182. De la Teja, *Revolution Remembered.*
183. Banquete is an unincorporated community in Nueces County, Texas (27°48'22" N, 97°47'46" W).
184. Nance, *Attack and Counterattack.*
185. Moore, *Savage Frontier.*
186. Ibid., 334.

Chapter 8

187. "General Adrián (Gaul) Woll," Sons of DeWitt Colony Texas, http://www.tamu.edu/faculty/ccbn/dewitt/woll.htm.

188. "Report from Gen. Adrian Woll to Gen. Isidro Reyes Concerning the Battle of Salado and the Dawson Massacre," September 20, 1842, Sons of Dewitt Colony Texas. http://www.tamu.edu/faculty/ccbn/dewitt/woll.htm.
189. Nance, *Attack and Counterattack*.
190. Texas Historic Marker No. 5029000335.
191. 29°29'360"N, 98°25'117"W.
192. Manuscript of the Mexican War by James Ramsay, "Eyewitness Descriptions: The Battle of Salado and Dawson Massacre," Sons of Dewitt Colony Texas, http://www.tamu.edu/faculty/ccbn/dewitt/salado.htm.
193. Morrell, *Flowers and Fruits from the Wilderness*.
194. Nance, *Attack and Counterattack*.
195. "Captain 'Black' Adam Zumwalt in the Battle of Salado-Dawson Massacre," Sons of Dewitt Colony Texas, http://www.tamu.edu/faculty/ccbn/dewitt/badam3.htm.
196. Castañeda received a grave wound in the Battle of Salado Creek.
197. "Report from Gen. Adrian Woll to Gen. Isidro Reyes."
198. Sowell, *Rangers and Pioneers of Texas*.
199. "Miles S. Bennet for the Cuero Star and Houston Post, 1898," Sons of Dewitt Colony Texas, http://www.tamu.edu/faculty/ccbn/dewitt/salado.htm.
200. "Early Days in Texas by Nathan Boone Burkett," Sons of Dewitt Colony Texas, http://www.tamu.edu/faculty/ccbn/dewitt/nathanmem.htm.
201. Utley, *Lone Star Justice*.
202. "Brazos," in Miller, *Life of Robert Hall*, 54.
203. Nance, *Attack and Counterattack*.
204. "Mathew Caldwell," Sons of Dewitt Colony Texas, http://www.tamu.edu/faculty/ccbn/dewitt/caldwellmathew.htm.
205. Robenalt, *Historic Tales from the Texas Republic*.
206. Ibid.
207. Miles S. Bennet, "Events Leading to and the Battle of Salado." Sons of DeWitt Colony Texas, http://www.tamu.edu/faculty/ccbn/dewitt/saladobennet.htm.
208. "Brazos," in Miller, *Life of Robert Hall*, 547.
209. Bennet, "Events Leading to and the Battle of Salado."
210. Ibid.
211. William Savage, a member of the author's family, was killed in the Dawson Massacre.
212. Nance, *Attack and Counterattack*.
213. "Brazos," in Miller, *Life of Robert Hall*, 54.
214. Robenalt, *Historic Tales from the Texas Republic*.

215. Battle of Arroyo Hondo, Texas State Historical Marker No. 5325000332, 29°25'183"N, 99°10'754"W.
216. Hondo Creek where it meets Quahi Creek was the site of the Battle of the Arroyo Hondo in 1842. The battle occurred following the third in a series of three invasions by Mexican forces in 1842 to reclaim territory lost during the 1836 Texas Revolution. The marker is near Hondo, Texas, in Medina County on Farm to Market Road 462, six and a half miles north of U.S. 90.
217. Moore, *Savage Frontier*, vol 4.
218. Bennet, "Events Leading to and the Battle of Salado."
219. Ramos, *Beyond the Alamo*.
220. "Brazos," in Miller, *Life of Robert Hall*, 54.
221. Robenalt, *Historic Tales from the Texas Republic*.

Chapter 9

222. Sowell, *Rangers and Pioneers of Texas*.
223. Gesick, *Under the Live Oak Tree*.
224. John Lindsay McCrocklin is a member of the author's family.
225. Gesick, *Under the Live Oak Tree*.
226. Moore, *Savage Frontier*.
227. 27°29'17.55"N 99°28'45.75"W.
228. Pierce, *Texas Under Arms*.
229. "Brazos," in Miller, *Life of Robert Hall*, 54.
230. Wolf, *Texas Splendid Expendables of 1842*.
231. Gesick, *Under the Live Oak Tree*.
232. Duval, *Adventures of Big-Foot Wallace*.

Chapter 10

233. Elizabeth York Enstam, "Women and the Law," *Handbook of Texas Online*, http://www.tshaonline.org/handbook/online/articles/jsw02.
234. Adele Lubbock Briscoe Looscan, "The Women of Pioneer Days," in *Comprehensive History of Texas*, 1:649–68.
235. 29°43'57"N 97°45'13"W.
236. Fehrenbach, *Comanches*, 276.
237. Kluger, *Seizing Destiny*.

238. "The Treaty of Annexation–Texas: April 12, 1844," The Avalon Project, http://avalon.law.yale.edu/19th_century/texan05.asp.
239. "Brazos," in Miller, *Life of Robert Hall*, 54.
240. Luther, *Fort Martin Scott*.
241. Reid, *Scouting Expeditions of McCulloch's Texas Rangers*.
242. "Brazos," in Miller, *Life of Robert Hall*.
243. Smith, *Frontier Defense in the Civil War*.
244. Luther, Fort Martin Scott.
245. 30°5'561"N, 98°26'038"W.
246. 29°30'004"N, 97°45'393"W.
247. Texas State Historical Marker No. 5187001412.
248. Haley, *Diary of Michael Erskine*.
249. Sanderlin, "Cattle Drive from Texas to California."
250. Olmsted, *Journey Through Texas*.

Chapter 11

251. "This Week in Texas Methodist History August 30: Reverend John McGee's Son Killed by Indians August 31, 1855," *Texas Methodist History*, August 29, 2009, http://txmethhistory.blogspot.com/2009_08_01_archive.html.
252. Luther, *Camp Verde*.
253. Utley, *Frontiersmen in Blue*.
254. Pease to Smith, June 20, 1855.
255. Luther, Camp Verde.
256. Cutrer, *Ben McCulloch*, 67.
257. Luther, Camp Verde.
258. "Brazos," in Miller, *Life of Robert Hall*, 54.
259. Santleben, *Texas Pioneer*.
260. Davis to Doss, May 12, 1855.
261. General Persifor Smith, with copy, to Colonel Emilio Langberg, December 6, 1855, *Congressional Serial Set*.
262. Shearer, "Callahan Expedition."
263. Governor E.M. Pease to James H. Callahan, July 25, 1855, *Congressional Serial Set*, 82.
264. Sansom, "Callahan's Raid in Mexico."
265. Ibid.
266. 28°29'30.32"N 100°55'10.19"W.

267. Minor, *Turning Adversity to Advantage*; The Lipan Apache Tribe: History-Timeline, http://www.lipanapache.org/History/timeline.html.

Chapter 12

268. A filibuster or freebooter is someone who engages in an unauthorized military expedition into a foreign country to foment or support a revolution.
269. Rippy, "Border Troubles Along the Rio Grande."
270. *Reports of the Committee of Investigation*, 12–13.
271. Redonet, "Underground Railroad."
272. Barr, *Black Texans*.
273. Ibid.
274. Barr, *Black Texans*; Guinn, *Our Land Before We Die*.
275. Tyler, "Fugitive Slaves in Mexico."
276. Wilkins, "Mexico's Legacy."
277. *Comisión Pesquisidora de la Frontera del Norte*.
278. Cunningham and Hewitt, "Lovely Land Full of Roses and Thorns," 387–425.
279. Rippy, "Border Troubles Along the Rio Grande."
280. Tyler, "Callahan Expedition of 1855."
281. The English term *filibuster* derives from the Spanish *filibustero*, itself deriving originally from the Dutch *vrijbuiter*, 'privateer, pirate, robber' (also the root of English *freebooter*). The Spanish form entered the English language in the 1850s, as applied to military adventurers from the United States then operating in Central America and the Spanish West Indies.
282. Fornell, "Texans and Filibusters in the 1850s."
283. "Byronic Hero," Dictionary.com, http://www.dictionary.com/browse/byronic-heroJanuary 4, 2017.
284. Christiansen, *Romantic Affinities*.
285. Manuel Guerra, "Henry, William R.," *Handbook of Texas Online*, http://www.tshaonline.org/handbook/online/articles/fhehg.
286. Ibid.

Chapter 13

287. Pease to Smith, June 21, 1855.
288. Heitman, *Historical Register and Dictionary of the United States Army*, 493.

289. Haralson, "Greyhound General."
290. Collins, *Texas Devils*.
291. Shearer, "Callahan Expedition," 433.
292. 29°51'N, 99°06'W.
293. "Bandera Pass Cemetery," http://www.rootsweb.ancestry.com/~txbander/ceme-banderapass.html; Sowell, *Rangers and Pioneers of Texas*. There are some historians that doubt the veracity of this story, but the graves remain nonetheless.
294. "Pavo Real," Texas Beyond History, http://www.texasbeyondhistory.net/pavoreal/site.html.
295. Luther, *Camp Verde*.
296. Colt 1851 navy revolver, http://www.armscollectors.com/mgs/colts_navies_part_1.htm.
297. Flayderman, *Flayderman's Guide*.
298. "Sharps Rifle," Wikipedia, http://en.wikipedia.org/wiki/Sharps_rifle.
299. Moore, *Texas Rising*, 304.
300. Crabapple Creek near Enchanted Rock, 30°26'35"N 98°50'15"W; Camp Enchanted Rock, 30°30.06'N 98°54'W.
301. Ivey, *Texas Rangers*.
302. Porter, *Black Seminoles*.
303. Ivey, *Texas Rangers*.
304. Wilkins, *Defending the Texas Borders*.
305. Born in Tipton County, Tennessee, Ed Burleson, Jr. (1826–1877) was the son of Edward Burleson Sr. and Sarah Owen.
306. Bandera, 29°44.052'N 99°4.596'W; Wilkens, *Defending the Texas Borders*.
307. Collins, *Texas Devils*.
308. Ibid.
309. "Leona Springs," the Edwards Aquifer website, http://www.edwardsaquifer.net/leona.html.
310. Crook and Crook, "Fort Lincoln, Texas."
311. 29°21.681'N 099°17.036'W.
312. Weddle, *San Juan Bautista*.
313. "General Adrian (Gaul) Woll," Sons of DeWitt Colony Texas, http://www.tamu.edu/faculty/ccbn/dewitt/woll.htm.
314. Hughes, Sitgreaves and Franklin. "Map Showing the Line of March."
315. McGraw, Clark and Robbins, *Texas Legacy*.
316. Hughes, *Memoir Descriptive of the March*.
317. Much detail of this route is provided in Nance, "Brigadier General Adrian Woll's Report."
318. "Paso del Águila," Handbook of Texas, https://www.tshaonline.org/

handbook/online/articles/rkp21. After the Texas Revolution and during the decade of the Republic of Texas, commerce between the towns and villages in northern Coahuila and the Texans was forbidden by Mexican authorities. A clandestine trade did continue, however, between San Antonio and the Mexican settlements, particularly those near the Rio Grande. Replacing the guarded main crossing sites near Presidio del Río Grande was a smuggler's trail that followed a more direct, though northerly, course to San Antonio. The trail left San Fernando de Rosas and crossed the Rio Grande thirty miles upriver from the old presidio at a ford near the mouth of the Rio Escondido. General Adrián Woll followed the upper portion of this trail when he raided San Antonio in 1842, and General Isidro Reyes positioned his forces at "El Paso del Águila" when he suspected that the Texans might retaliate by attacking Presidio del Río Grande or San Fernando de Rosas.

319. The small cinder cone volcanoes extruded from the cretaceous bedrock of this region. The diminutive basalt cones were a dark mass on the horizon that served as a beacon on the approach to the Leona.

320. "Callahan's Expedition: Indians and Mexicans Punished for Depredations," *Galveston Daily News*, Sunday, January 8, 1893.

Chapter 14

321. 29°10.887'N 99°45.795'W.
322. Sansom, "Callahan's Raid in Mexico."
323. Smith to Cooper, September 22, 1855.
324. Utley, *Lone Star Justice.*
325. Ford, *Rip Ford's Texas.*
326. Ibid.
327. J.S. McDowell, "Diary," *Galveston Daily News*, January 8, 1893.
328. Shearer, "Callahan Expedition."
329. Gesick, *Under the Live Oak Tree.*
330. Sansom, "Callahan's Raid in Mexico."
331. Shearer, "Callahan Expedition."
332. Wilkins, *Defending the Texas Borders.*
333. McDowell, "Diary."
334. Sansom, "Callahan's Raid in Mexico."
335. Sowell, *Rangers and Pioneers of Texas.*
336. "Coahuila y Sus Hombres / Los Indios Bárbaros del Norte," *El Siglo*

de Torreón, December 12, 2004, http://www.elsiglodetorreon.com.mx/noticia/123878.coahuila-y-sus-hombres-los-indios-barbaros-del-norte.html.

337. McGraw, Clark and Robbins, *Texas Legacy*. The route also led across a wide expanse of thorn brush later called the Brasada. The Spanish word *brasada* refers to something burned or burning, such as embers or hot coals. It was commonly used in the nineteenth century to refer to the dense south Texas thorn scrub, perhaps because of the burning heat of the ground in that area in summer, noted in several early travelers' journals. The Brasada was roughly bounded on the north by the *Lomería Grande* and on the east by the Texas coastal prairies.

338. Sansom, "Callahan's Raid in Mexico."

339. Thompson. *Fort Duncan, Texas*.

340. Steve Dial, "Battles for the Nueces Strip," Texas Beyond History, http://www.texasbeyondhistory.net/forts/clark/Battles.html.

341. 28.947451'N 100.624234'W

342. Sowell, *Rangers and Pioneers of Texas*.

343. Sansom, "Callahan's Raid in Mexico."

344. Wilkins, *Defending the Texas Borders*, 52.

Chapter 15

345. A Mexican alcoholic drink made by fermenting sap from the maguey (*Agave americana*).

346. Crimmins and Freeman, "Fort Duncan."

347. Crimmins and Freeman, "W.G. Freeman's Report on the Eighth Military Department."

348. Olmsted, *Journey Through Texas*.

349. Texas State Marker No. 14217.

350. Schober, "Historia."

351. McDowell, "Diary."

352. Historically, this has come to be known as "a separate crossing."

353. 28°39.758'N 100°29.998'W.

354. Wilkins, *Defending the Texas Borders*, 52.

355. McDowell, "Diary."

356. Sansom, "Callahan's Raid in Mexico."

357. McDowell, "Diary."

358. "Mexican War (1846–1848) and the Indian Wars," The Alamo

Battalion–San Antonio Citadel Club, http://www.citadelsanantonio.org/mexWar.html. It was at this time that Lieutenant Davant of the U.S. Army drowned in the crossing of the Rio Grande.
359. *Texas State Gazette*, October 20, 1955.
360. William Martin Davant was a graduate of the U.S. Military Academy at West Point in 1854. He attended from July 1, 1849, to July 1, 1854. Following graduation, he was appointed as a brevet lieutenant of mounted riflemen under Captain John G. Walker. He served on the frontier at Fort McIntosh, Texas (1854–January 1855). Then, he served at Fort Duncan, Texas (January–October 1855), with temporary "grazing duty" at Fort Inge). On March 3, 1855, he was promoted to full second lieutenant.
361. McDowell, "Diary."
362. Callahan to Pease, October 13, 1855.
363. Adams, "Embattled Borderland."
364. Winfrey and Day, *Indian Papers of Texas and the Southwest*, 5:170.
365. Cremony, *Life Among the Apaches*.
366. Collins, *Texas Devils*.
367. Missall and Missall, *Seminole Wars*.
368. Murray, "Unconquered Seminoles."
369. Latorre and Latorre, *Mexican Kickapoo Indians*.
370. Thybony, "Black Seminoles."
371. Kenmotsu and Wade, *American Indian Tribal Affiliation Study*.

Chapter 16

372. McDowell, "Diary."
373. 28°36'0"N 100°42'0"W.
374. Sansom, "Callahan's Raid in Mexico."
375. Ibid.
376. Sowell, *Rangers and Pioneers of Texas*.
377. Ibid.
378. Ibid.
379. Ibid.
380. Collins, *Texas Devils*.
381. Sumpter, *Jesse Sumpter Reminiscences*.
382. Sowell, *Rangers and Pioneers of Texas*.
383. This heroic youth was carried for that long distance by Captain William

A. Pitts, who placed the unconscious boy in his saddle and rode behind him on the same horse, holding him in his arms. This scene, with bullets whizzing from a pursuing foe, and the agonized father (Captain Nat Benton, with an arm broken), wrought almost into frenzy by what he considered the death wound of his only child, involuntarily calls to mind the legend of Damon and Pythias, found in Brown, *Indian Wars and Pioneers of Texas.*

384. Ibid.
385. Sansom, "Callahan's Raid in Mexico."
386. Ibid.
387. Sidney Burbank, Report to the adjutant general, October 9, 1855, *Congressional Serial Set.*

Chapter 17

388. *Comisión Pesquisidora de la Frontera del Norte*; Brown, *History of Texas*, 2:370–71.
389. Shearer, "Callahan Expedition."
390. Collins, *Texas Devils.*
391. Glasrud and Weiss, *Tracking the Texas Rangers.*
392. Shearer, "Callahan Expedition."
393. Cox, *Texas Rangers.*
394. Sowell, *Rangers and Pioneers of Texas.*
395. Sumpter, *Jesse Sumpter Reminiscences.*
396. Callahan, "Capt. Callahan's Address to the People of Texas."
397. Shearer, "Callahan Expedition."
398. "Return of Captain Callahan's Expedition," *San Antonio Herald*, October 16, 1855.
399. Sansom, "Callahan's Raid in Mexico."
400. Callahan to Pease, October 13, 1855.
401. Sumpter, *Jesse Sumpter Reminiscences.*
402. Brown, *Papers.*
403. Sansom, "Callahan's Raid in Mexico."
404. Ibid.
405. Ibid.
406. Haecker and Mauck, *On the Prairie of Palo Alto.*
407. Sansom, "Callahan's Raid in Mexico."
408. Ibid.

409. Matthews, *U.S. Army on the Mexican Border.*
410. Sumpter, *Jesse Sumpter Reminiscences*; Warren, "Early History of Eagle Pass"; Pingenot, *Paso del Águila.*
411. Sumpter, *Jesse Sumpter Reminiscences.*
412. Sansom, "Callahan's Raid in Mexico."
413. Sowell, *Rangers and Pioneers of Texas.*
414. McDowell, "Diary."
415. Ibid.
416. "U.S.-Mexican General Claims Commission."
417. Sansom, "Callahan's Raid in Mexico."
418. "Claims Against the United States, Class II, Callahan's Party," *Congressional Serial Set.*
419. Ibid.
420. Sansom, "Callahan's Raid in Mexico."

Chapter 18

421. Callahan reported on the aftermath of his retreat from Piedras Negras: "On the morning of the 7th we camped three miles from Eagle Pass, and the 8th resumed our march towards San Antonio. My company is now on its way to Fredericksburg to await your orders as its time of service expires on the 20th."
422. Callahan, "Letter from Capt. Callahan to Governor Pease."
423. "Return of Captain Callahan's Expedition."
424. "Letter from Captain Callahan."
425. United States Senate, *Letter from the Secretary of War*, 114.
426. Mexico, *Comisión Pesquisidora.*
427. Rippy, "Border Troubles Along the Rio Grande"; Olmsted, *Journey Through Texas.*
428. Texas Ranger (pre–Civil War) military rolls.
429. "The Callahan-Blassingame Incident," U.S. GenWeb Project, http://www.rootsweb.ancestry.com/~txblanco/blass.htm.
430. 30.09280'N 98.41670'W.
431. Brown, *Indian Wars and Pioneers of Texas.*

Afterword

432. "Phillips and Callahan Family Lines in Arkansas, Texas, and Oklahoma," http://freepages.genealogy.rootsweb.ancest ry.com/~rayphill/familycallahan.htm; Rubin Richard Dillard, "Home Page: Information about Woodson Blassingame," Genealogy.com, http://www.genealogy.com/ftm/w/a/g/Nelda-Wagner/WEBSITE-0001/UHP-0339.html.
433. L.W. Kemp in *Frontier Times*, June 1934, reprinted in Blanco County News, *Heritage of Blanco County*, 52.
434. "Calvin Blasengame's Letter," http://www.rootsweb.ancestry.com/~txblanco/blass3.html.
435. "The Callahan-Blassingame Incident."
436. Josh Harkinson. "Coming Home to Texas." *Mother Jones*. June 20, 2011. (http://www.motherjones.com/mojo/2011/06/texas-history-blasingame-callahan-perry), accessed 1.4.2017.
437. "The Callahan-Blassingame Incident."
438. Tyler, "Callahan Expedition of 1855."
439. Emilio Langberg letter to editor, *Bejareño*, in *Texas State Times*, November 17, 1855.
440. Shearer, "Callahan Expedition."
441. Ibid.
442. J.N. Almonte to W.L. Marcy, August 15, 1855, in Shearer, "Callahan Expedition," 433.
443. *Reports of the Committee of Investigation*.
444. *San Antonio Herald*, Tuesday, August 14, 1855.
445. Guerra, "Henry, William R."
446. Sowell, *Rangers and Pioneers of Texas*.

BIBLIOGRAPHY

Archaeological Reports

Adams, R.E.W. "Archaeological Investigations at the Gateway Missions." In *The Archaeology and Ethnohistory of the Gateway Area, Middle Rio Grande, Texas.* Final report to the National Endowment for the Humanities, University of Texas–San Antonio, 1997.

Campbell, Thomas Nolan. *The Indians of Southern Texas and Northeastern Mexico: Selected Writings of Thomas Nolan Campbell.* Texas Archeological Research Laboratory in cooperation with the Department of Anthropology and the Institute of Latin American Studies, University of Texas–Austin, 1988.

Dimmick, Gregg J. *Sea of Mud: The Retreat of the Mexican Army after San Jacinto, An Archeological Investigation.* Austin: Texas State Historical Association, 2004.

Duke, Alan R. "Artifacts from San Jacinto." *Houston Archeolgical Society Newsletter*, no. 43 (1974): 4–7.

Haecker, Charles M., and Jeffrey G. Mauck. *On the Prairie of Palo Alto: Historical Archaeology of the U.S.-Mexican War Battlefield.* College Station: Texas A&M University Press, 1997.

Hall, G.D. *Leona River Watershed, Uvalde County, Texas: An Archeological and Historical Survey of Areas Proposed for Modification.* Austin: University of Texas, 1974.

Hester, Thomas R. "The Archeology of the Lower Rio Grande Valley of Texas." In *An Exploration of a Common Legacy*, edited by Marlene Elizabeth Heck, 66–81. Austin: Texas Historical Commission, 1978.

———. "The Discovery and Study of the Mexican War Mass Grave at Reseca de la Palma." *Bulletin of the Texas Archeological Society* 86 (2015): 237–47.

Hindes, V. Kay, Mark R. Wolf, Grant D. Hall and Kathleen Kirk Gilmore. *The Rediscovery of Santa Cruz de San Sabá: A Mission for the Apache in Spanish Texas*. Austin: Texas State Historical Association and Texas Tech University, 1995.

Ivey, James E., Cristi Assad, Erwin Roemer and Jack D. Eaton. *An Archaeological and Historical Survey of Walnut Creek, Seguin, Texas*. Archaeological Survey Report. Center for Archaeological Research, University of Texas–San Antonio, 1977.

Kenmotsu, Nancy Adele, and Mariah F. Wade. *American Indian Tribal Affiliation Study*. Phase I, *Ethnohistoric Literature Review*. Austin: Texas Department of Transportation and National Park Service, 2002.

Luther, Joseph. Big Foot Wallace Site, 41BN252. TexSite form approved 2012. Texas Archeological Research Laboratory (TARL).

———. "Boneyard: The Ancient History of the Upper Guadalupe River." Paper presented to Society of American Archeology Society of American Archeology (SAA) 79th Annual Meeting, Austin, April 24, 2014.

———. "Boneyard—An Ethno Archeology Project." *Texas Archeology* 56, no. 2 (Spring 2012): 916–17.

———. Boneyard/LaRivera, 41KR22. TexSite revisit form approved 2012. Texas Archeological Research Laboratory (TARL).

———. Camp Verde, 41KR111. TexSite revisit form approved 2013. Texas Archeological Research Laboratory (TARL).

———. "Lipan Apaches in the Texas Hill Country." *HCAA News* 13, no. 5 (July 2012): 5–6.

Mounger, Maria A. "Mission Espíritu Santo of Coastal Texas: An Example of Historic Site Archeology." Master's thesis, Department of Anthropology, University of Texas, Austin, 1959.

Nelson, George S. *Preliminary Archaeological Survey and Testing of Fort Inge, Texas.* Uvalde, TX: Uvalde County Historical Commission, 1981.

Perttula, T.K. *Archeological Investigation of Mexican-American War Battlefields in Texas*. Austin: Department of Antiquities Protection, Texas Historical Commission, 1996.

Potter, Daniel, and Jack D. Eaton. *Archeological Survey of Property for the Proposed Eagle Pass International Bridge, Maverick County, Texas*. San Antonio: University of Texas Center for Archaeological Research, Texas Antiquities Committee, 1990.

Ricklis, Robert A. *Archeological Investigations at the Spanish Colonial Missions of Espíritu Santo (41GD1) and Nuestra Señora del Rosario (41GD2)*. Corpus Christi, TX: Coastal Archeological Studies, 2000.

Tennis, Cynthia L. *Archaeological Investigations at the Last Spanish Colonial Mission Established on the Texas Frontier: Nuestra Señora del Refugio (41RF1)*. Archaeological Survey Report No. 315. San Antonio: University of Texas Center for Archaeological Research, 2002.

Turner, Ellen Sue, and Thomas R. Hester. *A Field Guide to Stone Artifacts of Texas Indians*. Boulder, CO: Taylor Trade Publishing, 2013.

Ullrich, Kristi M., Antonio L. Figueroa, Jennifer L. Thompson, Anne A. Fox, Johanna M. Hunziker, Steve A. Tomka, and Cynthia M. Munoz. *Archeological Investigations at Mission Espíritu Santo (41GD1), Goliad County, Texas*. Archival series 3, Texas Archeological Research Laboratory, the University of Texas–Austin, and Archaeological Report 356, Center for Archaeological Research, University of Texas–San Antonio, 2005.

Weinstein, Richard A., ed. *Archaeological Investigations at the Guadalupe Bay Site (41 CL 2): Late Archaic Through Historic Occupation Along the Channel to Victoria, Calhoun County, Texas*. 2 vols. Prepared for Galveston District, U.S. Army Corps of Engineers. Baton Rouge, LA: Coastal Environments, 2002.

Ziga, Adriana Muñoz. "Archival Research of the History of the Francisco Flores Ranch." *Journal of Texas Archeology and History* 1 (2014): 127–47.

Articles

Austerman, Wayne R. "Arms of the El Paso Mail." *Gun Report*, January 25, 1980.

Callahan, James H. "Capt. Callahan's Address to the People of Texas." *New York Times*, October 26, 1855.

———. "Letter from Capt. Callahan to Governor Pease." *Washington American*, Thursday, November 1, 1855.

El Béjareño (San Antonio, Tex.), Saturday, September 1, 1855; Saturday, October 13, 1855; Saturday, December 1, 1855.

[Hunter, J. Marvin]. "Capt. Ben McCulloch." *Frontier Times* 23, no. 4 (December 1945): 4–39.

———. "Jack Hays, the Texas Ranger." *Frontier Times* 4, no. 6 (March 1927): 19.

James Callahan to Governor E.M. Pease, October 13, 1855. Printed in the *Texas State Gazette*, October 20, 1855.

Luther, Joseph. "The Battle of Walker's Creek." *Kerrville Daily Times*, June 3, 2011.

———. "The Callahan Expedition." *Kerrville Daily Times*, February 27, 2010.

———. "The Penetaka Comanche." *Kerrville Daily Times*, July 23, 2010.

McDowell, J.S. "Diary." *Galveston Daily News*, January 8, 1893.

McKee, Floyd. "Recounting the Tale of Seguin's First Cattle Drive." *Seguin Gazette*, May 24, 2015.

Moore, Stephen. "Ranger Mathew 'Old Paint' Caldwell." *Texas Ranger Dispatch* 11 (Summer 2003): 1–6.

New Orleans Picayune. "The Late Foray into Mexico." October 24, 1855.

Sansom, John W. "Callahan's Raid in Mexico." *Hunter's Magazine*, April–May 1911.

Texas State Times. "Callahan's Fight." October 13, 1855.

Thybony, Scott. "The Black Seminoles: A Tradition of Courage." *Smithsonian Magazine* 22, no. 5 (1991): 90–101.

Warren, Harry. "Early History of Eagle Pass." *Eagle Pass Guide*, November 1905.

Wilkins, Ron. "Mexico's Legacy: A Refuge for Fugitive Slaves and Black Job-Seekers; New Perspectives on the Immigration Debate." *Black Commentator*, no. 182 (May 4, 2006).

Young, Lee. "Analysis and Review: The Seminole Freedman by Kevin Mulroy." *Texas Ranger Dispatch* 28 (Spring 2009): 4–13.

Books

Adams, John A., Jr. *Conflict and Commerce on the Rio Grande, Laredo, 1775–1955.* College Station: Texas A&M University Press, 2008.

Alexander, Bob. *Six-Shooters and Shifting Sands: The Wild West Life of Texas Ranger Capt. Frank Jones*. Denton: University of North Texas Press, 2015.

Alonso, Ana María. *Tejano Legacy: Rancheros and Settlers in South Texas, 1734–1900*. Albuquerque: University of New Mexico Press, 1998.

———. *Thread of Blood: Colonialism, Revolution, and Gender on Mexico's Northern Frontier.* Tucson: University of Arizona Press, 1995.

Anderson, Gary Clayton. *The Conquest of Texas: Ethnic Cleansing in the Promised Land, 1820–1875*. Norman: University of Oklahoma Press, 2005.

Austerman, Wayne R. *Sharps Rifles and Spanish Mules: The San Antonio–El Paso Mail, 1851–1881*. College Station: Texas A&M University Press, 1985.

Baker, DeWitt Clinton. "Fannin's Massacre—Account of the Georgia Battalion." Chapter 64 in *A Texas Scrap-Book: Made Up of the History, Biography, and Miscellany of Texas and Its People*, 242–50. New York: A.S. Barnes, 1875.

Baker, T. Lindsay, and Julie P. Baker, eds. *Till Freedom Cried Out: Memories of Texas Slave Life*. College Station: Texas A&M Press, 1997.

Bancroft, Hubert H. *History of Mexico*. 6 vols. San Francisco: History Company, 1886–87.

———. *History of the North Mexican States and Texas.* 2 vols. San Francisco: History Company, 1886–89.

Banta, Seth. *Buckelew, The Indian Captive; or, The Life Story of F.M. Bucklew While a Captive Among the Lipan Indians in the Western Wilds of Frontier Texas, as Related by Himself.* Mason, TX: Mason Herald, 1911. Reprinted in *The Garland Library of Narratives of North American Indian Captivities*, vol. 107. Washington, D.C.: Office of American Studies, Smithsonian Institute, 1977.

Banta, William, and J.W. Cadwell. *Twenty-Seven Years on the Frontier; or, Fifty Years in Texas*. Austin: B.C. Jones & Company, 1893.

Barr, Alwyn. *Black Texans: A History of Negroes in Texas, 1528–1971*. Austin: Jenkins, 1973.

Berlandier, Jean L. *Indians of Texas in 1830*. Edited by John C. Ewers and translated by Patricia Reading Leclerq. Washington, D.C.: Smithsonian Institute, 1969.

———. *Journey to Mexico During the Years 1826 to 1834*. Vols. 1 and 2. Translated by Sheila O. Ohlendorf. Denton: Texas State Historical Association, 1980.

Biesele, Rudolph L. *The History of the German Settlements in Texas, 1831–1861.* Austin: Von Boeckmann-Jones, 1930.

Binkley, William C., ed. *Official Correspondence of the Texas Revolution, 1835–1836*. 2 vols. New York: D. Appleton and Company, 1936.

Blanco County News. *Heritage of Blanco County Texas*. Dallas: Curtis Media, 1987.

Bradle, William R. *Goliad: The Other Alamo*. Gretna, LA: Pelican Publishing, 2007.

Brady, Cyrus Townsend. *Border Fights & Fighters: Invaders and Indian Wars in Texas and in the South.* New York: McClure, Phillips & Company, 1902.

Brands, H.W. *Lone Star Nation: The Epic Story of the Battle for Texas Independence.* New York: Anchor Books, 2004.

Breeden, James O. *A Long Ride in Texas: The Explorations of John Leonard Riddell.* College Station: Texas A&M University of Press, 1994.

Britten, Thomas A. "The Indian Wars of Texas: A Lipan Apache Perspective." In *Texas and War: New Interpretations of the State's Military History*. Edited by Alexander Mendoza and Charles David Grear, 17–37. College Station: Texas A&M University Press, 2012.

———. *The Lipan Apaches, People of Wind and Lightning*. Albuquerque: University of New Mexico Press, 2009.

Brown, Charles H. *Agents of Manifest Destiny: The Lives and Times of the Filibusters*. Chapel Hill: University of North Carolina Press, 1980.

Brown, Gary. *Hesitant Martyr of the Texas Revolution: James Walker Fannin*. Danvers, MA: Taylor Trade Publications, 2000.

Brown, John Henry, ed. *The Encyclopedia of the New West*. Marshall, TX: United States Biographical Publishing Company, 1881.

———. *History of Texas from 1685 to 1892*. 2 vols. St. Louis, MO: L.E. Daniell Publisher, 1893.

———. *Indian Wars and Pioneers of Texas*. St. Louis, MO: L.E. Daniell Publisher, 1896.

Caldwell, Clifford, and Ron Delord. *Texas Lawmen, 1835–1899: The Good and the Bad*. Charleston, SC: The History Press, 2012.

Calore, Paul. *The Texas Revolution and the U.S.-Mexican War: A Concise History*. Jefferson, NC: McFarland, 2014.

Campbell, Randolph B. *An Empire for Slavery: The Peculiar Institution in Texas, 1821–1865*. Baton Rouge: Louisiana State University Press, 1991.

———. *The Laws of Slavery in Texas: Historical Documents and Essays*. Compiled by William S. Pugsley and Marilyn P. Duncan. Austin: University of Texas Press, 2010.

Casteñeda, Carlos E., trans. *The Mexican Side of the Texan Revolution, 1836: By the Chief Mexican Participants*. Dallas: P.L. Turner Company, 1928.

Castro Colonies Heritage Association. *The History of Medina County, Texas*. Dallas: National Share Graphics, 1983.

Ceballos-Ramírez, Manuel, and Oscar J. Martínez. "Conflict and Accommodation on the U.S.-Mexican Border, 1848–1911." In *Myths, Misdeeds, and Misunderstandings: The Roots of Conflict in U.S.-Mexican Relations*. Edited by Jaime E. Rodríguez O. and Kathryn Vincent, 136–37. Lanham, MD: Rowman & Littlefield Publishers, 1997.

Chance, Joseph E. *José María de Jesús Carvajal: The Life and Times of a Mexican Revolutionary*. San Antonio: Trinity University Press, 2006.

Chebahtah, William, and Nancy McGown Minor. *Chevato, the Story of the Apache Warrior Who Captured Herman Lehmann*. Lincoln: University of Nebraska Press, 2007.

Christiansen Rupert. *Romantic Affinities: Portraits from an Age, 1780–1830*. New York: Random House, 1989.

Chubb, Cutis. *Biography of the Old Blanco County Courthouse*. Blanco, TX: Captured Rainwater Company, 1999.

Collins, Michael L. *Texas Devils: Rangers and Regulars on the Lower Rio Grande, 1846–1861*. Norman: University of Oklahoma Press, 2008.

Cox, Mike. *Gunfights & Sites in Texas Ranger History*. Charleston, SC: The History Press, 2015.

———. *The Texas Rangers*. Vol. 1, *Wearing the Cinco Peso 1821–1900*. New York: Forge Books, 2009.

Cremony, John C. *Life Among the Apaches*. San Francisco: Roman & Company, 1868.

Crimmins, M.L. *Old Fort Duncan: A Frontier Post*. Bandera, TX: Frontier Times, 1938.

Crockett, David. *Col. Crockett's Exploits and Adventures in Texas Wherein Is Contained a Full Account of His Journey from Tennessee to the Red River and Natchitoches, and Thence Across Texas to San Antonio; Including Many Hair-Breadth Escapes; Together with a Topographical, Historical, and Political View of Texas…Written by Himself*. New York: Wm. H. Graham, Tribune Building, 1839.

Cude, Elton R. *The Wild and Free Dukedom of Bexar*. San Antonio: Munguia Printers, 1978.

Cutrer, Thomas W. *Ben McCulloch and the Frontier Military Tradition*. Chapel Hill: University of North Carolina Press, 1993.

Davenport, Harbert. *Notes from an Unfinished Study of Fannin and His Men, with Biographical Sketches, 1936*. Edited by David Maxey. Austin: Texas State Historical Association, 2002.

Davis, William C. *Lone Star Rising: The Revolutionary Birth of the Texas Republic*. New York: Free Press, 2004.

———. *The Texian War of Independence 1835–1836*. Oxford: Osprey Press, 2003.

De Cordova, Jacob. *Texas: Her Resources and Her Public Men; A Companion for J. De Cordova's New and Correct Map of the State of Texas*. Philadelphia: J.B. Lippincot and Company, 1858.

De La Peña, José Enrique. *With Santa Anna in Texas: A Personal Narrative of the Revolution*. College Station: Texas A&M University Press, 1997.

De la Teja, Jesús. *A Revolution Remembered: The Memoirs and Selected Correspondence of Juan N. Seguín*. Austin: State House Press, 1991.

———. *Tejano Leadership in Mexican and Revolutionary Texas*. College Station: Texas A&M University Press, 2010.

De León, Arnoldo. *The Tejano Community, 1836–1900*. Albuquerque: University of New Mexico Press, 1982.

Dennis, T.S., and Lucy S. Rea Dennis. *The Life of F.M. Buckelew, the Indian Captive*. Bandera, TX: Hunter's Printing House, 1925.

DePalo, William A., Jr. *The Mexican National Army, 1822–1852*. College Station: Texas A&M University Press, 1997.

DeShields, James T. *Border Wars of Texas, Being an Authentic and Popular Account, in Chronological Order, of the Long and Bitter Conflict Waged Between Savage Indian Tribes and the Pioneer Settlers of Texas*. Tioga, TX: Herald Company, 1912.

———. *Tall Men with Long Rifles, as Told to Him by Creed Taylor During the Texas Revolution*. San Antonio: Naylor Company, 1971.

Dimmick, Gregg. *Gen. Vicente Filisola's Analysis of José Urrea's Military Diary: A Forgotten 1838 Publication by an Eyewitness to the Texas Revolution*. Austin: Texas State Historical Association, 2009.

Duval, John C. *The Adventures of Big-Foot Wallace: The Texas Ranger and Hunter*. Whitefish, MT: Kessinger Publishing, 2010.

———. *Early Times in Texas; or, the Adventures of Jack Dobell*. Austin: Gammel, 1892. New edition, Lincoln: University of Nebraska Press, 1986.

Eastman, Seth. *A Seth Eastman Sketchbook, 1848–1849*. Introduction by Lois Burkhalter. Austin: University of Texas Press, 2003.

Ehrenberg, Herman. *Texas und Seine Revolution*. Leipzig, DE: Wigand, 1843. Abridged and translated by Charlotte Churchill. *With Milam and Fannin, Adventures of a German Boy in Texas' Revolution*. Austin: Pemberton Press, 1968.

Emory, William Hemsley. *Report on the United States and Mexican Boundary Survey*. 2 vols. Washington, D.C.: Nicholson, 1857–59. Reprint, Austin: Texas State Historical Association, 1987.

Fagan, Brian M. *The Little Ice Age: How Climate Made History, 1300–1850*. New York: Basic Books, 2001.

Fehrenbach, T.R. *The Comanches: The Destruction of a People*. New York: Knopf, 1974.

———. *Fire and Blood: A History of Mexico*. New York: Da Capo Press, 1995.

———. *Lone Star: A History of Texas and the Texans, From Prehistory to the Present*. New York: Da Capo Press, 2000.

Field, Joseph E. *Three Years in Texas: Including a View of the Texas Revolution and an Account of the Principal Battles*. Boston: Abel, Tompkins and Cornhill, 1836.

Filisola, Vicente. *Memoirs for the History of the War in Texas*. Abridged and translated by Wallace Woolsey. Austin: Eakin Press, 1985.

Fitzsimon, Reverend Laurence J. *History of Seguin*. San Antonio: C.H. Jackson Directory Company, 1938.

Flanagan, Sue. *Sam Houston's Texas.* Austin: University of Texas Press, 1964.

Flayderman, Norm. *Flayderman's Guide to Antique American Firearms and Their Values*. 9th ed. Iola, WI: Gun Digest Books, 2007.

Foote, Henry Stuart. *Texas and the Texans; or, Advance of the Anglo-Americans to the South-west; Including a History of Leading Events in Mexico, from the Conquest by Fernando Cortes to the Termination of the Texan Revolution*. Philadelphia: Thomas, Cowperthwait & Company, 1841.

Ford, John S. *Rip Ford's Texas*. Edited by Stephen B. Oates. Austin: University of Texas Press, 1963.

Fulton, Maurice Garland, ed. *Diary & Letters of Josiah Gregg: Excursions in Mexico and California, 1840–1847*. Norman: University of Oklahoma Press, 1941.

Gammel, H.P.N., ed. *The Laws of Texas, 1822–1897*. Vols. 1–3. Austin: Gammel Book Company, 1898.

Gesick, E. John. *Under the Live Oak Tree: A History of Seguin*. Seguin, TX: Tommy Brown Printing, 1995.

Glasrud, Bruce A., and Harold J. Weiss. *Tracking the Texas Rangers: The Nineteenth Century*. Denton: University of North Texas Press, 2012.

Glasrud, Bruce A., ed. *African Americans in South Texas History*. College Station: Texas A&M University Press, 2011.

Green, Rena Maverick, ed. *Memoirs of Mary A. Maverick*. San Antonio. Alamo Printing, 1921. Reprint, Lincoln: University of Nebraska Press, 1989.

Green, Thomas J. *Journal of the Texian Expedition Against Mier*. 1845. Reprint, Austin: Steck Company, 1935.

Greer, James K. *Texas Ranger: Jack Hays in the Frontier Southwest*. College Station: Texas A&M University Press, 1993.

Gregg, Josiah. *Commerce of the Prairies: The Journal of a Santa Fe Trader*. Philadelphia: Lippincott, 1844.

Guinn, Jeff. *Our Land Before We Die: The Proud Story of the Seminole Negro*. New York: J.P. Tarcher/Putnam, 2005.

Gwynne, S.C. *Empire of the Summer Moon: Quanah Parker and the Rise and Fall of the Comanches, the Most Powerful Indian Tribe in American History*. New York: Scribner, 2010.

Haas, Michelle M., comp. *Massacre: The Goliad Witnesses*. Ingleside, TX: Copano Bay Press, 2014.

Haley, J. Evetts. *The Diary of Michael Erskine*. Midland, TX: Nita Stewart Haley Memorial Library, 1979.

Haley, James L. *Apaches: A History and Culture Portrait*. Norman: University of Oklahoma Press, 1997.

———. *Sam Houston*. Norman: University of Oklahoma Press, 2002.

Hardin, Stephen L. *The Alamo 1836: Santa Anna's Texas Campaign*. Oxford: Osprey Publishing, 2001.

Haynes, Sam W. *Soldiers of Misfortune: The Somervell and Mier Expeditions*. Austin: University of Texas Press, 1990.

Hefter, J. *The Mexican Soldier 1837–1847: Organization, Dress & Equipment*. Edited and expanded by P.R. Wilson. Oklahoma City: Virtual Armchair General, 2013.

Herring, Patricia Roche. *Gen. José Cosme Urrea: His Life and Times, 1797–1849*. Norman, OK: Arthur H. Clark Company, 1995.

Hicks, Major James E. *Notes on United States Ordinance*. Vol. 1, *Small Arms, 1776–1946*. Mount Vernon, NY: American Library Service, 1946.

Hopewell, Clifford. *Remember Goliad—Their Silent Tents*. Austin: Eakin Press, 1998.

Hughes, W.J. *Rebellious Ranger: Rip Ford and the Old Southwest.* Norman: University of Oklahoma Press, 1964.

Hunter, J. Marvin. *Horrors of Indian Captivity: Authentic and Thrilling Sketches of Tragedies That Occurred on the Texas Frontier during Indian Times*. Bandera, TX: J. Marvin Hunter, 1954.

———. *Pioneer History of Bandera County.* Bandera, TX: Hunter's Printing, 1922.

Huson, Hobart. *Capt. Philip Dimmitt's Commandancy of Goliad, 1835–1836*. Austin: Von Boeckmann-Jones, 1974.

Ingmire, Frances T. *Texas Frontiersmen, 1839–1860: Minutemen, Militia, Home Guard, Indian Fighters.* St. Louis, MO: Ingmire Publications, 1982.

———. *Texas Rangers: Frontier Battalion, Minute Men, Commanding Officers, 1847–1900*. St. Louis, MO: Ingmire Publications, 1982.

Ivey, Darren L. *The Texas Rangers: A Registry and History*. Jefferson, NC: McFarland, 2010.

James, Marquis. *The Raven: A Biography of Sam Houston*. Austin: University of Texas Press, 1988.

Jenkins, John Holland. *Papers of the Texas Revolution 1835–1836*. 10 vols. Austin: Presidial Press, 1973.

———. *Recollections of Early Texas: The Memoirs of John Holland Jenkins.* Austin: University of Texas Press, 1958.

Jiménez, Melchor Sánchez. *La Breve Historia de Piedras Negras*. Piedras Negras, MX: H. Ayuntamiento Constitucional, 1990.

Johnson, Frank W. *A History of Texas and Texans*. Chicago: American Historical Society, 1914.

Johnson, Nicholas. *Negroes and the Gun: The Black Tradition of Arms*. Amherst, NY: Prometheus, 2014.

Kelton, Elmer. *Massacre at Goliad,* New York: Tom Doherty Associates, 1965.

Kennedy, William. *The Rise, Progress and Prospects of the Republic of Texas*. Fort Worth, TX: Molyneaux Craftsmen, 1841. Reprinted, Charleston SC: Nabu Press, 2012.

Kluger, Richard. *Seizing Destiny: How America Grew from Sea to Shining Sea*. New York: Vintage, 2007.

Knowles, Thomas W. *They Rode for the Lone Star: The Saga of the Texas Rangers.* Dallas: Taylor Publishing Company, 1999.

Koury, Michael J. *Arms for Texas: A Study of the Weapons of the Republic of Texas.* Fort Collins, CO: Old Army Press, 1973.

Lack, Paul D. *The Texas Revolutionary Experience*. College Station: Texas A&M University Press, 1992.

Lamego, General Miguel A. Sanchez. *The Second Mexican-Texas War 1841–1843*. Hill Junior College Monograph 7. Waco, TX: Texan Press, 1972.

Lancaster, Jane F. *Removal Aftershock: Seminoles Struggles Survive West.* Knoxville: University of Tennessee Press, 1994.

Latorre, Felipe A., and Dolores L. Latorre. *The Mexican Kickapoo Indians.* Mineola, NY: Dover Publications, 2012.

Long, Jeffery. *Duel of Eagles*. New York: William Morrow, 1990.

Lozano, Alice Fay, and Shirley Boteler Mock. *My Black Seminole Ancestors Running to Freedom*. San Antonio: University of Texas Institute of Texan Cultures, 2004.

Lozano, Ruben Rendon. *Viva Texas: The Story of the Tejanos, the Mexican-Born Patriots of the Texas Revolution*. San Antonio: Alamo Press, 1985.

Luther, Joseph. *Camp Verde: Texas Frontier Defense*. Charleston, SC: The History Press, 2012.

———. *Fort Martin Scott: Guardian of the Treaty*. Charleston, SC: The History Press, 2013.

Marcy, Captain Randolph B. *The Prairie Traveler: A Handbook for Overland Expeditions*. New York: Harper Brothers, 1859.

———. *Thirty Years of Army Life on the Border*. New York: Harper & Bros., 1866.

Martin, J.C., and R.S. Martin. *Contours of Discovery*. Austin: Texas State Historical Association, 1982.

———. *Maps of Texas and the Southwest 1513–1900*. Albuquerque: Amon Carter Museum, University of New Mexico Press, 1984.

Maverick, Mary A. *Memoirs of Mary A. Maverick, a Journal of Early Texas*. Edited by Rena Maverick Green and Maverick Fairchild Fisher. San Antonio: Maverick Publishing, 2005.

May, Robert E. *Manifest Destiny's Underworld: Filibustering in Antebellum America*. Chapel Hill: University of North Carolina Press, 2002.

McDowell, Catherine W. *Now You Hear My Horn: The Journal of James Wilson Nichols, 1820–1887*. Austin: University of Texas Press, 1967.

Mendoza, Alexander, and Charles David Grear, ed. *Texans and War: New Interpretations of the State's Military History.* College Station: Texas A&M University Press, 2012.

Miller, Edward L. *New Orleans and the Texas Revolution*. College Station: Texas A&M University Press, 2004.

Miller, Robert L. *Life of Robert Hall: Indian Fighter and Veteran of Three Great Wars, Also Sketch of Big Foot Wallace*. Austin: Ben C. Jones, 1898. Reprint, Austin: State House Press, 1992.

Miller, Thomas L. *Bounty and Donation Land Grants of Texas, 1835–1888.* Austin: University of Texas Press, 1967.

Mills, Judith Austin. *How Far Tomorrow: Remembering the Georgia Battalion in Texas.* Austin: Plain View Press, 2011.

Minor, Nancy McGown. *The Light Gray People: An Ethno-History of the Lipan Apaches of Texas and Northern Mexico*. Lanham, MD: University of America Press, 2009.

———. *Turning Adversity to Advantage: A History of the Lipan Apaches of Texas and Northern Mexico, 1700–1900*. Lanham, MD: University Press of America, 2009.

Missall, John, and Mary Lou Missall. *The Seminole Wars: America's Longest Indian Conflict*. Gainesville: University Press of Florida, 2004.

Montejano, David. *Anglos and Mexicans in the Making of Texas, 1836–1986*. Austin: University of Texas Press, 1987.

Montgomery, Cora. *Eagle Pass: Life on the Isthmus*. Vol. 3. New York: G.P. Putman and Company, 1853.

———. *Eagle Pass; or, Life on the Border*. New York: Putnam, 1852. Reprint, Austin: Pemberton Press, 1966.

Moore, Stephen L. *Savage Frontier*. Vol 4, *Rangers, Rifleman, and Indian Wars in Texas*. Denton: University of North Texas Press, 2002, 2006, 2007 and 2010.

———. *Texas Rising: The Epic True Story of the Lone Star Republic and the Rise of the Texas Rangers, 1836–1846*. New York: William Morrow, 2015.

Morrell, Zenos N. *Flowers and Fruits from the Wilderness*. 3rd ed. Boston: Gould and Lincoln, 1872. Reprint, Irving, TX: Griffin Graphic Arts, 1966.

Moursund, John Stribling. *Blanco County Families for 100 Years*. Burnett, TX: Nortex Press, 1981.

———. *Blanco County History*. Burnet, TX: Nortex Press, 1979.

Mulroy, Kevin. *Freedom on the Border: The Seminole Maroons in Florida, the Indian Territory, and Coahuila, and Texas.* Lubbock: Texas Tech University Press, 1993.

———. *The Seminole Freedmen: A History*. Norman: University of Oklahoma Press, 2007.

Nance, Joseph Milton. *After San Jacinto: The Texas-Mexican Frontier 1836–1841.* Austin: University of Texas Press, 1963.

———. *Attack and Counterattack: The Texas-Mexican Border, 1842.* Austin: University of Texas Press, 1964.

———. *Heroes of Texas*. Waco: Texan Press, 1966.

Newcomb, W.W., Jr. *The Indians of Texas: From Prehistoric to Modern Times.* Austin: University of Texas Press, 1961.

Nofi, Alber A. *The Alamo and the Texas War for Independence.* New York: De Capo Press, 2009.

Obadele-Starks, Ernest. *Freebooters and Smugglers: The Foreign Slave Trade in the United States after 1808.* Fayetteville: University of Arkansas Press.

O'Connor, Kathryn Stoner. *The Presidio La Bahía del Espíritu Santo de Zúñiga, 1721 to 1846.* Austin: Von Boeckmann–Jones, 1966.

Olmsted, Frederick Law. *A Journey Through Texas; or, A Saddle Trip on the Southwestern Frontier.* New York: Dix, Edwards and Company, 1857.

Opler, Morris E. *The Lipan and Mescalero Apaches in Texas.* New York: Garland Publishing, 1974.

Ornish, Natalie. *Ehrenberg: Goliad Survivor—Old West Explorer.* Dallas: Texas Heritage Press, 1997.

Perry, Carmen. *With Santa Anna in Texas: A Personal Narrative of the Revolution / José Enrique de la Peña.* College Station: Texas A&M University Press, 1997.

Pettermann, Dana L., and Holly Kathryn Norton. *The Archaeology of Engagement: Conflict and Revolution in the United States.* College Station: Texas A&M University Press, 2015.

Pierce, Gerald S. *Texas Under Arms: The Camps, Posts, Forts, & Military Towns of the Republic of Texas, 1836–1846.* Austin: Encino Press, 1969.

Pingenot, Ben E. *Historical Highlights of Eagle Pass and Maverick County.* Eagle Pass, TX: Eagle Pass Chamber of Commerce, 1971.

———. *Paso del Águila: A Chronicle of Frontier Days on the Border as Recorded in the Memoirs of Jesse Sumpter.* Compiled by Harry Warren. Austin: Encino Press, 1969.

Porter, Kenneth W. *The Black Seminoles: History of a Freedom-Seeking People.* Gainesville: University Press of Florida, 1996.

Procter, Ben H. *The Battle of the Alamo*. Austin: Texas State Historical Association, 1986.

Pruett, Jakie L., and Everett B. Cole Sr. *Goliad Massacre: A Tragedy of the Texas Revolution*. Austin: Eakin Press, 1985.

Ramos, Raúl A. *Beyond the Alamo: Forging Mexican Ethnicity in San Antonio, 1821–1861*. Chapel Hill: University of North Carolina Press, 2008.

Reid, Samuel C., Jr. *The Scouting Expeditions of McCulloch's Texas Rangers*. Philadelphia: Zieber, 1847. Reprint, Freeport, NY: Books for Libraries Press, 1970.

Reid, Stuart. *The Texan Army 1835–46*. Oxford: Osprey Publishing, 2003.

Reilly, Robert M. *United States Military Small Arms, 1816–1865*. Baton Rouge: Eagle Press, 1970.

Rickey, Don, Jr. *Forty Miles a Day on Beans and Hay*. Norman: University of Oklahoma Press, 1963.

Rives, George L. *The United States and Mexico, 1821–1848*. 2 vols. New York: Charles Scribner's Sons, 1913

Robenalt, Jeffery T. *Historic Tales from the Texas Republic: A Glimpse of Texas Past*. Charleston, SC: The History Press, 2013.

Robinson, Sherry. *I Fought a Good Fight: A History of the Lipan Apaches*. Denton: University of North Texas Press, 2013.

Robles, Vito Alessio. *Coahuila y Texas en la Época Colonial*. 2nd ed. Mexico City: Editorial Cultura, 1938.

Rodríguez, Jaime E.O., and Kathryn Vincent, eds. *Myths, Misdeeds, and Misunderstandings: The Roots of Conflict in U.S.-Mexican Relations*. Lanham, MD: Rowman & Littlefield, 1997.

Roell, Craig H. *Matamoros and the Texas Revolution*. Austin: Texas State Historical Association, 2013.

———. *Remember Goliad! A History of La Bahía*. Austin: Texas State Historical Association, 1994.

Rose, Victor M. *The Life and Services of Gen. Ben McCulloch*. Philadelphia: Pictorial Bureau of the Press, 1888.

Santleben, August. *A Texas Pioneer: Early Staging and Overland Freighting Days on the Frontiers of Texas and Mexico*. Edited by I.D. Affleck. New York: Neale Publishing Company, 1910.

Scarborough, Annie Cecil. *The Pass of the Eagle: The Chaparral Region of Texas*. Austin: San Felipe Press, 1968.

Schilz, Thomas. *The Lipan Apache in Texas*. El Paso: Texas Western Press, 1987.

Schwartz, Rosalie. *Across the Rio to Freedom: U.S. Negroes in Mexico*. El Paso: Texas Western Press, 1974.

Scott, Robert. *After the Alamo*. Plano: Republic of Texas Press, 2000.

Sivad, Doug. *The Black Seminole Indians of Texas*. Boston: American Press, 1984.

Smith, David Paul. *Frontier Defense in the Civil War: Texas' Rangers and Rebels*. College Station: Texas A&M University Press, 1992.

Smith, F. Todd. *From Dominance to Disappearance: The Indians of Texas and the Near Southwest, 1786–1859*. Lincoln: University of Nebraska Press, 2005.

Smith, S. Comton. *Chile con Carne; or, Camp and the Field*. New York: Miller & Curtis, 1857.

Smith, Thomas T. *Fort Inge: Sharps, Spurs and Sabers on the Texas Frontier, 1849–1869*. Austin: Eakin Press, 1993.

———. *The Old Army in Texas: A Research Guide to the U.S. Army in Nineteenth-Century Texas*. Austin: Texas State Historical Association, 2000.

———. *The U.S. Army and the Texas Frontier Economy, 1845–1900*. College Station: Texas A&M University Press, 1999.

Smithwick, Noah. *The Evolution of a State or Recollections of Old Texas Days*. Austin: University of Texas Press, 1983.

Sowell, A.J. *Early Settlers and Indian Fighters of Southwest Texas*. Austin: Ben C. Jones & Company, 1900.

———. *Incidents Connected with the Early History of Guadalupe County*. Town Book of Seguin. Seguin, TX, n.d.

———. *Rangers and Pioneers of Texas: With a Concise Account of the Early Settlements, Hardships, Massacres, Battles, and Wars, by Which Texas Was Rescued from the Rule of the Savage and Consecrated to the Empire of Civilization*. Austin: State House Press, 1991.

Spellman, Paul N. *Forgotten Texas Leader: Hugh McLeod and the Texan Santa Fe Expedition*. College Station: Texas A&M University Press, 1999.

Stillman, D.B. *Wanderings in the Southwest in 1855*. Edited by Ron Tyler. Spokane, WA: Arthur H. Clark Company, 1990.

Stout, Jay A. *Slaughter at Goliad: The Massacre of 400 Texas Volunteers*. Annapolis, MD: Naval Institute Press, 2008.

Stout, Joseph. *Schemers and Dreamers: Filibustering in Mexico, 1848–1921*. Fort Worth: Texas Christian University Press, 2002.

Sullivan, Roy F. *The Texas Revolution: Tejano Heroes*. Bloomington, IN: Author House, 2011.

Sumpter, Jesse. *Jesse Sumpter Reminiscences, 1902–1906*. Austin: Encino Press, 1969.

Taylor, Creed. *Tall Men with Long Rifles: The Glamorous Story of the Texas Revolution, as Told by Capt. Creed Taylor, Who Fought in the Heroic Struggle from Gonzales to San Jacinto*. Edited by James T. De Shields. San Antonio: Naylor Company, 1971.

Teja, Jesús F. de la, ed. *A Revolution Remembered: The Memoirs and Selected Correspondence of Juan N. Seguín*. Annotated ed. Austin: Texas State Historical Association, 2002.

Thompson, Jerry. *Cortina: Defending the Mexican Name in Texas*. College Station: Texas A&M University Press, 2007.

Thompson, R.A. *Fort Duncan, Texas: Rock of the Rio Grande Line of Defense*. Austin: Nortex Press, 2004.

Thrall, Homer S. *A Pictorial History of Texas*. St. Louis, MO: Thompson, 1879.

Thrapp, Dan L. *The Conquest of Apacheria*. Norman: University of Oklahoma Press, 1979.

Todish, Timothy J. *Alamo Sourcebook, 1836: A Comprehensive Guide to the Battle of the Alamo and the Texas Revolution*. Austin, TX: Eakin Press, 1998.

Tucker, Spencer C. *The Encyclopedia of the Mexican-American War: A Political, Social, and Military History*. Santa Barbara, CA: ABC-CLIO, 2012.

Tyler, Ronnie C., and Lawrence R. Murphy. *Santiago Vidaurri and the Southern Confederacy*. Austin: Texas State Historical Association, 1973.

———. *The Slave Narratives of Texas*. Austin: Encino Press, 1974.

Unger, Sebastian. *Tribe: On Homecoming and Belonging*. New York: Twelve, 2016.

Utley, Robert M. *Frontiersmen in Blue: The United States Army and the Indian*. New York: Macmillan, 1973.

———. *Lone Star Justice: The First Century of the Texas Rangers*. New York: Oxford University Press, 2002.

Vestal, Stanley. *Bigfoot Wallace*. Boston: Little, Brown, 1942.

Vigness, David M. *The Revolutionary Decades: The Saga of Texas, 1810–1836*. Austin: Steck-Vaughn, 1965.

Wade, Maria F., and Don E. Wade. *The Native Americans of the Texas Edwards Plateau, 1582–1799*. Austin: University of Texas Press, 2002.

Walter, Tamra L. *Espíritu Santo de Zúñiga: A Frontier Mission in South Texas*. Austin: University of Texas Press, 2007.

Webb, Walter Prescott. *The Texas Rangers*. Boston: Houghton Mifflin, 1935. Reprint, Austin: University of Texas Press, 1982.

Weber, David J. *The Mexican Frontier, 1821–1846: The American Southwest Under Mexico*. Albuquerque: University of New Mexico Press, 1982.

Weddle, Robert S. *San Juan Bautista: Gateway to Spanish Texas*. Austin: University of Texas Press, 1968.

Weinert, Willie Mae. *An Authentic History of Guadalupe County*. Seguin, TX: Seguin Conservation Society, 1976.

———. "Callahan, James H., 1812–1856." In *Historical Sketches as Published in the Seguin Enterprise, 1936–1938*. Seguin, TX: Seguin Enterprise newspaper, 1938.

Wharton, William H. *Texas: A Brief Account of the Origin, Progress and Present State of the Colonial Settlements of Texas, Together with an Exposition of the Causes Which Have Induced the Existing War with Mexico.* Kindle ed. N.p.: Amazon Digital, 2012.

Wilbarger, J.W. *Indian Depredations in Texas*. Facsimile ed. Austin: State House Press, 1991.

Wilkins, Frederick. *Defending the Texas Borders: Texas Rangers, 1848–1861.* Austin: State House Press, 2001.

———. *The Legend Begins: The Texas Rangers, 1823–1845*. Austin: State House Press, 1996.

Williams, Clayton. *Never Again: Texas 1848–1861*. San Antonio: Naylor Company, 1969.

Williams, Jack, and Robert Hoover. *Arms of the Apacheria: A Comparison of Apachean and Spanish Fighting Techniques in the Later Eighteenth Century*. Greeley: University of Colorado, 1983.

Williams, J.W. *Old Texas Trails*. Edited by Kenneth F. Neighbors. Burnet, TX: Eakin Press, 1979.

Williams, R.H. *With the Border Ruffians: Memories of the Far West, 1852–1868.* Lincoln, NE: Bison Press, 1982.

Winders, Richard Bruce. *Sacrificed at the Alamo: Tragedy and Triumph in the Texas Revolution*. Military History of Texas Series, no. 3. Austin: State House Press, 2004.

Winfrey, Dorman H., and James M. Day, eds. *The Indian Papers of Texas and the Southwest*. 5 vols. Austin: Pemberton Press, 1966.

Wolf, Rusty. *The Texas Splendid Expendables of 1842 (Based Upon the True Story of the Mier Expedition)*. N.p.: Lulu.com., 2008.

Wooster, Robert. *The American Military Frontiers: The United States Army in the West, 1783–1900*. Albuquerque: University of New Mexico Press, 2009.

———. *Soldiers, Sutlers, and Settlers: Garrison Life on the Texas Frontier*. College Station: Texas A&M University Press, 1987.

Wooten, Dudley Goodall ed. *A Comprehensive History of Texas*. 2 vols. Dallas: Scarff, 1898. Reprint, Austin: Texas State Historical Association, 1986.

Yoakum, Henderson K. *History of Texas from Its First Settlement in 1685 to Its Annexation to the United States in 1846*. 2 vols. New York: Redfield, 1855.

Journals

Adams, David B. "Embattled Borderland: Northern Nuevo León and the Indios Bárbaros, 1686–1870." *Southwestern Historical Quarterly* 95, no. 2 (October 1991): 205–20.

Addington, Wendell G. "Slave Insurrections in Texas." *Journal of Negro History* 25 (1950): 408–34.

Barker, Eugene C. "The African Slave Trade in Texas." *Quarterly of the Texas State Historical Association* 6, no. 2 (1902): 145–58.

———. "Texan Revolutionary Army." *Quarterly of the Texas State Historical Association* 9 (1906): 227–61.

Barton, Henry W. "The Problem of Command in the Army of the Republic of Texas." *Southwestern Historical Quarterly* 62 (1958–59): 299–311.

Benedict, J.W. "Diary of a Campaign Against the Comanches." *Southwestern Historical Quarterly* 32 (1929): 300–310.

Binkley, William C. "The Activities of the Texan Revolutionary Army after San Jacinto." *Journal of Southern History* 6 (1904): 340.

Bollaert, W. "The Geography of Texas." *Journal of the Royal Geographical Society* 20 (2006): 113–35.

Bridges, C.A. "The Knights of the Golden Circle: A Filibustering Fantasy." *Southwestern Historical Quarterly* 44, no. 3 (1941): 287–302.

Bugbee, Lester G. "The Old Three Hundred: A List of Settlers in Austin's First Colony." *Quarterly of the Texas State Historical Association* 1, no. 2 (1897): 108–17.

Crimmins, M.L., and W.G. Freeman. "Fort Duncan." *Southwestern Historical Quarterly* 52, no. 4 (April 1949): 444–47.

———. "W.G. Freeman's Report on the Eighth Military Department." *Southwestern Historical Quarterly* 52, no. 4 (April 1949): 54–58

Crook, Cornelia, and Garland Crook. "Fort Lincoln, Texas." *Texas Military History (Quarterly Publication of the National Guard Association)* 4, no. 3 (Fall 1964): 160.

Cunningham, Bob, and Harry P. Hewitt. "A Lovely Land Full of Roses and Thorns: Emil Langberg and Mexico, 1835–1866." *Southwestern Historical Quarterly* 98, no. 3 (1995): 387–425.

Davenport, Harbert. "Men of Goliad." *Southwestern Historical Quarterly* 43 (1939): 1–41.

Davis, Robert S. "Goliad and the Georgia Battalion: Georgia Participation in the Texas Revolution, 1835–1836." *Journal of Southwest Georgia History* 4 (1986): 64–69.

Dunn, Roy S. "The KGC in Texas, 1860–1861." *Southwestern Historical Quarterly* 70, no. 4 (1967): 543–73.

Dunn, William E. "The Founding of Nuestra Señora del Refugio, the Last Spanish Mission in Texas." *Southwestern Historical Quarterly* 25 (January 1922): 174–84.

Ellenberger, Matthew. "Illuminating the Lesser Lights: Notes on the Life of Albert Clinton Horton." *Southwestern Historical Quarterly* 88 (April 1985): 363–86

Elliot, Claude. "Georgia and the Texas Revolution." *Georgia Historical Quarterly* 28 (1944): 1–19.

Fornell, Earl W. "The Abduction of Free Negroes and Slaves in Texas." *Southwestern Historical Quarterly* 60, no. 3 (1957): 369–80.

———. "Texans and Filibusters in the 1850s." *Southwestern Historical Quarterly* 59, no. 4 (1956): 411–28.

Friend, Llerena B. "W.P. Webb's Texas Rangers." *Southwestern Historical Quarterly* 74, no. 3 (1971): 293–323.

Gesick, John. "The 1855 Callahan Raid into Mexico: Pursuing Indians or Hunting Slaves?" *Journal of Big Bend Studies* 19 (2007): 47–63.

———. "Texas Ranger James Callahan's Raid into Mexico to Pursue Indian Raiders, 1855." *Journal of Big Bend Studies* 19 (2007): 47–63.

Goggin, John M. "The Mexican Kickapoo Indians." *Southwestern Journal of Anthropology* 7 (1951): 314–27.

Hardin, Stephen L. "A Hard Lot: Texas Women in the Runaway Scrape." *East Texas Historical Journal* 29 (1991): 35–45.

Hendricks, Sterling Brown. "The Somervell Expedition to the Rio Grande, 1842." *Southwestern Historical Quarterly* 23, no. 2 (1919): 112–40.

Kelley, Sean. "Mexico in His Head: Slavery and the Texas-Mexico Border, 1810–1860." *Journal of Social History* 37, no. 3 (Spring 2004): 709–23.

Kinsall, Al. "Fort Duncan: Frontier Outpost on the Rio Grande." *Journal of Big Bend Studies* 11 (1999): 93–107.

Koch, Lena Clara. "The Federal Indian Policy in Texas, 1846–1860: The Rangers and Frontier Protection." *Southwest Historical Quarterly* 29, no. 1. (1925): 259–86.

Looscan, Adele B. "The Old Mexican Fort of Velasco." *Quarterly of the Texas State Historical Association* 1 (1898): 282–84.

Luther. Joseph. "The Boneyard—An Ethno Archeology Project." *Texas Archeology* 56, no. 2 (2012): 16–17.

———. "Finding Bigfoot." *Texas Archeology* 58, no. 3 (2014): 17.

Nance, Joseph Milton. "Adrián Woll: Frenchman in the Mexican Military Service." *New Mexico Historical Review* 33 (1957–58): 177–86.

———. "Brigadier General Adrian Woll's Report on His Expedition into Texas in 1842." *Southwestern Historical Quarterly* 58, no. 4 (April 1955): 528–32.

Nichols, James David. "The Line of Liberty: Runaway Slaves and Fugitive Peons in the Texas-Mexico Borderlands." *Western Historical Quarterly* 44, no. 4 (2013): 413–33.

Nielsen, George R. "Mathew Caldwell." *Southwestern Historical Quarterly* 64 (1961): 478–502.

Opler, Morris E. "Myths and Legends of the Lipan Apache Indians." *Memoirs of the American Folklore Society* 36 (1940).

Porter, Kenneth W. "Negroes and Indians on the Texas Frontier, 1834–1874." *Southwestern Historical Quarterly* 53, no. 2 (1949): 151–63.

———. "The Seminole in Mexico, 1850–1861." *Hispanic American Historical Review* 31, no. 1 (1951): 1–36.

Presley, James. "Santa Anna in Texas: A Mexican Viewpoint." *Southwestern Historical Quarterly* 62, no. 4 (1959): 489–512.

Reeve, Frank D. "The Apache Indians in Texas." *Southwestern Historical Quarterly* 50 (1946): 189–219.

Rippy, J. Fred. "Border Troubles Along the Rio Grande, 1848–1860." *Southwestern Historical Quarterly* 23, no. 2 (1919): 91–111.

———. "Some Precedents of the Pershing Expedition into Mexico." *Southwestern Historical Quarterly* 24, no. 4 (1921): 292–316.

Robertson, James M. "Captain Amon B. King." *Southwestern Historical Quarterly* 29 (October 1925): 147–50.

Sanderlin, Walter S.A. "Cattle Drive from Texas to California: The Diary of M.H. Erskine, 1854." *Southwestern Historical Quarterly* 67, no. 3 (July 1963–April, 1964): 397–412.

Scarborough, Jewel Davis. "The Georgia Battalion in the Texas Revolution: A Critical Study." *Southwestern Historical Quarterly* 63 (1960): 511–32.

Shearer, Ernest C. "The Callahan Expedition, 1855." *Southwestern Historical Quarterly* 54 (1951): 430–51.

Smith, Ruby Cumby. "James W. Fannin, Jr., in the Texas Revolution." *Southwestern Historical Quarterly* 23, no. 2 (1919): 79–90.

Smith, Thomas T. "U.S. Army Combat Operations in the Indian Wars of Texas, 1849–1881." *Southwestern Historical Quarterly* 99, no. 4 (1996): 501–31.

Sprague, John T. "Journal of a Wagon Train Expedition from Fort Inge to El Paso Del Norte in 1850." *Military History of the West* 25, no. 1 (Spring 1995): 69–105.

Traylor, Maude Wallis. "Those Men of the Mier Expedition." *Frontier Times* 16 (1938–39): 299–309.

Turner, F.H. "The Mejía Expedition." *Quarterly of the Texas State Historical Association* 7 (July 1903): 1–28.

Tyler, Ronnie C. "The Callahan Expedition of 1855: Indians or Negros?" *Southwestern Historical Quarterly* 70 (1966–67): 574–85.

———. "Fugitive Slaves in Mexico." *Journal of Negro History* 57, no. 1 (1972): 1–12.

Weddle, Robert S. "San Juan Bautista: Mother of Texas Missions." *Southwestern Historical Quarterly* 71 (1968): 542–63.

Letters

Davis, Jefferson, secretary of war, to J.E. Doss, William G. Thomas and Charles A. Campbell of Fredericksburg, May 12, 1855. Congressional Series of United States Public Documents, Volume 1515, Claims of the State of Texas, No. 21, p. 85.

Houston, Sam, to James W. Fannin, March 11, 1836. http://www.tamu.edu/faculty/ccbn/dewitt/andrew3.htm#fannin%20letter.

Morris, Robert, to James W. Fannin, February 6, 1836. Archival Communications Fannin and Goliad Aug. 1835-Mar 1836. http://www.tamu.edu/faculty/ccbn/dewitt/goliadofficial.htm.

Pease, Governor E.M., to General T.F. Smith, June 21, 1855. *Military Papers, 1855–1890*. Archives, Texas State Library, Austin.

Pease, Governor E.M., to Persifor F. Smith, major general, June 20, 1855. Archives, Texas State Library, Austin.

Robinson, James, to James Fannin, March 6, 1836, and February 13, 1836. Archival Communications Fannin and Goliad Aug. 1835–Mar 1836. http://www.tamu.edu/faculty/ccbn/dewitt/goliadofficial.htm.

Santa Anna, Antonio López, to José Urrea, Bexar, March 3, 1836, and March 23, 1836. http://www.tamu.edu/faculty/ccbn/dewitt/goliadurrea.htm.

Smith, Percifer F., to Samuel Cooper, September 22, 1855. Congressional Series of United States Public Documents, Volume 1515, Claims of the State of Texas, No. 30, p. 90.

Urrea, José, to the Mexican minister of war and marine, March 21, 1836. General José Urrea's Report of the Battle of Coleto Creek. http://www.tamu.edu/faculty/ccbn/dewitt/goliadmex.htm#urrearep.

Official Government Documents and Library Archives

"Agreement of James Campbell, Arthur Swift, Matthew Caldwell, to Pay Joseph S. Martin a Promissory Note for the Land upon Which Walnut Springs Would Be Founded." Gonzales County Record of Deeds. Vol. A., p. 113. Located in the Gonzales County Courthouse, 1838.

Affleck, J.D. "History of John C. Hays." Pts. 1–2. Typescript in Archives Collection, University of Texas Library.

Barker Texas History Center. *Fort Duncan Papers*. University of Texas–Austin.

Brown, John Henry. *Papers*. Barker Texas History Center, University of Texas–Austin, 1880–92.

Brown, Samuel T. "Account of the Georgian Battalion at Goliad." Written for the *Texas Almanac*, 1859.

Burleson, Edward, Jr. *Papers*. Dolph Briscoe Center for American History, University of Texas–Austin.

Comal County Court Records, October 4, 1856.

Comal County Probate Court Records, April 27, 1858, and September 1, 1858.

Comisión Pesquisidora de la Frontera del Norte. New York: Baker & Godwin, 1875.

Committee of Twenty. *Texas Citizens Circular Regarding the Proceedings of a Meeting to Discuss the End of Slave Trafficking*. Seguin, TX, August 26, 1854. Series 6, Early Statehood Era, 1848–1860. Early Texas Documents Collection, 1790–1923. University of Houston Libraries.

Congressional Serial Set. Washington, D.C.: GPO, 1880.

David Crockett, Burleson Family Papers, 1860–1898. Dolph Briscoe Center for American History, University of Texas–Austin.

The Federal Writers Project. *Slave Narratives: A Folk History of Slavery in the United States from Interviews with Former Slaves*. Vol. 16, *Texas Narratives, Part 3*. Washington, D.C.: Library of Congress, 1943.

Ford, John S. "John C. Hays in Texas." Typescript. Barker Texas History Center, University of Texas–Austin, 1879.

———. "Memoirs." Typescript. Barker Texas History Center, University of Texas–Austin, 1836–96.

Frederick Wilkins Papers. "Defending the Frontiers—The Texas Rangers, 1848–1861." N.d., MS 283, University of Texas–San Antonio Libraries Special Collections.

Gonzales County Historical Commission. *Gonzales County History*. Colleyville, TX, 1986.

Guadalupe County Clerk's Records. A record of the acts and transfers which founded the town. Various dates.

Heitman, Francis B. *Historical Register and Dictionary of the United States Army*. 2 vols. Washington, D.C.: GPO, 1903. Reprint, Urbana: University of Illinois Press, 1965.

Hughes, George W., Lorenzo Sitgreaves and William B. Franklin. "Map Showing the Line of March of the Centre Division, Army of Mexico, under the Command of Brigr. Genl. John E. Wool, from San Antonio de Béxar, Texas, to Saltillo, Mexico." In *Report of the Secretary of War, Communicating a Map Showing the Operations of the Army of the United States in Texas and the Adjacent Mexican States on the Rio Grande*. Senate Ex. Doc. No. 32, 31st Cong., 1st sess. Washington, D.C.: Government Printing Office, 1850.

Hughes, Major George W. *Memoir Descriptive of the March of a Division of the United States Army, Under the Command of Brig. Gen. John E. Wool, from San Antonio de Béxar, in Texas, to Saltillo, in Mexico*. Senate Exec. Doc. 32, 31st Cong., 1st sess. Washington, D.C.: Government Printing Office, 1850.

Matthews, Matt M. *The US Army on the Mexican Border: A Historical Perspective*. Long War Series Occasional Paper. Fort Leavenworth, KS: Combat Studies Institute Press, 2007.

McCulloch, Ben. *Ben and Henry Eustace McCulloch Family Papers, 1798–1961*. Center for American History, University of Texas–Austin.

"Muster Roll. Capt James C. Winn's 3rd. Co. Georgia Battalion 1st Regiment Texas Volunteers from 31st. December to 29th. February 1836." Dolph Briscoe Center for American History, University of Texas–Austin.

Pease, E.M. *Pease Executive Record Book 35*. Texas State Archives and Library Commission, Austin.

Piedras Negras Claims: In the American and Mexican Joint Commission; Pedro Tauns (no. 679) and others v. the United States. Argument for the United States. Washington, D.C., 1871.

Reports of the Committee of Investigation Sent in 1873 by the Mexican Government to the Frontier of Texas. Translated from the official edition made in Mexico, 1873. New York: Baker & Godwin, 1875.

Swanson, D.A. "Fort Clark, Texas: A Bootstrap on the Nueces Strip to Headquarters of the Military District Nueces." Unpublished manuscript on file at Fort Clark Museum, 1985.

Texana Collection, MS 288. University of Texas–San Antonio Libraries Special Collections.

Texas Adjutant General's Office. *Report of the Adjutant-Gen. of the State of Texas for the Period Ending December 15, 1910*. Charleston, SC: Nabu Press, 2012.

Texas Adjutant General's Records, 1838–1889. Dolph Briscoe Center for American History, University of Texas–Austin.

Texas Ranger (pre–Civil War) military rolls. Military rolls, Texas Adjutant General's Department. Archives and Information Services Division, Texas State Library and Archives Commission.

U.S. Bureau of Indian Affairs. *Indian Wars and Local Disturbances in the United States, 1782–1898.* Washington, D.C.: Department of the Interior, 1921.

"U.S.-Mexican General Claims Commission." In A.H. Feller, *The Mexican Claims Commissions, 1923–1934: A Study in the Law and Procedure of International Tribunals*, 322. New York: MacMillan Company 1935.

U.S. Senate. *Letter from the Secretary of War.* 45th cong. 2nd sess., Ex. Doc. 19. Washington, D.C.: Government Printing Office, n.d.

Vicente Filisola and José Francisco Urrea Manuscripts, MS 334. University of Texas–San Antonio Libraries Special Collections, San Antonio.

Selected Internet Sites

Allen, Richard, et. al. The Georgia Battalion Project—Refugio, Goliad, and San Jacinto: The Georgia Battalion in the Texas Revolution, 1835–1836. http://georgiabattalion.com/about-us.

Barnard, Joseph H. Dr. Joseph H. Barnard's Revised Roll of Fannin's Men. https://tshaonline.org/supsites/fannin/hd_ttr4.html.

Daily National Intelligencer of Washington, D.C. "Expelling the Mexicans, Austin, Texas." November 8, 1854. http://files.usgwarchives.net/tx/freestone/texas/gennews.txt.

Davenport, Harbert. Notes from an Unfinished Study of Fannin and His Men with Biographical Sketches, 1936. https://tshaonline.org/supsites/fannin/hd_home.html.

Eagle Pass Public Library. Timeline of Eagle Pass History. http://www.eaglepass.lib.tx.us/fortduncan.html.

Family Tree of James Hughes Callahan. http://www.rootsweb.ancestry.com/~txblanco/callahan.htm.

Fannin Battleground State Historic Site. http://www.visitfanninbattleground.com/index.aspx?page=984.

Hindes, Kay E. "Historic Camps and Crossings on the Medina and San Antonio Rivers." *Texas Beyond History*, 1995. http://www.texasbeyondhistory.net/st-plains/images/he6.html.

Lipan Apache Tribe of Texas. http://www.lipanapache.org/Communitypages.html#.Va0_o_lViko.

Lively Garland R. "Colonel James Walker Fannin's Regiment at Goliad." Military History Online. http://www.militaryhistoryonline.com/19thcentury/articles/fanninsregiment.aspx.

———. "Gonzales: Crucible of the Texas Revolution." Military History Online. http://www.militaryhistoryonline.com/19thcentury/articles/gonzales.aspx.

Murray, Dru J. "The Unconquered Seminoles." Florida History: Native Peoples. http://funandsun.com/1tocf/seminole/semhistory.html.

Nacimiento, Mexico Anishinabe Reservation. http://www.anishinabe-history.com/reservations/nacimiento.shtml.

"Organismo del EjércitoMéjico." The Second Flying Company of Alamo de Parras. http://www.tamu.edu/faculty/ccbn/dewitt/adp/history/1836/the_battle/the_mexicans/ejercito.html.

Phillips, Dalton Ray. Our Callahan Family. http://freepages.genealogy.rootsweb.ancestry.com/~rayphill/callahanfamily.pdf.

Santos, Richard. "U.S. Army Describes Rio Grande Area in 1847." March 30, 2011. http://www.elcaminorealdelostejas.org/news/82.

Schober, Otto. "Historia." *Tu Ciudad*, June 4, 2010. Piedras Negras: La Frontera Fuerte de México. Official government website. http://www.piedrasnegras.gob.mx/2010/06/historia.

Sons of DeWitt Colony Texas. http://www.tamu.edu/faculty/ccbn/dewitt/dewitt.htm.

Stopka, Christina. Partial List of Texas Ranger Company and Unit Commanders. Texas Ranger Research Center. http://www.texasranger.org/ReCenter/Capt.s.pdf.

Texas Almanac, 1859. Table of Distances. University of North Texas Libraries, Texas Historical Foundation. http://texashistory.unt.edu/ark:/67531/metapth123765/m1/146/.

Texas State Historical Association. *Handbook of Texas Online*. https://tshaonline.org/handbook.

Texas State Historical Association. Online Republic of Texas Military Records. https://tshaonline.org/supsites/military/rep_link.htm.

Texas State Historical Association. Republic Claims. http://www.tsl.state.tx.us/arc/repclaims/index.php.

Washington, Lewis M.H. "Fannin and His Command: Comprising a Brief Sketch of the Organization, Military Operations and Massacre of Col. James W. Fannin and His Regiment, in the Revolutionary Struggle of

Texas—1835 and '36." Sons of DeWitt Colony Texas. http://www.tamu.edu/faculty/ccbn/dewitt/goliadwash.htm.

Theses and Dissertations

Beach, Lola Doyle. "History of Gonzales County in the Nineteenth Century." Thesis, University of Texas, 1930.

Dixon, Frederick Kemp. "History of Gonzales County in the Nineteenth Century." Thesis, University of Texas, 1964.

Gassner, John C. "African American Fugitive Slaves and Freemen in Matamoros, Tamaulipas, 1820–1865." Thesis, University of Texas–Pan American, 2005.

Haralson, James Brent. "Greyhound General: A Military Biography of Major General John G. Walker, CSA." Thesis, Texas Tech University, 2005.

Jennings, Nathan Albert. "Riding to Victory: Mounted Arms of Colonial and Revolutionary Texas, 1822–1836." Thesis, University of Texas–Austin, 2013.

Maestas, Enrique Gilbert-Michael. "Culture and History of Native American Peoples of South Texas." PhD diss., University of Texas–Austin, 2003.

Moellering, Max Arwerd. "A History of Guadalupe County, Texas." Thesis, University of Texas–Austin, 1938.

Moore, Robert Lee. "History of Refugio County." Thesis, University of Texas, 1937.

O'Neal, John William. "Texas, 1791–1835: A Study in Manifest Destiny." Thesis, East Texas State University, 1969.

Perez, Aminta Inelda. "Tejano Rangers: The Development and Evolution of Ranging Tradition, 1540–1880. PhD diss., University of Iowa, 2012.

Redonet, Georgia. "The Underground Railroad: A Study of the Routes from Texas to Mexico." Curriculum unit, University of Houston, Houston.

Sellers, Rosella R. "The History of Fort Duncan, Eagle Pass Texas." Thesis, Sul Ross State College, 1960.

Talley, Michael J. "Leadership Principles Applied to the Goliad Campaign of 1836." Thesis, U.S. Army Command and General Staff College, Fort Leavenworth, KS, 2002.

Tijerina, Andres A. "Tejanos and Texas: The Native Mexicans of Texas, 1820–1850." Ph.D. diss., University of Texas at Austin, 1977.

Tyler, Ronnie Curtis. "Slave Owners and Runaway Slaves in Texas." Master's thesis, Texas Christian University, 1966.

INDEX

A

Alabama Greys 22, 25
Alamo 28, 34, 35, 37, 81, 87, 96, 168
Alarcón, Martín de 81
Alavez, Colonel Telesforo 53
Alavez, Señora Francita 53, 70
alcalde of Piedras Negras 138
Alcerrica, Augustín 67
Alsbury, William Wirt 97, 98, 101
Álvarez, President Juan N. 163
American outlaws 77
Ampudia, General Pedro de 98
Andrade, Captain Salas 60
Andrews, Joseph W. 43
Angel of Goliad 53, 70
Apacheria 79
Apaches 102, 106, 108
Aransas River 42
Archer, Branch T. 19
Arista, General Mariano 81
Arroyo Hondo 93
Atascosito Road 39
Austin's 1840 map of Texas 81
Austin, Stephen F. 19, 23, 70, 74, 81, 170
Ayers, Lewis 39

B

Balcones Escarpment 79
Balderas, Captain Luis 67
Bandera 119, 123, 141
Bandera County 122
Bandera Pass 110, 119
Banquete 83
Barbee, Dr. John Gaston 153
Barnard, Joseph H. 70
Barwell 63
Bastrop 102
Batallón de Tres Villas 170
Battle of Agua Dulce 32
Battle of Coleto 52, 55
Battle of Mier 98
Battle of Piedras Negras 147
Battle of Refugio 55, 91
Battle of Rio Escondido 148
Battle of San Jacinto 54
Bejar Defenders 88, 89
Benavides, Plácido 25, 32
Bennett, Miles 89
Benton, Benjamin Eustace 130, 134, 145, 155
Benton, Captain Nathaniel 130, 145
Berlandier, Jean Louis 81
Bidais 80
Bird, Captain James 84, 91
"Black Bean Incident" 98
black Seminole 116
Blanco Cemetery 160, 162
Blanco County 107, 157
Blanco River 106, 159
Blassingame, Calvin 160, 161
Blassingame, Luther 160
Blassingame, Mary 162
Blassingame, Woodson 160
Boerne 111
"Boneyard" 80
Branch, Umphries 74
Brazos River 18, 19, 22
Brooks, John Sowers 22, 34, 41
Brown, John Henry 160
Brown, Samuel T. 63

Bugg, Zack 143
Bullock Uriah J, 22
Burbank, Captain Sidney 137, 148
Burkett, N.B. 89
Burleson, Aaron 149
Burleson, Captain Ed 130
Burleson, General Edward 96
Burleson, Lieutenant Ed, Jr. 123
Burnet, David 21

C

Caldwell, Captain Matthew "Old Paint" 74, 78, 87, 93
Caldwell County 102
California Trail 108
Callahan 63, 79, 81, 102, 138, 161
Callahan, Carolina 102
Callahan, Catherine 102
Callahan Expedition 114, 128, 129, 131, 134, 155, 158
Callahan, James 133, 159, 162
Callahan, James Hughes 15
Callahan, James Sanford 102
Callahan, John A. 102
Callahan, Wesley Hughes 102
Callahan, William Milford 102, 160
Cameron 84
Campbell, Charles A. 111
Campbell, James 74
Camp Chacon 98
Camp Crabapple 122
Camp Davant 110
Camp Enchanted Rock 122
Camp Houston 106
Camp Verde 110
Canales, Antonio 83
Cañón de Uvalde 78
Capote Ranch 107
Carroll, Parson 91
Castañeda, Captain Francisco 88
Castroville 93
Chacon Creek 97
Chadwick, Joseph M. 22, 41
Chandler, F.W. 106
Cherokees 90
Cibolo Creek 87
Clopton, H.K. 145
Clopton, W.H. 156
Coahuila, Mexico 113
Coahuila y Tejas 18
Cocos 80
Coleto Creek 52
Collins, Robert 17
Colonia Militar de Guerro 141
Colt model 1849 pocket revolver 121
Colt Navy .36 caliber revolver 121
Colt Paterson revolvers 86
Columbia 23
Comancheria 79
Comanches 32, 72, 77, 78, 80, 81, 102, 104, 106, 108, 120, 131, 137, 139
Comfort 111
Committee of Safety and Correspondence 23
Consultation 23, 169
Copano 25, 52, 53, 61, 64, 68
Córdova, Colonel Vicente 90
Corpus Christi 104
Cos, General Martin Perfecto de 31
Cox, Mike 14
Crockett, David 35
Cuero 84
Curry's Creek 111

D

Davant, Second Lieutenant William M. 139
Davis, Jefferson 111
Dawson Massacre 92, 100
Dawson, Nicholas M. 92
Day, James Milford 76
Day, Sarah Medissa 97, 101
Department of Texas 105
Derby, Jim 131
Dimmitt, Captain Phillip 26
Dimmitt's Landing 34
Doss, J.E. 111
Duval, Burr 56
Duval, John C. 64

E

Eagle Pass 122, 128, 131, 132, 135
Edson, Lieutenant J.H. 119
Edwards Plateau 81
Ehrenberg, Herman 57
Eighth United States Infantry 125
El Camino Real 126
Elm Creek 135
El Ronco 81
Encina 125
Erskine, Michael H. 107

F

Fannin, James W., Jr. 19, 36, 52, 68, 167
Federal Constitution of 1824 20
filibuster 117
First Regiment of Infantry of Texas 76
First Regiment of Texas Mounted Volunteers 105
First U.S. Infantry 106
Fisher, Captain William S. 98

Flaco, Lipan chief 97
Flores, Manuel 74
Flores Ranch 86
Ford, John Salmon "Rip" 76, 116, 129
Fort Clark 108, 128
Fort Defiance 28, 33, 34, 40, 52, 55, 68
Fort Duncan 116, 148
Fort Inge 125, 127, 128, 131, 184
Fort Lincoln 125
Fort Lipantitlán 32, 171
Fort Martin Scott 104, 106, 123, 157
Fort Velasco 19
Francis, William C. 39
Frazer, Hugh McDonald 55
Fredericksburg 80, 106, 111, 123, 157
Freeman, Lieutenant Colonel William Grigsby 136
Frio River 80

G

Gadsden, Ambassador James 162
Garay, Colonel Francisco 44, 49, 51, 68
Garza, Carlos de la 39, 50, 52
Georgia Battalion 15, 18, 25, 26, 41, 43, 53, 63, 64, 67, 68, 167, 172
Gillespie County 123
Gillespie, Robert Addison 87
gold rush 106
Goliad 18, 21, 26, 81, 84, 167
Goliad Massacre 145
Gonzales 35, 36, 72, 74, 84, 102
Gonzales Minutemen Company 80, 84
Gonzales Rangers 78
Gonzales-Seguin Rangers 76
Gonzalez County Militia 76
Grant, James 169
Green, Thomas Jefferson 92
Gregory, John 145, 153
Guadalupe County 107
Guadalupe River 52, 54, 73, 74, 80, 84, 107, 111, 119, 123, 130
Guerra, Luis 25
Guerrero 125

H

Hall, Robert 73, 76, 93, 104
Hammock, Pierce 54
Hardee, Captain William J. 133
Harney, Colonel William S. 125
Harris, Wesley 134, 145
Hays, Captain Jack 76
Hays, John Coffee 76, 96
Hemphill, Judge John 94
Henry, Captain William R. 118, 129, 130, 141, 163
Hicks, Fabian 134
Highsmith, Benjamin 57
Hinds, Eli Clement 106, 160
Holland, Captain Benjamin 60
Holland, Hal 134, 145
Holloway, William 156
Holt, David 52
Holzinger, Lieutenant Colonel Juan José 54
Horton, Colonel Albert 57
Houston, First Lieutenant Tom 130
Houston, Sam 23, 35, 96, 169
Howard, Major George 78
Hughes, Benjamin Franklin 64
Hughes, James 101

J

John Horse 141
Johnson Creek 81
Johnson, Francis (Frank) W. 23
Johnson, Thomas 160, 162
Johnson, William S. "Mallheel" 160
Johnston, General Albert Sidney 78
Jones, Captain Augustus H. 88
Jones, William E. 106, 159
Jones, Willis 134, 145, 156
Junction 81

K

Karnes, Colonel Henry W. 78
Kennimore, John C.P. 54
Kent, David 57
Kentucky Mustangs 56
Kentucky volunteers 28
Kerr County 110
Kerrville 80, 111, 130
Kickapoos 106, 122, 131, 141
Kimble County 81
King, Captain Amon B. 28
King, Henry 130, 134, 145
King, Wilburn H. 119
Kinneman, John 63
Kiowas 106, 139
Kyle, First Lieutenant William 130, 144

L

La Bahía 62, 64
LaFayette Battalion 21
La Maroma 142
Lamar, President Mirabeau B. 22

La Navaja 141
land bounties 17
Langberg, Colonel Emil 116, 138, 150, 162
Laredo 31, 97
Laredo Road 97
Las Moras Creek 131, 132
Las Moras Springs 80
Lavaca Bay 53
Lavaca River 84
Leal, Manuel 78
Leona River 125, 126, 127, 128, 129, 131, 133
Leona Springs 127
Leon Springs 80
Lindsey, A.M. 106
Lipan Apaches 80, 81, 111, 113, 114, 116, 123, 131, 139, 142, 159, 162
Lipantitlán 83
Llano County 122
Llano Estacado 81
Llano River 80, 81
Lockhart 102
Lockhart, Charles 76
Lomería Grande 81
Lone Star flag 17
Longstreet, Major James 125
López, Esteban 40
Los Angeles 108
Los Diablos Tejanos 110
Los Indios Bárbaros del Norte 132
Luckie, Samuel 94
Luntzel, Christopher 139

M

Macon, Georgia 15
Macon Messenger 15
Madero, Captain Evaristo 143
Maldonado, Colonel Juan Manuel 137
Manahuilla Creek 57
Martin, Joseph S. 74
Matamoros 23, 31, 32, 105, 169
Matamoros Expedition 21, 24, 28
"Matamoros Fever" 23
Maverick, S.A. 159
Mayan Indians 31
Mayeyes 80
Mays, Sam 52
McCormick, James 134
McCrocklin, Jesse Lindsay 97
McCulloch, Ben 74, 76, 105
McCulloch, Henry E. 74, 76, 80, 87, 96
McCulloch's Expedition 106
McDowell, J.S. 130, 138, 153
McGee, Jouette Fletcher 109
McGee, Reverend John 109
McKinney, Collin 23, 169
McLean, Ephraim 96
McLeod, Lieutenant Hugh 15
McRae, Cole 150
Medina River 93, 97, 141
Menchaca, Lieutenant Colonel Manuel 143
Mexía, José Antonio 25
Mexican-American War 111
Mexican bandidos 78
Mexican expeditionary army 29
Mexican War 105
Mexico City 100
Mier 98
Mier Expedition 83, 98
Milledgeville, Georgia 17
Miller, William P. 67
Mission Concepción 97
Mission River 25, 44, 46
Mission Santa Cruz de San Sabá 81
Mitchell, Asa 159
Mitchel, Major Warren J. 21
Mobile Greys 57
model 1840 flintlock musket 86
Monclova, Coahuila 23
Moore, Colonel John Henry 80
Moral, Colonel Sebastain Moro del 88
Morales, Colonel Juan 58
Mordicai, James B.F. 54
Morrell, Reverend Z.N. 88
Mountain Home 81
Murphy, Corporal James B. 47

N

Nacimiento, Coahuila 116, 141
Nacogdoches Mexicans 90
Navarro, José Antonio 74
Navarro, Luciano 74
Neely, James 54
Neighbors, Robert S. 111
New Orleans 53
New Orleans Greys 21
New York Times 148
Nichols, James W. 76, 77
Nueces River 77, 79, 83, 97, 108, 133
Nueces Strip 133
Nuestra Señora de la Candelaria 79
Nuestra Señora del Refugio Mission 25, 169
Nueva Villa de Herrera 137
Nuevo León 116, 118
Núñez, Colonel Gabriel 49, 58

O

Old Three Hundred 19
Olmsted, Frederick Law 137

P

Paso del Águila 137
Paso de las Piedras Negras 132
Paso de los Adjuntos del Río Escondido 138
Patino, Captain Miguel 143
Patton, Ben F. 134, 153
Patton, Charles A. 131
Pease, Governor E.M 110
Pedernales River 80
Perote Prison 100
Perry, Cicero Rufus 97
Perry, Edward 47, 50
Piedras Negras 111, 135, 137, 138, 142, 145, 158, 163
Piedras Negras burned 152
Pinta Trail 80, 106
Pittsburgh Land Company 106
Pittsburg, Texas 106
Pitts, Captain William A. 146
Pitts, General John D. 106
Pitts, J.D. 119
Polk, President James K. 104
Ponton, Andrew 72
Portilla, Colonel Nicolás de la, 66
Prairie Lea 102
Presidio del Río Grande 125
Presidio La Bahía 27
Presidio Monclova Viejo 141
Presidio San Juan Bautista 125
Pretalia, Captain Rafael 42

Q

Quelluna, Chief 81
Quemado 132
Quihi 108
Quinoñes, Agatón 78

R

Ramírez, Captain Antonio 67, 137
Ramírez y Sesma, General Joaquín 31
Randall, Willis 92
Ranger corps 84
Raymondville 32
Read, Second Lieutenant Charles A. 130
Red Rovers 56
Refugio 26, 28, 40, 81, 84
Reid, Lieutenant Charles 156
Republic of Texas 21, 34, 103, 171
Republic of the Rio Grande 21
Republic of the Sierra Madre 118
Republic of Yucatán 21
Reyes, General Isidro 85
Rio Blanco 159
Rio Escondido 125, 137, 142
Rio Grande 94, 97
Rio Grande Defenders 88
Rio San Antonio 142
Robinson 170
Rodgers, J.B. 47
Rodríguez, Captain Nicolas 32
Roemer, Ferdinand von 72
Ross, Captain Shapley P. 78
Ruiz, Colonel José Francisco 81
Runaway Scrape 36
runaway slaves 116, 137

S

Sabinal 108
Salado Creek 87
Salas, Colonel Mariano 58
Salazar, Gaspar 137
Saltillo 29, 31
San Antonio 80, 82, 85, 87, 170
San Antonio Herald 158, 163
San Antonio River 26, 34, 52
San Antonio Sentinel 159
San Felipe 23
San Fernando 123
San Fernando de Rosas 112, 113, 125, 126, 131, 138, 139, 142
San Juan Bautista Mission 29
San Lorenzo de la Santa Cruz 79
San Luis Potosí 29
San Marcos 104
San Marcos River 80, 102
San Patricio 32, 84
Sansom, John W. 113, 128, 134, 138
Santa Anna, General Antonio López de 20, 29, 163
Santa Fe Expedition 101
Santos, Don Guadalupe de los 42
Sauer family cemetery 162
Saunders, Judge X.B. 149
Schmidt, August 113, 123, 131, 156
Scott, General Winfield 90
Seco Creek 125
Second Division of the Mexican Army Corps 85
Second Dragoons 133
Seguin 80, 82, 84, 86, 107
Seguín, Erasmo 74
Seguín, Juan N. 74, 89, 94
Seguin Ranger Station 76
Seguin, Texas 73, 76
Seminoles 122, 131, 141
Shackelford, Captain Jack 40
Shackelford, John 70
Sharpe, Captain John 38

Sharps model 1851 carbine 121
Shiller, Brent 143
Siete Leyes 20
Sisterdale 111
slave owners of San Antonio 116
Smith, Augustus 145
Smith, General Persifor F. 110
Smith, Tom 54
Smithwick, Noah 101
Smugglers' Trail 125
Somervell Expedition 83, 96
Somervell, General Alexander 95
Sowell, A.J. 74, 76, 134
Stewart, Thomas 54
Sumpter, Jesse 150, 155
Sutherland, Jno. [John] 159
Swift, Arthur 74

T

Tatum, Joseph 52
Taylor, Creed 88
Taylor, General Zachary 104
tejanos 39, 74
Tejas 80
Terms of the Capitulation 61
Texas army 172
Texas Declaration of Independence 18, 76
Texas Rangers 76, 156
Texas State Cemetery 164
Thomas, William G. 111
Ticknor, Captain Isaac 22
Tom, Hughes 134, 152
Tonkawas 80, 81, 106
Tornel Decree 20
Travis, Colonel William B. 33
Treaties of Velasco 81
Treaty of Annexation 103
Treaty of Guadalupe Hidalgo 105
Troutman, Joanna 17, 167
Tumlinson, Captain John J. 84
Tyler, President John 103

U

United Mexican States 20
United States Mounted Rifle Regiment 152
Urrea, General José de 31, 35, 39, 52, 60
Urrutia, Captain José de 121
U.S. First Infantry 110
U.S. model 1817 common rifle 22
U.S. Mounted Rifles 110
Uvalde 125, 127, 128, 131, 133

V

Vanguard Brigade 31
Vásquez Expedition 83
Vásquez, General Rafael 81
Velasco 18, 167
Victoria 32, 38, 50, 52, 54, 56, 81
Victoria, Guadalupe 67
victoriana guardes 39
Vidaurri, General Santiago 118
Villa Fuente 149

W

Wadsworth, Captain William A.O. 22
Walker, Captain John G. 119, 128, 152
Walker, Samuel H. 76, 96
Wallace, Major Benjamin C. 21
Wallace, William "Big Foot" 87, 96, 98, 100, 133
Walnut Springs 74
Ward, William 17, 68, 167
Washington-on-the-Brazos 28, 34, 171
Watson, John M. 161
Westover, Captain Ira 26
Wharton, William H. 19
Wichitas 106
Wilcox, J.A. 159
Wild Cat 122, 141
Wilkinson, William Cubelo 54, 63
Wilson, Joseph 52
Winn, Captain James C. 22
Woll, General Adrián 85
Woll's Road 125
Woods, Samuel E. 51
Wool, General John E. 125
Worth, Major General William Jenkins 105
Wyatt, Peyton S. 41

Y

Yucatán Activo Battalion 31

Z

Zapata, Andrés 137
Zaragoza, Coahuila 113, 125, 141
Zavala, Lorenzo de 21
Zumwalt, Adam 72, 84

ABOUT THE AUTHOR

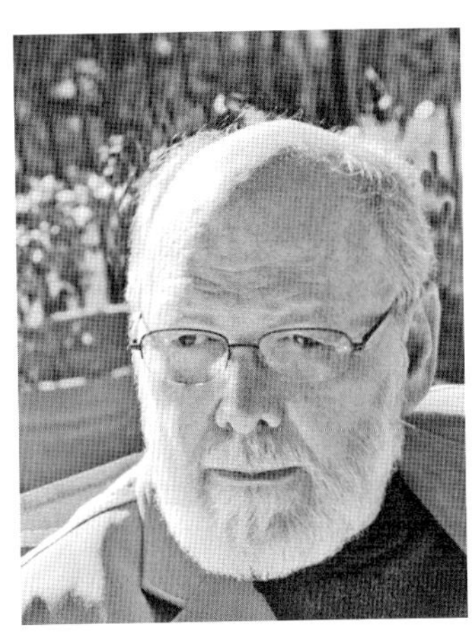

Photo by Debra Johnson.

Joseph Neal Luther is a sixth-generation Texan who lives in Kerrville, Texas. He earned his doctorate at Texas A&M University and is a professor emeritus of the University of Nebraska–Lincoln, where he taught for twenty-three years, serving as associate dean of the College of Architecture. He also taught for ten years at Eastern Washington University. An enthusiastic historical archaeologist, Dr. Luther is a member of the national Society for Historical Archaeology and the Society for American Archaeology and has given papers at their national conferences. Locally, he is an active member of the Texas State Historical Association, Texas Archeological Society, Southern Texas Archaeological Association, Wild West History Association and the West Texas Historical Association. Dr. Luther has written two books of historical archaeology: *Camp Verde: Texas Frontier Defense* (2012) and *Fort Martin Scott: Guardian of the Treaty* (2013) both published by The History Press. *James Callahan* is his third book on nineteenth-century Texas history.